Musical Theatre Script and Song Analysis Through the Ages

Musical Theatre Script and Song Analysis Through the Ages

James Olm

methuen | drama
LONDON • NEW YORK • OXFORD • NEW DELHI • SYDNEY

METHUEN DRAMA
Bloomsbury Publishing Plc
50 Bedford Square, London, WC1B 3DP, UK
1385 Broadway, New York, NY 10018, USA
29 Earlsfort Terrace, Dublin 2, Ireland

BLOOMSBURY, METHUEN DRAMA and the Methuen Drama logo
are trademarks of Bloomsbury Publishing Plc

First published in Great Britain 2022

Cover design: Rebecca Heselton
Cover image: Paper © Compack Background/ Shutterstock. Music: George
Gershwin autographed manuscript page of 'Roll Dem Bones' from *Porgy and Bess*,
1935 © Granger Historical Picture Archive / Alamy Stock Photo

A catalogue record for this book is available from the British Library.

A catalog record for this book is available from the Library of Congress

ISBN:	HB:	978-1-3501-9933-0
	PB:	978-1-3501-9932-3
	ePDF:	978-1-3501-9934-7
	eBook:	978-1-3501-9936-1

Typeset by Integra Software Services Pvt. Ltd.
Printed and bound in Great Britain

To find out more about our authors and books visit www.bloomsbury.com
and sign up for our newsletters.

To Arthur Giron: my mentor
and inspiration.
To Leah, Rachel, and Jameson:
my never-ending cavalry.

Contents

Foreword

When I was Head of the Graduate Playwriting Program at Carnegie Mellon University in the 1980s, the Music Department and the Drama Department decided to join forces and create a new major. It would be called the Composer-Playwright Fellowship. Informally, faculty members from both departments began referring to this unknown person as "The Genius Stephen Sondheim candidate" who had facility with both words and music. We knew that to find this gifted gal or guy somewhere in the United States would be a miracle. But we did.

Influential in the development of this new major was my colleague Charlie Willard, a powerhouse musical theatre expert. You will benefit from his wisdom in the pages to come. A gentleman, Charlie represented the Kurt Weill Estate before his early death in a boating accident.

Carnegie Mellon, once known as Carnegie Tech, established the first drama degree in America in 1914. Since then, it has earned a strong reputation for graduating the best professionals in their fields; be it design, directing, acting, musical theatre, or story tellers on TV, screen, and stage. To update our current students, I polled our accomplished Hollywood writers, such as Steve Bochco (*Hill Street Blues*), John Wells (*China Beach*), Charley Peters (*Three Men and a Little Lady*), and asked them how we could improve our graduate curriculum to make them more competitive. They all responded in the same vein – "Do nothing. We do what we do because of the solid, classical education we got." An outstanding example of this mentality favoured Stephen Schwartz, who in a philosophy class was gripped by the theatrical concept of Christ addressing crowds as a clown in *Godspell*. Later, his imagination was set in motion when in a history class he focused on the Charlemagne family and created *Pippin*. Side by side, Carnegie-Mellon celebrates the Sciences and the Arts. The University's faculty is encouraged to work in the disciple we teach. When I was asked to co-author the book of the epic Broadway musical, *Amazing Grace*, I attempted to share the step-by-step decision-making with my students.

It's tough to get into Carnegie Mellon; teams travel far and wide across the land auditioning, reading manuscripts, hearing tapes, judging stamina and the nature of the applicant's passion. We received around two hundred applicants for the new Composer-Playwriting Fellowship. Since we commit to a student for life, we prize how a student lives his or her life. Our winner of the first Composer-Playwright Fellowship, James Olm, is a son of the Midwest. Here's an image of him: on summer weekend nights he increased his income by playing piano and singing with his former wife on the tourist ship *Vista Star* on Lake Superior. Jim's talent for affection is fed by music of faith, soaring love feelings, as in his passionate *The Magdalene*, and his scores for my plays *St. Frances in Egypt* and *Flight* (the story of the Midwestern Wright Brothers) – published by Samuel French, script and score.

While I worked with Jim on my plays – with his music – I visited his classes. The impulse to teach is much akin to the relationship of the composer-playwright to his audience. Jim is a born teacher. He has been very careful in the selection of his subject matter, touching his audiences. As he has implemented the principles Charlie Willard taught him, which sometimes mirror mine, which are pathways to the heart, he now has written this book to help you make manifest the unspeakable, uncover the buried, and, above all, give voice to those who cannot sing.

Arthur Giron, Playwright
Former Head, Graduate Playwriting Department
Carnegie-Mellon University

Acknowledgements

The basic vernacular and *lyric* theory that will be covered in this book came directly from Mr Charles Willard, former Broadway producer, touring company manager, and professor at Carnegie-Mellon University. He died in 1991 in a boating accident. I had the privilege of being his student from 1986 to 1988.

Other vernacular that is based in playwriting came directly from New York playwright Mr Arthur Giron, who was former chair of the Playwriting Program at Carnegie-Mellon University. He has been my teacher, mentor, and cherished close friend since 1986.

During the course of developing the new musical theories, Mr Richard Burk, Coordinator of Acting at Casper College, was an incredible sounding board for me. As a cherished and trusted friend, he was always there to be able to bounce off ideas – good or bad.

A big thank you goes to Mr Dom O'Hanlon and Ms Meredith Benson for giving me the needed support and trust throughout this publishing process.

Introduction

Ouch. We all have suffered through musicals that haven't worked: either by watching them, performing in them, working backstage on them, directing them, or writing them. Sometimes, this failure to engage us is just one aspect or part of the show, and other times it is a complete and utter breakdown.

What is interesting is that many times, we can feel this major failure within a show, but can't totally articulate why it has achieved such grandiose badness. Oh sure, we can all recognize obvious flaws: an actor who badly misrepresents a character role, a costume that doesn't fit the period, miscues in lighting or volume, a musician missing a note in their part, or a director misrepresenting the intent of the book. However, many times, we can't quite articulate why a show sputters, or dies. Likewise, we all can recognize a wonderfully fresh and exciting show, yet not totally understand why it is so successful. There is something humanly visceral inside each of us that takes over. It becomes more emotional and abstract. For us, that successful blend of emotion and energy in a show is translated in an undefined gut feeling. It's instinctual. It's experiential and life-moving. It's everything that theatre and art is supposed to be.

Hopefully, this book will help you articulate those abstract feelings in concrete and very real analytical ways. It will introduce you to a new vernacular that will help you describe what we all feel but have trouble disseminating or articulating. It will give you a roadmap to the musical's innermost being and heartbeat.

This book will take you through a step-by-step process of how to analyse a musical, first by introducing new terminology, and then by using many different musicals as examples to help you understand the terminology and their functions within a musical. The book then ends by analysing landmark musicals through musical theatre historical periods, so that you can start to apply what you've learned in very concrete ways.

You will probably notice that I do not use specific examples of quoted lyrics in this book. This is only due to the fact that acquiring copyright permission for over 106 lyric examples was just too cost prohibitive. I encourage all of you to examine each described song lyric online or in script form so that you can actually see the complete connection between the lyrics and its energies.

Keep in mind that watching movie musicals is not advised as a way to analyse musicals unless they are actual taped productions of stage performances. I believe the theories in this book do apply to movie musicals, however sometimes not as efficiently. The difference is that in a movie, there isn't the live interaction between the actors and the audience. As you learn about musical analysis, you will realize that in a live musical performance, there is a kinetic exchange of energies between the actors and the audience that doesn't translate well through the screen. This lack of kinetic energy exchange is why many of us don't like movie musicals as much as live performances. Another reason is that they tend to change the librettos of movie musicals from the original Broadway shows. Generally, I advise people not to watch the movies, although I do use *The Sound of Music* movie in many examples in this book. It's actually one movie that I believe is better than the stage script! Truly, the only way to analyse a musical correctly is through study: script reading and score listening.

The result of reading and understanding this book is that it will hopefully change your way of thinking about musicals: how you direct them, how you perform in them, how you compose and write them, how you design and teach them, and finally, when watching them as an audience, how you enjoy them, and why you enjoy them. Hopefully, you will never look at a musical in the same way again. Ever.

1

Some Basic Terminology

The musical machine

We live in a car world. There are luxury and economy cars, fast and slow cars, sexy and practical cars, and gadget-filled and stripped-down cars. In essence, there is a car for every need and desire. However, we all buy cars for one main reason, and one reason only – to have the vehicle transport us from one place to another. Cars can get us to our destination in many different ways and fashions. It all depends on the kind and quality of the car. Generally speaking, the poorer the car runs, the less enjoyable the ride. The nicer the car runs, the more enjoyable the trip. A car with a broken radio, a shaky rearview mirror, or a stuck window will still get you to your destination safely, but it will be a bit annoying. A car with a flat tyre, a slipping clutch, or an engine with an oil leak, will also get us to our destination, but the trip will sputter or slow down at best. This would be a more unpleasant journey. A car with the transmission falling out, an engine block cracking, or a radiator breaking will totally stall the car out. This will be a detestable trip, and one that all of us would like to try to avoid.

The musical is like a car – plain and simple.

Like a car, the musical is a machine, and it transports us from our reality to an entirely different world. In this world, the musical takes us on a journey through the character's experiences, to a final, set destination – the conclusion or resolution of the story. Like a car, the musical has an incredible amount of parts: actors, technicians, songs, directors, dialogue, choreographers, lyrics, musicians, story, and dance, just to name a few. When all of these parts fit together perfectly and are correctly calibrated, the musical production will take you on an utterly pleasant and wonderful journey to that final, prescribed destination. However, many times a musical might have "a shaky rearview mirror" or "a stuck window." That musical's trip overall could still be quite pleasant, but it would include a few minor irritations while watching it. Add a flat tyre, or a slow oil leak, and the musical becomes less tolerable, more difficult to sit through and watch. With a broken transmission, the musical journey will not be worth taking, and your date will be furious with you for spending so much money on a piece of junk.

The key to a good musical trip (and a great social life) is to have all of the elements of the musical, both structural and through production, clearly aligned well in a unified fashion. The vision and the focus must be consistent with the structure of the musical. The question becomes how we grasp and articulate those important musical elements and then translate them into a language that is accessible to all people involved in the production. Does this sound like a daunting task? Well, ok, it is. However, it is not impossible.

The dramatic question

The dramatic question in a musical is one overall question that we as an audience want answered by the end of the show. It is what keeps the musical machine running. It is the gasoline and the accelerator. It is the question that keeps the audience glued to their seats. It is this lingering question that keeps us all turning to the next page of the book in order to find out what happens at the end. It can be as simple as "Will the boy and girl get together and live happily ever after?" or as complex and philosophical as "Will feminism take root and survive in a patriarchal society?" It is a question that answers the plot of the show, but it also tends to go beyond. Other terms that people use that are similar to the dramatic question are super-objective, motivational force, primary objective, ultimate goal, and dramatic impetus.

I prefer the term dramatic question to these other terms because a dramatic question *demands response*. It demands an answer. It demands action. It demands *resolution*. A term like super-objective or dramatic impetus sounds theoretical and lays flat. It doesn't demand anything. The dramatic question forces you to continue down the road to a conclusion.

Every story has to have a character or characters to root for. If this does not exist, audiences will begin to ask, "Why am I watching this?" That response is the kiss of death, and one that will cause most performing artists to dive into deep depression. Generally, the characters we root for will be found within the body of the dramatic question. Since they are the ones that we care for, we also want to know what will happen to them. Audiences tend to identify with those characters and live through them vicariously. This is a primary visceral response and desire of an audience. If we care about a character, then the dramatic question will ultimately reveal itself and demand resolution – thus, a happy audience, and no depressed artists.

The dramatic question drives the musical. Because of this, it is very important to spend a lot of time and energy focusing on and analysing what this question is. When you are figuring out the dramatic question, truly be careful to follow your gut feeling. As you read the script and listen to the music and lyrics of the show, be sure to take the time to assess what you are unconsciously feeling. Ask yourself why you are continuing to turn the pages. What do you want to find out? Whom are you rooting for? What do you want to happen for the character(s) at the end of the show? Focus in on those questions, and the dramatic question will naturally flow out of this.

There is no one exact, perfectly worded, and correct dramatic question. This is an important point. Decades of class discussions have shown me that in any musical, the students' wording of the dramatic question will vary from year to year and that many times their dramatic question is better than mine! They all end up saying the same thing, but in a slightly different way. This is good! This is what makes new productions of an old show interesting – a slightly different perspective and slant on the interpretation of the product. However, it must stay true and in alignment with the intent of the show and its creators. You must be meticulous in your creating of the dramatic question, so that it is very specific in what you are trying to articulate in the show.

Here is a potential dramatic question for Meredith Willson's *The Music Man*:

Will Marian find her true love in Harold Hill, and will the people of River City grow to find new excitement in their boring lives?

You'll notice that I choose to not only include the romantic aspect of the show, but also include the entire community of River City in the question. The community is a huge part of the show, and we tend to love them and care for them. We want the town to be happy and to be pulled out of their humdrum existence.

For Andrew Lloyd Webber's *The Phantom of the Opera*:

Will the Phantom or Raoul win the heart of Christine?

Yes, there is an entire cast of players and workers within the opera house. However, in this musical, the main focus is Christine, The Phantom, and Raoul. We really are fairly uninvested in any of the other characters. Don't get me wrong – all of the characters are important and integral to the success of the musical. However, they function to focus on the dilemma between the three main characters.

In this next example, I'm using the movie musical instead of the Broadway production because I believe this is the one movie that is actually better than the stage show – Rodgers and Hammerstein's *The Sound of Music*. One could easily state the dramatic question to be:

> *Will Maria and Captain Von Trapp get together and live happily ever after?*

This on its own makes sense and points to what we would like to see happen with the main characters. But, in this musical, that type of dramatic question seems shallow, considering the challenges that face the characters. Maria is not only falling in love with the Captain, but she is also questioning her life direction, especially spiritually. The dramatic question more appropriately could be:

> *Will Maria find and accept her true, God-given path in life?*

Some musicals are structured in a unique way, and you need to go no further than the shows of Stephen Sondheim. One of my all-time favourite musicals is *Sunday in the Park with George*. This show actually has two dramatic questions – one for each act.

> Act I: *Will George choose Dot or art?* / Act II: *Will George find his own unique inspiration and voice in art?*

Another uniquely structured musical is *The Last Five Years*. In this show, one character is living chronologically forward in time, while the other character is chronologically living backwards in time. Therefore, we already know the beginning and the end of the show early on. This makes for a different kind of dramatic question:

> *What causes a seemingly good relationship to break apart?*

Finally, discussing the dramatic question brings up another interesting thought. *Why have a dramatic question?* My firm belief about theatre has always been that we as an audience and we as theatre professionals are involved with this art to make a difference in society. This difference can be as simple as to lighten the load of an audience member through entertainment and escapism. It can also be as monumental as leaving the theatre learning something new about ourselves and society, and thus changing our ways for the betterment of that calling. We have an instinctual desire to better ourselves, and theatre is a way to explore those possibilities by living through alternative experiences of the characters on stage. Therefore, I believe we attend theatre and perform theatre in the desire to change and improve our own personal situations. Having a dramatic question forces us to address a situation, care for the people involved in that situation, and then demand an answer or resolution for them at the end. Moreover, we demand the same thing from our own lives and ourselves.

Distance

If the dramatic question tells us who to follow, who to root for, and to what end result we would like to see happen in the show, then the distance of the show is the route and journey that the characters take in order to reach that desired resolution. It is the body and heart of the musical. The distance is "the road trip" itself. It is *how* we get to the end of the show – the action, the crossroads, the scenery along the way, the turns we take, the bumps we hit, and the surprises that we come across. The distance keeps us interested, and it maintains our desire to reach the final destination/conclusion. If there isn't enough distance in the show, the musical will be over way too fast, or it will feel slow and cumbersome because there isn't enough there to keep our interest. The audience will become impatient, frustrated, and eventually will want to leave the show before it is over.

From a structural standpoint, the best musicals and dramas have greater distances between where the characters are presently, and where those characters need to be at the end of the show. The distance of the show is increased in a variety of ways, usually by using obstacles. The obstacles can be physical or mental in nature. They can be through other characters. They can be structured through time, weather, and terrain. They can be mental/emotional obstacles where characters inadvertently fall in love, or they have emotional baggage from a horrific past. Obstacles are anything that poses a challenge or hurdle for the character and makes it more difficult for the character to reach his/her goal or end result.

In *My Fair Lady*, the dramatic question is *"Will Eliza become a lady and have a lasting emotional relationship with Higgins?"*

The entire show is based on obstacles. Eliza is a poor flower girl – she has no money. She has no social influence, no manners, or etiquette. Most importantly, she speaks with a cockney accent and therefore cannot speak in "perfect English." Eliza also has a time constraint on her – she is expected to learn the ways of language and etiquette in six weeks' time, while being brutally mentored by the hard-hitting, immorally driven, rude, and no-nonsense authoritarian Higgins. That in itself is a prescription for failure and still we are rooting for her, hoping for the happy outcome.

Yet those obstacles aren't enough to juggle. Alfie Doolittle enters the scene to profit from his daughter, Eliza, and Higgins must deal with that. Eliza and Higgins start developing some strange sense of emotional connection that Higgins ignores, just as Freddy falls head over heels in love with Eliza. Karpathy, the expert linguist from Hungary, shows up at the ball at the same time Eliza is trying to pass off as being a "Lady." All of these obstacles add tension and distance to the answering of the dramatic question.

In *Kinky Boots*, the dramatic question is "*Will Charlie and the factory workers of Price and Son overcome their fears of sexuality differences in order to embrace a new direction in shoe production that will save their factory?*"

Charlie is facing the dilemma of whether or not he should close the factory, putting all the factory workers' jobs at risk. He is dealing with the obstacle of financial trouble – how he will meet his bills and payroll. He has time obstacles – a deadline for the closing of the factory and a deadline getting the boots ready for the Italian showcase. He has the obstacles of the workers themselves reacting to the inevitable closing. Charlie's solution is to produce drag queen boots, and to bring in Lola as designer. This isn't a Kum Bah Yah moment for the workers, needless to say.

Thus begins the emotional obstacles. Workers are dealing with their own emotional baggage on sexual prejudice. Lola is not getting support from the factory workers and, eventually, even Charlie. Both Lola and Charlie are dealing with the baggage of their fathers' upbringing. All of these emotional obstacles are difficult to address and rectify, and push the final, end result further and further away from resolution.

A musical that has more obstacles and longer distances within it will be a musical that is more interesting and exciting to the audience, and will help propel the musical to the desired resolution.

The absolute Cardinal Rule of Energies

It's in the music and the lyrics. **It's in the music and the lyrics.** IT'S IN THE MUSIC AND THE LYRICS!

Remember this simple and very important rule, and all of the world will be good. Musicals are musicals because of the music and lyrics. Period. Yes, it is the synthesis of singing, acting, and dancing into one performance medium, but what makes the musical a musical is due to the music and lyrics. It is that musical sharing, a kind of kinetic energy connection, between the actors and the audience that differentiates the musical from any other performance art form, including dramatic theatre. This sharing of kinetic energy is the heartbeat of the musical, and the part of the musical that audiences will fully remember, more than anything else. As long as it involves music, it becomes incredibly memorable – from ballads, to reprises, to dance numbers, to glorious underscoring at the end of a show. It is the music and lyrics, which give the show its depth, warmth, emotional drive, and heartbeat.

An example that I love to use to further this point is *The King and I*. How many of you remember Tuptim? Lady Thiang? Pretty easy to remember, right? Now, how about Kralahome? Huh? Who is he? Many people don't remember this wonderful and important character, even though he is involved with many scenes throughout the show. The point of this is Tuptim and Lady Thiang both have songs that they sing while Kralahome does not. Because of this basic difference, Tuptim and Lady Thiang are more memorable. The music and the lyrics put a focus on these characters because they need to be brought into light. That is why the lead characters traditionally have more songs and dances. It is Anna and the King's story that we must follow and focus on – not Kralahome's. If Kralahome has a bunch of songs, the focus is then redirected to him versus the others, and that creates confusion to the audience. Who are we to follow? Is Kralahome a part of the dramatic question?

This is not to say that the libretto isn't important. On the contrary, a weak libretto kills a musical. The libretto must blend into and out of the music and lyrics with seamless motion. It must be incredibly consistent in its character development with the music and lyrics. Many times, it is the depth and breadth of the characters, as well as the "story line." The libretto is the other arm and leg of the musical and should be treated as such. When creating a new musical, sometimes it is the libretto that should dictate the next song, not the other way around. Sometimes songs just don't fit in right to the momentum of the show, and it's the librettist's job to point that out. Other times, a specific song is the designing moment of the show, and the libretto needs to work around that, developing new scenes to merge the two. It is that fine, collaborative balance between the three – the music, lyrics, and story – that creates the next great masterpiece.

Charles Willard came up with some incredible energy theories when it comes to the musical and its understanding and analysis. These energies are formulated, incorporated, and personified through the music and lyrics of each song in a musical. They also can be sent out through dance, or through music underscoring. These energies define who one roots for, who one despises, who one remembers, and who one forgets. These energy forces stay amazingly consistent when created and produced well, and if followed religiously, will aid you in achieving a more focused, consistent, and powerful production. Likewise, if you misinterpret the energies of a show, the musical will begin to breakdown, like a car having a new tyre but it is the wrong model. This is why close, considerate, and meticulous analysis is so necessary when you are preparing, writing, or producing for a musical.

Therefore, as you read on now, and learn about each specific energy, **you must always base your analysis on the Cardinal Rule of Energies.** Yes, it is important to have the story, the book, the dialogue be congruent with the energies of the characters, but ultimately, the energies must be found and defined in the music and lyrics of that character – NOT the story or the character descriptions.

Dance can also be a major contributor of energy in characters, but only under two conditions: one, that the dance has music underscoring in it and, two, that the choreography has first correctly analysed the energies of the characters *through the music and lyrics*. In other words, dance is a secondary medium to focus character energy: totally dependent upon, and under the umbrella of, the initial music and lyric analysis.

Energies can be attached to one character, a group of characters, or even to an entire community of people. As long as they sing quite a bit, they can be an energy. Even an entire city or town of people in a musical can represent an energy. So remember: It's in the music and the lyrics. **It's in the music and the lyrics. IT'S IN THE MUSIC AND THE LYRICS!**

2

Need Energy in Lyric Analysis

N – Need energy

Every musical must have at least one Need energy character. Need energy characters – designated by the letter N – are the source of feeling, caring, and purpose in a show. These characters are the people that you root for in the story. They are also the ones who in some way fit into the show's dramatic question. We care about them enough to want to follow them through their journey in the show, and we ultimately want them to succeed in their journey. As stated in the Cardinal Rule of Energies, Need energy can be attached to one single main character, to an ensemble of characters, or even to an entire town or community of characters. As long as they sing quite a bit, they can be an energy.

N energy characters are quantified through the music and lyrics that they sing, as well as the dances they perform. N characters have very specific characteristics that justify their being. Generally, characters will not have all of the following characteristics, but they will strongly have a few, depending on their type of character, their needs, motivations, the plot line, and their journey.

Figure 1, the Need Energy Lyric Circle, is a list of characteristics to look for in Need energy characters *within the lyrics of their songs*. None in the circle is any more important than the other. All of them show a sign of a character or characters that have some type of real vacancy or powerlessness in their lives.

Yearning

Many N characters have an intense yearning for something. Their deep longing is what makes us want to feel for them, and care for them. Many times this yearning is unknown to the other characters on stage, left only for

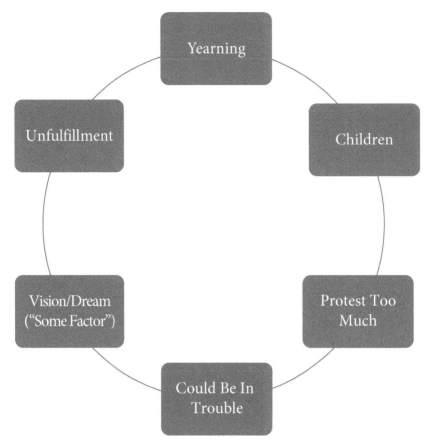

Figure 1 Need Energy Lyric Circle.

the audience to hear through a soliloquy in musical song. They will sing about their yearning, and usually it is in a very private moment when no one else can hear them. It can be a secret only known between the character and audience. Other times, his or her yearning can be straightforward to another individual – in essence a plea to a confidante or friend. However it is formulated, the audience is rooting for this character to receive an answer for his/her yearning. Some in the business might call this the "I Want" song, however, it tends to be deeper than a "want." It is more soulful, more an unfulfillment in life. It is the difference between "I want a car" and "I long to travel to distant lands."

A character(s) can be yearning for a better life, for the perfect partner, for peace in a chaotic world in which s/he lives. It can be a town that is longing for more in life, or a character who is trying to figure out why s/he was born. Whatever that yearning may be, if it is sung, then that character is N.

The Music Man

Marian the Librarian is a strong, intelligent, and independent woman. However, when she sings, she is singing about her yearning for "the perfect man" – My White Knight. Her yearning is sung either alone, or in confidence with Mrs Paroo. In asking not for a "*Lancelot*" nor "*an angel with wings*", she is looking, waiting, and wishing for a companion in life, because, in spite of the fact that she is financially secure, independent, and working, she still is longing for Mr Right to come along. We as audience members are privy to that personal information, and after she sings it to us, we are rooting for her to find Mr Right.

Next to Normal

Diana is suffering from mental illness – bipolar disorder. Her doctor has given her new medication, which zaps the life out of her. She then sings "I Miss The Mountains," which has her reminisce about how her life used to be and how much she yearns for the normalcy of that past life, which encompasses the clear air that "*cuts you like a knife.*" One cannot help but root for this poor woman who desperately wants to be normal, and just isn't given a good option.

Unfulfillment

Generally, unfulfillment goes hand in hand with yearning. Someone who has a deep-seated yearning in his or her life is generally someone who also feels unfulfilled. There is something missing in their lives that cannot be bought, sold, or bargained for. It is a feeling of lack of completeness in one's soul. It churns inside of the character and as hard as they try, they can't ignore it. This unfulfillment sometimes can't even be put into words. It is the restlessness within the soul that constantly is paining the character.

Pippin

Pippin is the son of King Charlemagne. After his narrated introductions, the first that we hear of him is his first song, "Corner of the Sky," in which he tries to explain his unfulfillment in life. Rivers know their place. Eagles know theirs. Pippin is seeking what eludes all of us: "Am I going to find out why I was put on this earth?"

Evita

Eva Duarte is a poor girl living in a small town in Argentina. She wants a better life for herself but doesn't have the means or privilege to ascertain it. After linking herself up to Agustin Magaldi, she talks him into taking her to Buenos Aires so she can follow her dream of being an actor. She will scrape, claw, and steal to try to achieve a fulfilling life, as she warns in the song "Buenos Aires" to "*stand back*" and notice her "*star quality!*"

A vision or a dream – the "Some Factor"

A major clue that is very helpful in deciphering unfulfillment and yearning is the "Some Factor." When people have a soulful yearning or incompleteness, usually it is accompanied by a wishing for, or dreaming of *something*. Interestingly enough, we almost always accompany it with a form of the word *some*. Just think for a moment about all the songs that come into mind with the word *Some* in the title: "Somewhere," "Somewhere Out There," "Somewhere Over the Rainbow," "Something Good." It's amazing! We all yearn for things to be different in our lives, and it always goes along with a dream or vision of how it can be better. And then *some* pops into the equation: sometime, someone, something, somewhere, somehow, someplace, someday, etc.

Using a form of the word "some" automatically leads the character to sing about their dream or vision in life. In other words, the answer to their "some" is the vision or dream. Dorothy in *The Wizard of Oz* sings about **some**where over the rainbow. Her unfulfillment is that she is not satisfied at home – the grass is greener somewhere else. So she dreams about this perfect spot where all of her yearning and unfulfillment will be quenched and satisfied.

The Music Man

Marian stands by her window and sings about the unknown man of her dreams in "Goodnight My **Some**one." She yearns deep down inside, wishing for this white knight in shining armour to appear in her life. Her vision is of this perfect companion who is out with the night stars, listening to her finally saying good night – to her "**some**one."

Many times, this song is a secret between the character and the audience. Once they confide their closest, most private secret to you, don't you just want to root for them like crazy? Of course you do, and if you don't, you're just a non-feeling, cold, heartless brute.

Little Shop of Horrors

Audrey is a sweet, naïve woman who has a major inferiority complex. She is victimized by a sadist dentist and is being abused by him daily. She has a dream of escaping away from Skid Row, to a life in the suburbs with a picket fence and Seymour mowing the yard. It's a simple life of peace and contentment. It's a place "*some*where *that's green.*"

To my recollection, I can only think of one song where *some* in the title is not a need song, and that is in *Gypsy*, with Mama Rose singing, "**Some** People." There, she is telling everyone that a specific type of life can be ok for "*some people*" but certainly not for her. At that point, she doesn't need anything. A tank couldn't stop her from doing what she sees fit to do. Therefore, she is not a N character.

Could be in trouble

Generally speaking, there is some trouble lurking with N energy characters – if not, their needs would be resolved immediately and therefore the show would be over. Obstacles always get in the way of our N characters achieving their resolution. This is what creates more *distance* in the story, and thus more interest. Trouble can be in many different forms, but we always know when we're in trouble, right?

Many times, you can find a clue to this type of song in a lament – that is, a song listing troubles. It can be many times comical, and why wouldn't it be? Don't you just want to laugh after a while when someone whines about all of their problems? An example of a lament would be the song "I'm Just a Girl Who Cain't Say No" from *Oklahoma!* Ado Annie sings about her troubles sticking romantically to only one man. Poor girl.

Another clue to this type of song is a plaint – a direct cry for help. A prime example is in *Oliver*, the song "Where is Love." How can you not feel for this boy crying out for love?

Les Misérables

Valjean, a poor man desperate for food, has stolen silver items from a church and is caught by the police. The Bishop of the church lies to the police, saying the silver was a gift to Valjean, thus giving him a second chance in life. This selfless act of true compassion by the Bishop forces Valjean to re-examine his own life and his present pathway to thievery and hate, by singing "What Have I Done?" He abhors his past actions and decides at that moment to take a new lease on life.

The Last Five Years

In "Nobody Needs to Know," Jamie is having an affair with another woman, and Catherine, his wife, does not know about it. In bed with his "new" love, he sings about how he must get up and continue his life with his wife Cathy, and how impossible it is to do that anymore, knowing how much he loves this other woman.

A Funny Thing Happened on the Way to the Forum

A comedic version of a trouble song would be "I'm Calm," sung by Hysterium. Hysterium is a chief slave with little backbone. He is constantly being manipulated by the mischievous and intelligent Pseudolus. Hysterium desperately tries to stay on top of things and to be in charge, but circumstances get worse and worse to the point where he sings "I'm Calm," trying to talk himself into not losing it. As the song plays out, we find that this is definitely what is happening – he's in trouble and he's one second from going crazy!

Protest Too Much song

A Protest Too Much song is a specially crafted N energy song that has the N character singing the opposite of what s/he is truly feeling. Many times, N characters can be singing about how good they are feeling, when really they aren't feeling okay at all. We actually do this a lot in our own lives. It is a safety mechanism that we humans use to protect ourselves from showing our inward hurt. Sometimes we do it without even realizing it.

Kiss Me Kate

An example of a Protest Too Much song would be "I Hate Men" from *Kiss Me Kate*, where Lilli Vanessi really doesn't hate all men – as a matter of fact, she is in love with Fred Graham. However, she says that she hates men because Fred has hurt her and she doesn't want to get hurt again.

Camelot

"C'est Moi" from *Camelot* is another good example. Lancelot is singing about how great he is, when we all know that what he is singing about is impossible for any man. No one is perfect, and it is in that bravado where we then can find weakness. Even though Lancelot is a great and powerful knight, he does have weaknesses – "love and desire" can be sparked in that man and it is with Gueneviere!

Children

Children almost always are N energy. The reasons are pretty obvious – they have no power. Our society puts children at the mercy of adults, no matter how determined or confident a child is. If they are under the legal age of adulthood, they have no vote, they can't make a living wage, they are inexperienced in life, and they are too immature to make important decisions. Even Annie in the musical *Annie*, who has incredible moxie and determination, is still a N character. She may believe that the "*sun will come out tomorrow*," but she has no power as to what her outcome is going to be. She is at the mercy of Mrs Hannigan, Rooster, Grace, and Daddy Warbucks – their rules, their powers, and their desires decide her fate.

Single characters and communities

As I've said previously, N energy can be personified in one, two, or many characters. The larger the number of N characters in a show, the more likely that these characters all have something in common. Many times, an entire community can be N energy – the "chorus" of the show. As long as they sing music, they can be considered for an energy in the show.

The Music Man

The entire town of River City is N energy. They are caught in the doldrums of nothing new and nothing different. They are bored doing the "same old same old." They hunger for something new, and they don't even know it. They are the typical unhappy couple who just list their basket of woes matter of factly: "cold and stubborn."

Then, as the musical continues, these community members break into smaller ensembles that more specifically portray their individual needs. The women need to be noseying around all the time at every little gossipy morsel of news, just so they can satiate their boredom and unimportance in life in "Pick-a-Little, Talk-a-Little."

The school board is another N ensemble. They are introduced to barbershop quartet music to fill with joy, their empty lives and their distaste for each other: "Sincere."

Finally, there are children, Winthrop, who learns about that new, special place where dreams happen: "Gary Indiana."

They all have individual N energy that fits their specific predicament in the show, yet all of them fall under the umbrella of the community of River City being N. They are all longing for something new, different, and exciting.

A Chorus Line

All of the actors who are auditioning for a role in the chorus line are N characters. They all desperately want to be called back and then cast for the show. In the powerful opening number, "I Hope I Get It," they lament about how badly they *need this job.* How could we possibly not feel for them all?

They each have their own stories to tell about themselves and why it is so important to dance. Through the songs that they sing, each gives a different perspective as to how they became a dancer and what motivated them to be where they are today.

Morales explains her horrors at the Performing Arts School where she wasn't connecting with a strict and non-compassionate drama teacher: "Nothing."

Sheila, Bebe, and Maggie describe their home troubles in the song "At the Ballet," where the only place of refuge and safety was when they attended and watched ballet.

Cassie desperately wants to show the director that she still has it as an older dancer in the song "The Music and the Mirror." All she ever needed was the chance to dance again …

Each character individually has their own needs of unfulfillment, yearning, and a desire to reach their dream. Together, they are a community of N.

Resolvability

Always remember that the N energy must be resolvable in some way. We want to root for our N energy characters and, therefore, we must be able to believe that there is a possibility for them to get what they need. If there isn't a morsel of believability to the final outcome of the show, then there really isn't any reason for us to watch it. We're always hoping for the happy ending, even though many times it doesn't end the way we want it to!

The survival question

As a final way to check and see if a character is N, you should ask yourself the ultimate question: "Will these characters survive on their own in this show?" In other words, do they have a need that truly will cripple them in life if they don't get the need resolved? You must first refer back to your dramatic question and see whom you truly are rooting for in the show. From there, then ask the above question. If they are truly in need, you *will* be able to assess the importance of their need. It really must feel life-or-death important for the need to be resolved. If it doesn't, more than likely, it is not N energy.

Do keep in mind that *all* characters in a show have "needs." We are human. Nobody is totally complete as an individual – just ask Lancelot! We all have those hidden secrets in our lives that make us vulnerable and need-worthy. The key is following the needs of the characters that *are highlighted musically and lyrically* in that specific show by the composer, lyricist, and librettist. We must follow that and focus on the people we're rooting for in the dramatic question.

3

Life Force Energy in Lyric Analysis

LF – Life Force energy

Balancing the N energy characters are at least one or more Life Force energy characters. Life Force energy characters – designated by the letters LF – are the ones who have the independence, power, and vision to be able to help and guide the N energy characters towards their unresolved problems. They lead the N characters to the ultimate solution. LF characters are strong, passionate, forward in motion, and committed to their lives. They don't have any real needs that will destroy them within the show. They have a clear vision of how to live their lives and they will in some way help the N characters onto the right (or wrong) path. LF characters can be good people or bad people ("anti-LF characters"), thus the N characters must assess who to align with in order to find resolution. Just like N energy, LF energy can be attached to one single main character, to an ensemble of characters, or even to an entire town or community of characters. As long as they sing and/or dance quite a bit, they can be an energy.

Like N energy, we quantify LF energy characters through the music and lyrics that they sing, as well as the dances they perform. Keep in mind that LF characters can have "needs" within a show, but those needs are not sung about and they certainly aren't what we are rooting for in the musical. Just like N characters, LF characters will not have all of the following characteristics listed, but they will strongly have a few, depending on their type of character, their powers, motivations, and the plot line.

Figure 2, the Life Force Energy Lyric Circle, is a list of characteristics to look for in Life Force energy characters within the lyrics of their songs. Again, none in the circle is any more important than the other. All of them show a sign of a character or characters that have real power and drive in the musical. They propel the need characters and the musical along.

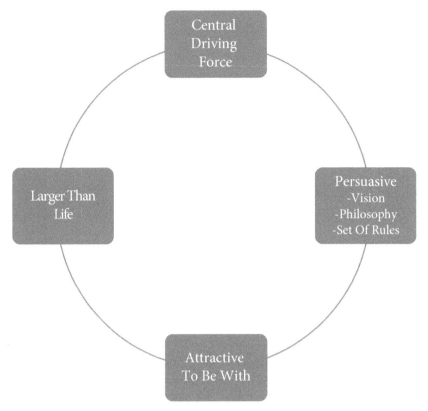

Figure 2 Life Force Energy Lyric Circle.

Central driving force

LF energy characters are absolutely positively the central driving force within a show. The minute they walk onto the stage, you know that you need to watch them and listen to them. They are self-assured, and they know where they belong and why. They have a magnetism, which causes the N characters to want to follow them immediately. They are directors. We know from watching the LF characters that they know where to go, what to think, how to do something, and where the action is. You just instinctively know that they are "where it's at" and therefore we will give them our attention. They in turn, will propel the musical along, giving it the momentum and direction.

The Fantasticks

A perfect example of the central driving force of a character is El Gallo. He glides onto the stage wearing a Zorro-type cape and hat, and literally sets up each scene and scenario that happens in the show. He's a narrator who helps guide all the other characters, as well as the audience. His first song, "Try To Remember" invites and encourages the audience to think back to a day when love was young and full of life. He wants us to follow him and to learn from him. Are we going to say no? Of course not. We're ready for the journey at hand.

Kinky Boots

Is there any question that Lola is a central driving force? She is the answer to Charlie Price's problems. With her direction, the factory can make boots for drag queens across the nation and world. It is just up to the factory employees to get on board with the programme. In "Land Of Lola," her explosive and charismatic persona, as well as her flamboyant apparel, automatically turns our heads towards her and makes us want to follow her the second she offers "*take my hand.*" She is a tour de force and there's no messing around with that lady of the stage!

Larger than life

LF energy characters are larger than life. They are larger than all other characters. This can be personified in many different ways. It can be through their position – that being a position of power – a president, a king or queen, the head of a household/parent, rich, athletic, physical, or one having social status. Whatever that power is, LF characters use it and N characters follow it. They can be magical, or hold special powers that no one else has, like a wizard or witch. They can also have great powers through their knowledge, education, experience, or wisdom. They are people that we look up to in some way. They have charisma, public speaking abilities, and are born leaders. Obviously, from the examples above, El Gallo and Lola also fit into this description. Usually, LF characters will have an abundance of LF characteristics.

The Phantom of the Opera

The Phantom is considered "a ghost." He is supernatural. He can make things happen inexplicably and devastatingly. He's evasive, unseen, and in the shadows. He magically appears in mirrors and sings to Christine in "The Mirror (Angel of Music)." How can anyone in that opera house fight that?

Another example is in the title song, "The Phantom of the Opera," when the Phantom sings about how his great powers over Christine continue to grow stronger *"inside your mind."* He has total power over her through some type of magic or telepathy. The power he has is the unknown, the inexplicable, and the shadows where no one can consciously figure out who or what he is.

The Light in the Piazza

Margaret is a strong woman and mother. She continues to care for her 26-year-old daughter Clara, who is developmentally challenged due to an accident. Given this fact, Margaret is a protective mother, wanting the absolute best for her child. She is powerful, smart, and wise, all by learning through experience. Most of all, she will always protect Clara, falling into that important maternal role during "Hysteria/Lullaby." Clara had gone into hysterics, trying to find Fabrizio. With her maternal instincts taking over, Margaret finds her, and calms her down by singing her a motherly lullaby. She is definitely the authority figure in the show.

Attractive to be with

The term "attractive" is much broader in context than just in *physical* attractiveness. LF characters tend to be "attractive," but more in an eye-catching way than a physical way. Yes, absolutely, LF characters can be physically attractive, and many times, they are, but it is more than that. It is the charisma that surrounds the individual, the power, and the leadership. I liken it to the way we all are attracted to a tornado or a tidal wave. They aren't necessarily pretty or handsome – they can be terrifying – but there is that sheer force of power that makes it irresistible for us to take our eyes off them. Who is not able to stare at El Gallo for a first time when he comes out in his Zorro-styled outfit in *The Fantasticks,* or when Curly enters, admiring the morning at the opening of the show *Oklahoma!*?

Miss Saigon

The Engineer is a hustler at Dreamland, a bar/brothel he owns in Saigon, Vietnam. He protects the women under his control, as long as they continue to make money for him. He's an "unconventional" entrepreneur – a sleazebag. Still, there is an attractiveness to him in the way he works things, and deals with things. He has power and he has the wit, and we can't keep our eyes off of him, in spite of the fact that he's a creep. His idea of the "American Dream" is not quite what we might have in mind – he twists it around, focusing on the ugliness and sinister part of it, to take advantage for his own gain.

Sunday in the Park with George

In the first act, George is the painter/artist George Seurat. He creates so much beauty in his paintings. Yet, he has a huge human flaw – he can't seem to give all of himself to Dot, his model and lover. It is difficult for him to balance his love of art with his love of Dot. He's perceived as being odd by the masses and they don't understand his paintings – his work. Yet, he still perseveres.

In "Opening Prelude to Sunday in the Park with George," we are mesmerized by what George can imagine and see. He can create incredible art from *"a blank page or canvas."* We are always attracted to what goes on in the mind of a genius – even though he may be at times difficult, rude, socially inadequate, self-centered, or kind.

Persuasive

LF characters are persuasive, and can be persuasive in both a positive and negative way. It is that power of persuasion that gets the unfulfilled N energy characters to go down that path of eventual solution. Absolutely, LF characters will use their power of persuasion hand in hand with their other powers – their attractiveness, their driving force, and their larger-than-life qualities. It is this power that must, at least in some way, answer to the N character's yearning and unfulfillment. In addition, it must be, or seem in some way to be, a possible solution to their dilemma.

Usually, when in the midst of persuasion, LF characters must be giving a credo of some type. Possibilities are:

- **Vision:** LF characters give their vision of how things will be if you follow their path. It can be a potential answer to the N character's "some factor" dream. If the N character is looking for that pot of gold at the end of the rainbow, LF characters have a vision that will tell them how to find it.
- **Philosophy or belief:** LF characters live a certain way, so therefore the N character should live that way too. If N characters are looking for confidence in how they should live, LF characters will show that confidence and persuade them to live with confidence too. LF characters live their **credo**, and set that example for everyone to see.
- **A set of rules:** LF characters oftentimes give N characters a set of rules – a code of operation – to abide by. They set the standard and they follow it in their own lives. They then persuade N energy characters to follow it too: "If you follow these rules, you will then be able to live the life that I lead."

The Music Man

The classic example is when Harold sings the song "Trouble." He's a salesman, but he can't get people to buy what he's selling – boy's band instruments and uniforms – unless they truly have a focused need and desire for it. Therefore, he concocts the notion that the billiard parlour in town will cause terrible moral problems for River City's youth. He persuades them to believe that they have a problem, even when perhaps they don't. By the end of the song, the entire town believes that they are turning into the "*Devil's playground.*"

Harold then gives them a vision of safety and moral citizenship by starting a boy's band in the song "Seventy-Six Trombones." The town imagines this boy's band as being the pinnacle of their town, the answer to all of their problems and dreams. Harold sets down the rules to achieve this – by appointing him as the leader of the band, to buy instruments to play, and to purchase uniforms. Suddenly, the River City residents become excited and energized with the whole idea of a boy's band – Harold Hill's persuasion is complete.

Gypsy

June has just left with Tulsa, which leaves Rose and Louise alone. Rose then, in her knock-down, boisterous, optimistic self, decides that she is going to make Louise a star. Louise isn't buying it. Rose then sings "Everything's Coming Up Roses," to convince Louise that everything is going to be fine, she will reach the stars and "*be great!*"

Here, Rose is not only giving Louise a vision, but she is also persuading her that it *will happen,* if she follows and trusts her. With a song and voice that big, how can you ignore it, let alone say no?

Single characters and communities

Just like N energy, LF energy can be personified through one character or more, as well as even an entire community. As long as they share common philosophies, beliefs, and visions, they can certainly be a community of LF. They must, however, sing a lot of music and/or dance a lot of music. The key is that characters are only considered for N energy or LF energy if they have a body of music to justify their existence in the overall plan of the show.

Brigadoon

The entire town of Brigadoon is made up of LF energy characters – they sing and dance to a ton of music. They are happy, complete, magical, attractive to be with, and full of the love and appreciation of life (except for Harry Beaton). Just in the opening song of "Brigadoon," when the fog lifts and this old town magically appears, you feel how enchanted and special the town is.

Even in that beginning magical moment, we feel that Brigadoon is a safe, wonderful place to live and find love. Individually, the characters and ensembles have their own stories to tell that explain their happiness and settled nature.

Fioni would like to have a love for life, but as she states in her song "Waitin' For My Dearie," she will not compromise and just marry any man. She's strong and self-assured.

Charlie, although he has known many a lass, will always be content in going home to his love, Bonnie Jean: "I'll Go Home to Bonnie Jean."

Meg is comfortable with many kinds of men and loves them all. She will seek out any available bachelor to court, similar to her mother in the story "My Mother's Wedding Day."

Cats

The entire group of cats is LF. Soooooooo much LF. Tooooooooo much LF! And that is why the show tends to drive a lot of people crazy. There is only one N energy character in the show, Grizabella, and she just isn't on stage enough to balance out the action and story. What we do have are a bunch of cats who really are satisfied in life, highly energetic, fun, and sassy.

Old Deuteronomy is the Leader cat – the most wise, one of the oldest, the most charming and gentle giant within the community. He leads them and gives them the set of rules for entering the Heaviside Layer. He also chooses the cat who will enter "The Journey to the Heaviside Layer."

Rum Tug Tugger is a Mick Jagger-type of cat who only eats and does what he wants, when he wants it. He has every girl cat scratching the claw bar in desire: "The Rum Tug Tugger." And there's nothing that any of the cats can do about that!

The Old Gumbie Cat is finicky as finicky can be. She decides what, when, who, and how, depending on her moment, as *she sits and sits.* At the end, she whisks away her large costume and goes into a massive, high-energy tap dance: "The Old Gumbie Cat."

In the LF community of cats, we are finding out about their personalities, traits, and desires, and frankly, they are charming. Most importantly, much to the chagrin of the story, they all really don't need anything, yet they are all being considered for the Heaviside Layer. That's an issue. Of course, we know it's going to be Grizabella, since she's the only cat who is ostracized and down on her luck. She's the only one who *needs* a second chance in life – all of the other cats will do just fine without it, so why would they want it in the first place?

Each LF character individually has already achieved their own fulfillment and groundedness in life. Together, they are a community of LF.

Unlike N energy, LF energy, however, can also be found in other dimensional planes through theatricality: a vision out there, a belief system, or the subconscious. There are very few instances of this type of LF (three shows to be exact at this point …) and so we will address those much later in the book. For now, let's just work on grasping the understanding of LF usages that are found in the majority of musicals.

The survival question

You can ask the same ultimate survival question when it comes to LF energy characters: "Will these characters survive on their own in this show?" The key here is " … in this show." If you ask this question about a LF character, your answer will always be yes. These characters are going to be ok – they will survive – whether or not they have some ongoing "need" in the show. These characters are fulfilled. They are the mentors. They will continue to go on about their lives regardless of whether the N energy characters follow along with them or not. They can be hurt, discouraged, or even frustrated at the end, but they will still *survive*. As in the end of "The Fantasticks," El Gallo says in his last lines that he did purposely hurt the families so that they learn about themselves and the harshness of life, but unfortunately for him, he hurt "*a little bit, too.*"

He's a survivor!

4

Alignment Energy in Lyric Analysis

A – Alignment energy

"Start your engines!" The Alignment energy, designated by the letter A, is when the engine of the car starts up and we know where we are heading on our journey. This is where we feel confident in the direction of the show. It is that "Ah ha!" moment where we finally know where we are going and why. We know what the musical is all about and we even can project a wanted conclusion to the show. That ending is what we are rooting for. *The A is not necessarily musical in nature.* It is where the LF and N energy characters intersect together in some way – they *align*.

In order for that alignment to occur, both the LF and N characters must have performed at least one song. This doesn't necessarily mean that a song or dance has to be performed in its entirety before the A comes into play. It does mean, however, that the LF and N characters have defined and represented their energy through music.

The A also states the dramatic question and the distance of the show. We now understand where the show is taking us but not necessarily how. That's what gives the show its interest and drive. We want to find out how the show will end, and how we will get there. It's basically saying, "This is the trip we're on, and c'mon along!"

The A is a gut feeling. Sometimes, the LF and N are introduced, and it still doesn't quite feel like we know where the show is going. We have an inkling, but we still need more time. Generally, in those cases, it just takes another song to solidify the idea. A rule of thumb is that the A needs to happen within the first twenty minutes of a show. If it doesn't happen by then, audiences tend to get antsy and start asking questions like, "Why am I watching this?" – the kiss of death to a writer.

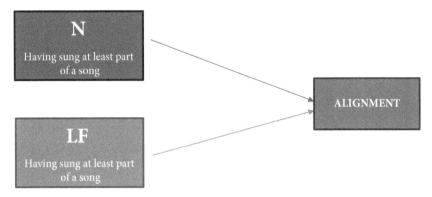

Figure 3 Alignment Energy.

The Light in the Piazza

In this wonderfully delightful musical, the show begins with Margaret and Clara, who are mother and daughter, visiting Florence in 1953. In the first song, "Statues and Stories," we see that Margaret is definitely in control of the tour, introducing Clara to the magical city of art and light. We notice that Clara is uncharacteristically social to strangers and her actions seem more child-like in nature. We also see that Margaret is very protective of her. In the song, we begin to understand this mother/daughter relationship, and with it, realizing that the protective Margaret feels like LF while the protected Clara feels like N. Suddenly, the wind magically blows off Clara's hat and floats gently through the air, right into the hands of an Italian stranger – a young man, age appropriate to Clara. Their eyes meet and immediately we understand love at first sight. Fabrizio introduces himself to Clara, singing his name. Clara enchantedly sings back hers. Immediately following that exchange, we watch Margaret trying to get Clara away from the stranger, but nothing is going to keep them apart. Clara gives Fabrizio their hotel name, and Margaret pulls her away and exits.

What we don't know at this point, is whether Fabrizio is LF or N. We get a sense that he is N due to his youth, exuberance, and lack of English communication, but that is not enough. It is, however, enough to know the alignment. The song "Il Mundo Era Vuoto" will finally define Fabrizio's N energy solidly.

The A happens right at the moment of love at first sight when Clara and Fabrizio sing their names, formally introduced by the magical hat. We know those two should belong together and we know that Margaret wants nothing of it. Their love is destiny – initiated by magic!

Les Misérables

Immediately at the beginning of the show, we see the plights and cruelness of the authorities over the criminals of the day. We learn that Valjean has been unjustly incarcerated for nineteen years due to his stealing of a loaf of bread, and then trying to escape from prison. Javert sees him as a criminal for life and will never see him as being free when his probation occurs. The "scarlet letter" of the yellow slip will always take away any freedom and rights that Valjean should have. The lines have been drawn immediately between Javert, the authoritarian LF character, and Valjean, the poor N character victim. What we aren't sure of yet is which way Valjean will go once he is "free." A Bishop saves him from hunger and gives him shelter and food – LF. Valjean responds to his generosity by fleeing in the night, stealing some of the church's silver. The authorities catch him, but the Bishop again saves him by stating that the silver was a gift and that in his rush to leave, Valjean forgot two silver candelabras. Once the authorities leave, the Bishop uses the moment with Valjean to teach him an important lesson in paying it forward, now that God has taken hold of his soul. It is at that moment that Valjean starts to become a changed man when he sings "What Have I Done?" The line has been drawn between good and evil, and he chooses good. We now want to know whether Valjean will find reconciliation and peace within himself and the world around him.

The A is when he sings "What Have I Done?" Of course, the crowd goes crazy after that song!

5

Growth Moment Energy in Lyric Analysis

GM – Growth Moment energy

The Growth Moment or GM is when we have arrived at our trip destination. (How ironic that GM also stands for General Motors.) It is the total source of satisfaction and resolve in a show. It is always found somewhere at the end of the show, although not always at the *very end* of the show. The GM gives the characters and audience members a sense of completeness. It is where the N characters are resolved and the LF and N characters come together in some way. Most importantly, the GM answers the dramatic question.

In many instances, the GM "drops the curtain." The GM can be the big climatic moment in the show where once it is over, the audience jumps to their feet and applauds with hoots and hollers of appreciation. Most of the time, the GM is musical in nature – a song – and that song will be a biggie. It takes the N energy in all its glory, and presto, resolves it. Most times, the N character(s) that we are rooting for are singing the GM song, since it is their realization and resolution.

Musically, the GM can be big or small. Typically, in older shows, it is that song at the end that finishes with a bang. Newer shows don't feel compelled to do that. In *Pippin*'s case, it has an anti-GM where the world of the main characters are stripped down to bare bones, including the disappearance of sets, lights, costumes, and even orchestra. Total silence. Nevertheless, Pippin, Catherine, and Theo accept their lot in life by standing together and holding firm to their beliefs. Just the opposite is "Home" from *The Wiz*, where Dorothy sings about her realization that there is "no place like home." This song has the booming ending, the blaring brass, and at the finale, the curtain falling with Toto running on to greet Dorothy back home. Done.

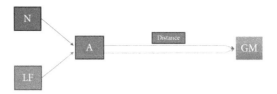

Figure 4 Growth Moment Energy.

The GM has a few possibilities or clues to look for when approaching the end of the show.

A feeling

The GM is definitely "a feeling." It is a sense of completion that both N characters and audience feel. It is that sense of finality and satisfaction that we get when we have finally accomplished a long-standing dream of ours. In *Brigadoon,* when Mr Lundie allows Tommy back into Brigadoon to be with Fiona at the end of the show, he tells us to always believe in the power of love. It's the moment to savour and cherish.

A change

In some way, a change happens during the GM. Usually, this is with the N characters, but not always. Sometimes, both the N and the LF characters have changed to a point. They have grown in their journey and cannot turn back to their old selves. "I used to be this way, but now I've changed." We may indeed not like the way the person has changed, however, the change has happened and this change has resolved the show. In *Kinky Boots*, to everyone's celebration, we see the factory workers come out one by one in flamboyant costumes topped with amazing kinky boots. They finally embraced change, and celebrated sexual freedom in the song "Raise You Up."

A celebration or victory

I think this one is self-explanatory. Many shows end with some type of celebration or victory in which the characters or entire cast come out to sing happily of the resolution. It can be a celebration of marriage, for example, "How Do You Solve a Problem Like Maria Reprise" in *The Sound of Music* movie, or a celebration of a life, for instance, "Long Live God/Prepare Ye The Way Reprise" in *Godspell*. Whatever it is, they sing about it and the N is resolved.

A surrender or admission

"I was wrong and I admit it." How many times have married couples or friends had incredibly intense arguments or breakups, and then finally, in the end, have an admission or surrender from one or both of them that breaks the ice and resolves the dispute? It can be the same thing with a GM. Rose, in the musical *Gypsy*, singing "Rose's Turn" is a classic example of finally admitting to her weaknesses and insecurities.

A new resolve

Here's the GM that many audience members loathe, but they have to accept it because it is indeed a GM that still resolves. A new resolve is where the characters don't get the resolution that they are yearning for. Instead, they gain new insight from the alternative resolution. "I can live a more enriched life now, even though this one didn't work out." It can be the ultimate bummer! When we are in trouble in life, sometimes the answers that we are begging for don't appear at the end in the form we wanted. The married couple ends in divorce. The couple doesn't get together in the end because they know in the long term that it just wouldn't stick. Usually, there is a change in those people and a wisdom that comes from that change.

This sometimes happens in musicals. We may not like the ending, but we do accept it because it is the right, more believable, and honest ending. In *West Side Story*, we want Tony and Maria to be able to hop on a bus and to live happily ever after somewhere else, but it just doesn't happen that way, does it? From Tony and Bernardo's deaths, the kids learn from it, and finally understand the senselessness of fighting and violence. In the end, they all lift Tony up and process out in unification with music underscoring – a bummer ending but a believable one, and one that does resolve the N.

It is important to take note that the GM does not mean that suddenly the N characters become LF. That is not correct. They do not become LF. The GM only means that the N is resolved and that the show is, in essence, over. The dramatic question is answered. Don't get confused by thinking that the energies then "switch." Character energies generally do not switch throughout the run of a musical, unless they are musicals that are specifically designed with that technique written right into the storyline. Those musicals are very uncommon. We will discuss this energy shift in detail later, when we talk about ground plans.

Codas

Sometimes, a GM happens but then the musical continues on for awhile. In this case, usually there are certain unresolved issues within the storyline that still need to be answered. It is this epilogue time after the GM that we call the coda of the musical. A good example is in the movie *The Sound of*

Music. The GM of the show is the marriage of Maria and the Captain. We are totally satisfied and feel the show is in its completion. Maria is resolved, and the children are resolved. However, the issue of the Nazis and war still linger on. We want our Trapp family to be safe and we don't want to see the Captain have to leave his family and fight for the Nazis. So the last twenty-five minutes of the movie resolves that issue. Take note that there are no new songs – only reprises – and the Nazis and nuns don't sing, so there really aren't any LF or N energy fights happening during this time. Thus, the main GM is the marriage. At the end of the coda, we hear the chorus singing "Climb Every Mountain" in the background while the Trapp family is hiking their way to freedom. This becomes another climax, but strictly a coda resolution – kind of like putting a cherry on top of a big sundae that's already been made.

The musical *Oklahoma!* is another example of this. The song "Oklahoma" actually is the GM of the show. Laurey and Curly are married – end of story. They celebrate with the song. However, we still have to deal with a missing piece of the puzzle, and that is Judd. So, the musical goes on and on and on to deal with that, and frankly, nobody cares. It's a coda, it ties up all the loose ends, and the married couple can finally leave to live happily ever after. Hopefully, this happens before the audience falls asleep, since the N energy was resolved miles earlier.

The Fantasticks

In *The Fantasticks*, the dramatic question of the show is "*Will Matt and Louisa learn the true realities of a mature and sustaining relationship?*" Both Matt and Louisa were pretty naïve and their world view was fairly sheltered. They both needed to learn and experience the world a little bit more before really taking their relationship seriously. Both are N characters. So, Henry and Mortimer, LF characters, have taken Matt to "experience the world" as well as El Gallo, LF, taking Louisa to watch and "see the world." Matt's experiences are painful and torturous. Louisa watches his experiences from afar – first seeing him in pain, and then seeing him through a mask that makes the scene delightful to her. Once it is over, Matt is discarded, unloaded back at home, broken down and alone. El Gallo abandons Louisa. They both find each other bruised, and willing to talk truthfully about their experiences and the world. They then sing "They Were You" to reaffirm their love in a genuine and eyes-wide-open way. The dramatic question is answered. Matt and Louisa's need is resolved.

This is an example of a quiet, thoughtful GM. It doesn't necessarily bring down the curtain, but it certainly is the resolution that the audience adores. A little coda follows with the fathers entering to welcome their kids back, and El Gallo singing a reprise of "Try to Remember," to end the show. Beautiful, quiet resolution.

Miss Saigon

In *Miss Saigon*, the dramatic question is "*Will Kim and Chris brave all of the adversities of the world to finally have a life together?*" Both Kim and Chris are N characters. The war is over, and Chris' friend John (LF) is now working for an organization that brings out-of-wedlock Vietnamese children back to their American veteran fathers. John has found Kim and her son Tam, and he arranges a meeting between them and Chris. Chris unfortunately is now married to Ellen (LF). As the story builds, meetings are missed, but Ellen and Kim finally do meet, and Ellen tells Kim that Chris is married to her. Crushed, Kim leaves. Ellen gives Chris a final ultimatum that it is either her or Kim, and Chris chooses Ellen. Chris finally connects with Kim, and in a moment of total anguish where she assures Tam that he will grow up to be American, Kim shoots herself. Chris finds her, holds her, and as she's dying, she sings in "The Finale" the question of how they ever got to this point. As she dies and Chris mourns her, the orchestra builds to a climax and ends the show.

The GM in this show is the song "The Finale" when Kim dies and Chris mourns her death. The curtain drops immediately afterward. It's a big, dramatic ending that does answer the dramatic question, but it doesn't necessarily end the way the audience would like to see it end. It's tragic. Kim's death does resolve her need and Chris' need, as sad as the ending is. Very powerful.

6

Basic Need and Life Force Energy Characteristics in Music Analysis

Music analysis overview

Trying to analyse music as N and LF energy is much harder and much more subjective in nature than in lyric analysis. Music is difficult to nail down into actual categories because music parallels emotions and both emotions and music are abstract. Lyrics have the advantage of clearly defining the intention of the character through verbal communication. Music doesn't have that advantage. To borrow a line from the movie *Close Encounters of the Third Kind*, when the music scientist is trying to communicate to the mother ship by playing the same notes that the mother ship is playing, he states in exasperation, "What are we saying to each other?"[1] Music has ambiguity, subtleness, and unexplainable emotional nuance. Articulating music can only be done in the abstract and in how we as individuals emotionally react to it. Just as emotions aren't black and white, neither too is music.

So how do we utilize and understand the power of music within N and LF energy, if music can only abstractly describe what a character is going through at that moment? Is there a concrete connection between music and the energies? Is there a way to listen to the music and have it help us support whether the character is N or LF energy? I believe so.

Music is pure truth

Music analysis must be character-based and character-driven – not the other way around. Whatever the character is feeling emotionally, the music should and will parallel those emotions. Where it gets really tricky, is when the character isn't being honest about his/her own feelings, or when the character is *unaware* of his/her own feelings. Just as we must analyse the lyrics and look into its subtext, we must also do that with the music. Music will not lie. Music is the character's ally to whatever emotional state she/he is in at that moment. Music is the companion of the lyrics and will not fight with them. Music is the heart and breadth of the character, so whatever the music is doing, it is singing/playing pure truth. It just may be that the character is *unaware* of that truth.

Before we attempt to analyse Need and Life Force energy characteristics in music, we all must first have a basic music reference point – an agreed-upon rubric to compare our analysis with. When we are talking about something as subjective as music, we need to keep our reference points very general in nature. So when we talk about a basic, fundamental, **stereotypical** N or LF energy song, what music characteristics could we all agree with in very general terms to create this rubric? I believe those characteristics are found in basic elementary music timbres.

Basic Need Energy Music Characteristics

N energy music very generally tends to be ballads. The music is following the unfulfillment and tentativeness of our N characters. They are longing for something, or they are in trouble and need help. All of these characteristics tend to lend themselves to a ballad-style song. They are slower in tempo, building on the dream or contemplativeness of the character. They tend to be love songs, or lament songs. Slower, more thoughtful songs give us time as audience members to really listen to and understand the lyrics. It allows us the time to truly soak in the N characters' dilemma and in turn, feel for them. These songs tend to start softly and eventually have a nice dynamic arc to them, where at the climactic moment we hear the pivotal emotional peak in both volume and journey.

Because of the soft nature of stereotypical N energy songs, orchestrations tend to be more string and woodwind prevalent, versus brass and percussion. The use of harp, bells, acoustic guitars, and brushes versus sticks in percussion all lend themselves well to N energy. Any instrument that softly blends in with the tenderness of the moment will be the more predominant instruments. "Some Enchanted Evening" from *South Pacific*, begins with strings alone,

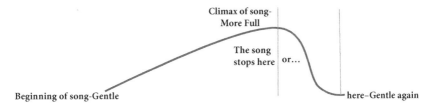

Figure 5 Traditional Slow Song Growth Arc.

while "I Dreamed a Dream" from *Les Misérables* starts with strings and an oboe, to grasp the intimacy of the moment. In "Still Hurting" from the *Last Five Years*, a lone simple piano part begins the song. All three then grow to a major climax by the end of the piece. They are all good examples of this traditional ballad.

In summary, the following seven basic characteristics are good indicators of traditional, *truthful* N energy music:

Ballad-style song
Ballads can be love songs, or songs that tend to be more personal in nature. They open your heart more. They tend to give us pause to really think about and feel for an individual. They take their time and offer us a breathing spot within the show where we really can reflect on characters and their inner workings.

Softer
Softer can mean both volume: pp, p, and mp, or it can also mean tactile: a song that is not "in your face." More subtle and nuanced.

Melodic
Any musical theatre composer would argue that all music is melodic, however, with Need songs, you can definitely count on the music being very melodic and beautiful in nature. It's the "opera aria" of the work. The melodies generally are more memorable, and easier to grasp, partly because they are slower and easier to pick up.

Legato
The music tends to flow more smoothly, like a gentle brook, versus the rushing rapids of a river. It's more tender.

Slower
The tempo tends to be slower in nature. This is due partly to the fact that we then can take our time comprehending what the N characters are going through and needing. If we lose track of that, we then lose track of why we are rooting for them.

Has a traditional growth arc in the song

A traditional growth arc is this intrinsic feeling of continuing growth and momentum in a piece. It starts quietly, reflectively, simply, and as the song continues, it begins to grow, perhaps in volume, fullness of orchestra, tempo, or even pitch and higher keys. It continues to grow into an emotional climax that generally is supported with volume and fullness that peaks at that moment. It will tend to have the singer in their strongest, highest vocal range, as well as in their loudest portion of the piece. The composer might also insert a modulation (key change) at this point and repeat the chorus one more time to climax the piece even more. A growth arc can end at this climax, or it can settle back down to a very simple, quiet, tender, and thoughtful ending.

Strings/woodwind/quieter acoustic instruments are prevalent

Instrumentation is key to supporting the emotion of the song. In a Need song, quieter instruments tend to be used because of all the timbre reasons above. They must reflect what the song is trying to get across. We must be able to hear every lyric the character is singing. The other main instrument families – brass and percussion – tend to be used more so for the climaxes and fortes of the songs. They tend to be splashes in the piece versus integral parts.

Need energy music as interpreted in dance

Because of these lighter, softer uses of music, N energy dance numbers tend to be more gentle, subtle, and romantic. There is a sense of emotional expression that mirrors the immense desire of fulfillment within N characters. Lone soliloquies or secret moments with a partner are prevalent. N energy dances tend to open a window to the soul of the characters that we are rooting for. It can be a secret moment that is only shared between that character and the audience.

Basic Life Force Energy Music Characteristics

Stereotypical LF energy songs tend to follow the characteristics of LF energy as a whole: bold, confident, rhythmic, powerful, strong, and passionate.

They tend to be faster in tempo, thrusting the music more forward in motion. An LF song is like a really good rock tune. You can't help but join in with foot tapping, clapping, and dancing. The songs take control over you – an attractiveness that lulls you into wanting to join them. There is also a feeling of grounding and satisfaction in the songs – much to do with their credo, philosophy, or belief – that gives the music a sense of confidence and thrust.

LF songs are orchestrated using the more powerful families of instruments: percussion, brass, and loud, aggressive electronic instruments. It's that "in your face" articulation that makes you take notice. The music demands attention, and splashes of brass and percussion gets that notice. Take note of the song "Seventy-Six Trombones" from *The Music Man* or "So You Wanted to Meet the Wizard" from *The Wiz*. Songs will grab your attention when the sounds of an entire brass section start blaring out at you. Simple physics! In the song "Footloose" from *Footloose*, right away you are slapped in the face with the glissando of the piano, the electric lead guitar blaring, and the tom toms banging a tribal beat. You have no choice but to take notice! And these songs never let up. They continue getting stronger until the end of the piece.

In summary, the following seven basic characteristics are good indicators of traditional, *truthful* LF energy music:

Rhythm/anthem song
If LF characters are the central driving force of a musical, their music must also reflect that. LF music must exude strong energy. Rhythm gives the music the strong beat and presence required to gain the audience's attention. It needs to move people along, and get them to follow. It is eye opening, vital, and powerful in its feel.

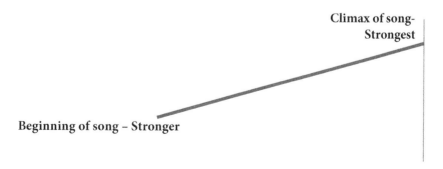

Figure 6 Traditional LF Growth Plane.

Anthems are proclamations of credo, philosophy, and belief. They are strong and mighty. They cannot be swayed. People will give up their lives before they give up their anthems. Think of when one of the US team wins a gold medal in the Olympics and "The Star Spangled Banner" is played.

Louder

Loud can mean both mf, f, and ff, or a song that is more "in your face." You aren't supposed to ignore the traditional LF song; so therefore, a strong, loud presence will attract your attention and focus you on the character singing.

Melodic, yet more rhythmic

Again, composers claim that all of their music is melodic, but you will find LF music has more balance between rhythm and melody. After all, LF characters know what they want in life and they go for it, so the rhythmic pulsating energy should be there. However, a great LF song will also have a great melody line too.

Attacking/articulate

This sits right alongside the rhythm. Surprising attacks or slams of bright instruments for affect is all about LF energy. We never want to lose track of who is singing – the central driving force of the song. Clarity and brightness are all necessary items in an articulate LF song. LF characters want to get their point across, and so does their music.

Faster

LF music doesn't want to give anyone the chance to get lulled into a sense of complacency or mellowness. Faster tempos mean higher energy.

More direct, "in your face" all the way through

LF music has a purpose and that is to persuade you to follow the character's wishes. The music will be more "in your face" so that you will pay attention and heed what they are saying – thus, louder, attacking, more rhythmic music. They demand to be listened to and reckoned with.

Brass/percussion/louder electronic instruments are prevalent

Instrumentation again is key to supporting the LF energy of the song. In a LF song, louder instruments tend to be used because of all of the reasons above. They must reflect what the song is trying to get across. We must be able to feel the energy of the LF character's central driving force. The other main instrument families – violins and woodwinds – tend to be used more so for "breathing areas" of the song where we rest the characters for a moment or the characters change their tactic for emotional effect.

Life Force Energy Music as interpreted in dance

Many times, the high-energy dance numbers are LF energy songs. This is due to the power of the rhythm, energy, syncopation, and thrust of the music. It's the kind of dance piece that can receive huge applause and screams afterwards. The tempos are quick and catching, the dance moves are high voltage and powerful, and they can be extremely celebratory in nature. Again, it's the attitude of the LF characters that dance is portraying, so the dances take control and run.

Basic Music Characteristics is only the beginning

If all N and LF energy music followed the above elementary patterns, the musical theatre world would be pretty darn boring and eventually clichéd and formulaic. Period.

However, these indicators are extremely prevalent in both old and new musicals. What we must realize, however, is that this is NOT the cardinal rule of N and LF energy music. There are incredible exceptions to this basic rule, and this is what makes music so absolutely fascinating, yet difficult to analyse. Nevertheless, in having these basic characteristics *as a foundation*, we now have a reference point and springboard for comparison with other music energy forms. In essence, we now are all on the same page. With this basic premise in mind, we're now ready to dig deeper into our characters and the music that accompanies them.

One might ask, "But what about a show like *The Fantasticks* or *You're a Good Man Charlie Brown* that only has three or four instruments – piano, harp, string bass, and percussion? How can you analyse music that is so trim and concise in its scope? All of the music sounds quiet, doesn't it?" Again, you have to look at the music within its own canvas. A Need song like "Much More" in *The Fantasticks* has that ballad style, is quiet in many parts, legato, slower, and has an arc to the song with a big climax at the end. The arrangement of the song mirrors those qualities – the piano is more melodic and legato in its accompaniment, the harp is more angelic and soft, and the bass is pizzicato. But an LF song like "It Depends On What You Pay" has the same small set of instruments, yet it gives us more rhythm in the song, more volume, more attack and articulation, faster, and is persuasively in your face the entire way through. The percussion and piano attack is quite different and the harp takes more of a backseat. So comparatively speaking, the analysis still works. One just has to keep it within its own musical parameters and proportional perspectives.

Note

1   *Close Encounters of the Third Kind* (1978), [Film] Dir. Steven Spielberg.

7

The Need Energy Music Circle of Truth

As stated before, characters, like all human beings, are complex creatures. Many times we tell the truth. We say exactly what we are feeling. Other times, we don't tell the truth – sometimes knowingly and other times unknowingly. Sometimes we say things just to get our own way, using tactics that aren't necessarily how we truly feel, but how the opposing character feels, therefore favourably reacting to what we say. We manipulate, we vacillate, and we change our minds – again knowingly or unknowingly. When music is composed for characters at a specific time, the music will always follow the characters' lead. The music will be as honest as the characters are honest. If characters are sharing their utmost secret, the music will reflect that. If characters are lying to someone or to themselves, the music will also reflect that. Whatever mindset the characters are in, the music will mirror that.

Music is always speaking the truth.

The Need Energy Music Circle of Truth consists of five different "character mindset" levels for Need characters. Under each level is a description of how the characters perceive and act upon their pure truth. These numerical levels are not in any way suggesting an order of depth in psychology or subtext, i.e. going from a shallow to a deep-seated psychological place. All are equal in their own way. What the levels do describe is where characters stand in regard to their own pure truth and whether characters are even *aware* of that pure truth. It is this information that clearly prescribes and justifies the necessary music that accompanies the character – whether the N song indeed *sounds like the traditional, basic N song or sounds like its traditional, basic LF opposite*. Hold tight – we'll get to this explanation in a bit.

N Energy General Music Characteristics	LF Energy General Music Characteristics
• Ballad-style song • Softer • Melodic • Legato • Slower • Has a traditional growth arc in the song • Strings/Woodwinds/Quieter acoustic instruments are prevalent	• Rhythm/Anthem song • Louder • Melodic, yet more rhythmic • Attacking/Articulate • Faster • More direct, in your face all the way through • Brass/Percussion/Louder electronic instruments are prevalent

Figure 7 N and LF Energy General Music Characteristics Table.

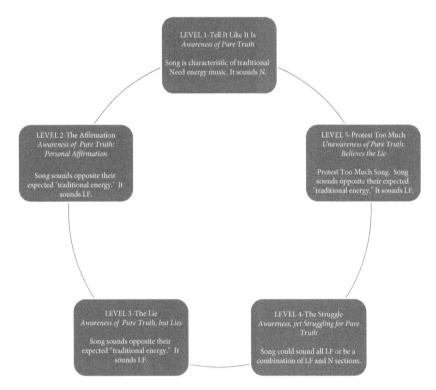

Figure 8 Need Energy Music Circle of Truth.

Level 1–Tell It Like It Is

This is the most common of the levels and the one that we should always begin with as a starting point after analysing the characters through lyric analysis and initial music listening. Level 1–Tell It Like It Is is where N characters are aware of their pure truth and then sing about it. In other words, the N characters know what they are missing in their lives, or why they are unfulfilled, or know that they are in trouble, or know that they need help. With this awareness, they sing about it truthfully, either to other characters or to the audience. They are in essence telling it like it is – they have this problem and they are wishing for or wanting a solution. They just aren't sure how to get it.

So how does the music reflect this state of character?

Level 1–Tell It Like It Is follows the Basic Need Energy Music Characteristics – ballad-style, softer, melodic, legato, slower, has a traditional growth arc in the song, and the strings and woodwinds are the dominant family of instruments. Perhaps it won't have all of these qualities, but it will have a lot of them. Again, we are looking at music in a very general, large canvas approach. Of course, all music is very complicated, both structurally and orchestrally in its arrangements. But, by assimilating all of this general information about a song, one can come up with character justifications as to whether the music in a song leans towards N or LF energy. We always have to look at the large brushstrokes of the canvas.

Cats

"Memory," sung by Grizabella, is a classic example of a Level 1–Tell It Like It Is song. Grizabella is an outcast, alone, looked down upon by the rest of the cat community. She sings about better days and dreams, wishing for another chance in life. She is desperate. The music reflects this pain beautifully in traditional Basic Need Energy Music Characteristics. It's a ballad, slow, legato, and its melody line has made it into the world hit that it is still today. The growth arc in the song is classic – starting very soft and descriptive, then growing and growing until the final key change where it hits this huge climactic ending – Grizabella's final plea to have someone touch her. The instrumentation follows this growth, beginning with soft, sparse instruments – a soft electric piano and solo clarinet – and then growing until the entire orchestra supports her, complete with horns and percussion. The song is following the growing emotions within Grizabella – first quiet and contemplative, lulling her back to a time of happiness and memory, and then by the end of the song, her emotions are full of desperation which requires the bigger, bolder sound.

Les Misérables

Fantine's "I Dream a Dream" is another classic example following the same characteristics as "Memory." Fantine is desperate too, needing love, help, and support. This song is also a ballad, slow, legato, and melodic. The music starts with quietly pulsating string instruments and acoustic guitar, but then continues growing to a full orchestral climax with timpani, cymbal rolls, and horns. These types of songs tend to be the memorable, loved songs of the show, and as stated above, the ones that become the hits. People relate to the vulnerability in these songs and delight in the growth climax. Audiences will always root for and relate to the oppressed characters. Songs like this allow the audiences to take a breath, and totally relate to these characters both in experiences and in emotion.

The Phantom of the Opera

"Think of Me" and "Wishing You Were Somehow Here Again" are both good, strong, typical examples of Level 1–Tell It Like It Is songs. They too reflect the traditional generic characteristics of need music. Christine's N songs are ballads, softer, smoother, and melodic in nature. The growth arcs are huge, with big, loud climactic finales, complete with full orchestration, forte, and vocally extreme high notes for Christine at the end. The instrumentation again is softer in nature, with strings and woodwinds taking the lead. At the finales, splashes of brass and percussion help with the climax. Christine's singing of "Think of Me" is expressing her lack of self-confidence as well as her subtextually needing Raoul to think of her. That unfulfillment is expressed through the emotional growth arc of the song, growing to a huge pleading climax at the end. "Wishing You Were Somehow Here Again" is expressing her loss of her father and her need to have him back with her. Again, she's opening up her heart to her utmost secret and that secret is quiet, tender, and emotionally melodic, with the huge growth arc paralleling her increased need for him at the end.

When starting your music analysis process, always first begin by seeing if each song fits Level 1–Tell It Like It Is. This is the most common level, the most traditional level, and the one that we tend to relate to most predominantly when listening to music. If the song doesn't fit this level, then you need to start going around the rest of the circle to try and find the level that does fit the song.

Levels 2–5

The rest of the levels, 2 to 5, are Need songs that sound like the Basic *Life Force* Energy Music Characteristics. What? How can that be? How can a N character have LF music characteristics? If characters are unfulfilled, hurting, lost, troubled, empty, or ignored, how could they possibly sing a song that is loud, attacking, fast, rhythmic, and in-your-face?

Consider these emotions: frustration, exasperation, helplessness, desperation, angst, revengefulness, hate, hurtful, and agony. How many of you would be quiet if you were suffering from this? And that is the point. We're complicated emotional creatures. This is why music is so wonderful for characters – it reaches those nuances and complexities in emotion when simple words no longer satisfy. We can be so hurting and unfulfilled that we lash out at someone or something. We can be so lost and scared in our lives that we actually laugh about it – we either do that or we allow ourselves to totally disintegrate into a pathetic pile of sorrow! How many times have you told a joke when something drastically cataclysmic has happened in your life? How many times have you been vicious because you've been hurt so badly and are so desperately in need of something? How many times have you laughed because something hurts so badly? How many times have you screamed at someone while you're crying uncontrollably? How many times have you laughed at a funeral? All of these circumstances and infinitely more, are reasons for having Need songs with Basic LF Music Characteristics.

Another consideration for these characteristics is for structural reasons. Musicals should have a balance between the numbers of N and LF songs in a show. Considering that the average musical has between twenty and twenty-six songs per show, there should be between ten and thirteen N songs and ten and thirteen LF songs each. If it doesn't, the musical may feel lopsided and therefore unbalanced, giving you a feeling like an unaligned steering wheel in a car. However, having ten to thirteen slow, ballad-style, Level 1– Tell It Like It Is Need songs in a show would kill the momentum of the show. Slower songs literally slow down shows, and if you have too many slow songs, the show progressively decelerates and dies. For all of these reasons, this is why we must have the following four other levels of music truths.

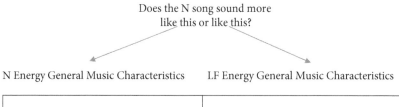

Does the N song sound more
like this or like this?

N Energy General Music Characteristics | LF Energy General Music Characteristics

N Energy General Music Characteristics	LF Energy General Music Characteristics
• Ballad-style song • Softer • Melodic • Legato • Slower • Has a traditional growth arc in the song • Strings/Woodwinds/Quieter acoustic instruments are prevalent	• Rhythm/Anthem song • Louder • Melodic, yet more rhythmic • Attacking/Articulate • Faster • More direct, in your face all the way through • Brass/Percussion/Louder electronic instruments are prevalent

Figure 9 Does the N Song Sound More Like This or Like This?

Level 2–The Affirmation

Level 2–The Affirmation is where characters are aware of their pure truth – their needs – and they sing about their woes in personal affirmation. They are singing about their state of being. They are at the cusp of peak emotional height. They are at the point of "I know this to be true" and "I'm going to complain about, scream about it, and be in-your-face about it." The characters are very matter of fact in this type of song. These songs tend to be more of desperation and angst. They are clawing their way up through their darkness, trying desperately to be honoured, respected, loved, treated well, fairly, and equally. But it is also the song which indicates that characters are more at their wit's end.

This is why the Level 2–The Affirmation song musically sounds like a traditional LF song. The emotions are so raw and unfiltered that the characters feel an incredible need to sing it from the rooftops. They don't want to be quiet about it – they hurt and they need to let it out.

Annie

"It's A Hard Knock Life" is a great example of a Level 2–The Affirmation song. It sounds like a LF song right from its opening sequence – the electric piano is sharply hitting chords to the beat, the tuba is bouncing in syncopation, and the percussion is hitting the beat on a closed high-hat. Immediately you feel the rhythm and want to be a part of it. All the kids are complaining about their troubled, oppressed lives, yet they have no answers for it. It's their *personal affirmation* of the fact that their lives SUCK! They are indeed singing in truth about their woes. Meanwhile, even though this song is about the abusiveness of children, we in the audience are still smiling, tapping our feet, and having a good time watching them being oppressed. Sick huh? The bottom line is, if they had written a Level 1–Tell It Like It Is song, the show would've stopped in its tracks with the audience bawling in their seats – not to mention the fact that everyone would never allow the evil Mrs Hannigan a chance at being comical. They would want her head and dead!

Rent

"Take Me or Leave Me" is another strong example of a Need song that characteristically sounds like a traditional LF song. Maureen and Joanne are singing their need through their angst, and that angst is reflected completely in the music through hard, rhythmic rock and roll syncopation, by the piano, electric bass, and closed high-hat with sticks. Maureen is lashing out at Joanne, telling her to accept her flirting as a part of her personality or to break up and leave the relationship. Both are fighting like cats and dogs for their position, meanwhile both are hurting inside and desperately not wanting to break up. They just want the other one to give in to their demands. They are being very truthful about their positions. As they really start to get into it, the song grows into a kind of gospel revival-tune-fight between the two, supported by a gospel rock band sound of electric organ, electric guitar, bass, drums, and piano. It's passionate and heart-felt, and neither are giving up. It's in your face because they are bold and, frankly, stubborn N characters!

Evita

Eva is a very complicated character. She has all the "qualities" of a LF character but she is really N and that is what makes her character so fascinating and difficult to analyse. She is the character that we are rooting for – we want the best for her. We want her to become the head of Argentina. We want her to be the voice of the people. We want her to be caring: to take care of the country in a good and honest way. In the song "Buenos Aires," we see her in action, acting like an extraordinary LF character. She emits energy, excitement, and charisma, and she is being honest about it, believing she could be the next upcoming star. The song explodes into action immediately with South American, bossa nova syncopation played by the piano, drums, xylophone, and electric bass. You can't help but move to this dance music! But we must keep in mind that Eva is scrappy as all get out, and she will do what she has to do in order to fulfil her deep-seated desire to claw up to the upper classes of privilege and power. It only makes sense that she sings and dances to a "LF sounding" song. She has to have that scrappiness and moxie to achieve her amazing obstacles of political power!

You will find many Level 2–The Affirmation songs in musicals. The Affirmation song is a great technique to keep the show driving along. Likewise, as stated previously, these types of songs are also based in human emotion that begs for loud, rhythmic, and articulate music. When I'm desperate, I don't want to be quiet about it. Look out world, you're gonna listen to me because I'm gonna yell my truth from the rooftops!

Level 3–The Lie

The Level 3–The Lie is exactly that – a lie. The N characters who sing a Level 3–The Lie song are aware of the pure truth in their situation, but *have to lie about it*. Generally, this is a song where the N characters are oppressed victims, totally without control in their lives, and they have to in essence sing a lie in order to continue to survive. Many times their lives depend on it. These characters have no power. They are controlled by outside forces (usually evil LF characters) and are generally in danger. The lie is not devious. It is a matter of survival. Therefore, they must act like all is good and happy, singing a song with a lot of energy, power, and support. This is why the music to these types of songs sound like the characteristics of LF music. These characters are singing that everything is ok, that their lives are fine, and they are proud to sing about it. The bigger the LF sound, the more they are covering up what they truly feel inside. It's all an act to please the oppressors.

These songs are also desperate in nature *subtextually*, yet come off as fun, wonderful, enjoyable songs to the listeners on stage and to the audience. Again, it is important to note that the characters who sing these songs are aware of the fact that they are telling a lie. They have to "fake" being fulfilled, happy people. But the underlying truth is one of devastation, sadness, emptiness, and a total feeling of hopelessness. They feel like they don't have any options in their lives and so they do what they do and lie about it, or else they die, literally or figuratively.

Jekyll and Hyde

Lucy singing "Good N' Evil" is a great example of a Level 3–The Lie. Lucy has to sing "Good N' Evil" because it is her only way to make money and survive. If she doesn't do this, she has no way of surviving day-to-day life. Her job is to make men in the bar happy and "satisfied." If she fails at this, she is then beaten by a pimp, The Spider. He allows no sob stories in his fine establishment. The Spider feels he's doing Lucy a favour by giving her a job.

The music starts off quiet and sinister, as if Lucy is subtextually hinting to us how she really feels in her life, supported by the string section, bass, and rolling cymbals with soft mallets. But not for long. It is as if she sees Spider hanging in the back of the place, getting more and more agitated that the room isn't getting lively and raucous. Therefore, she flips the switch and distorts the way she really feels with the notion of what is better – good or evil. The music makes an abrupt shift to this lie supported by the sudden entrance of cabaret-esque drumming. After that, it's all about a lively cabaret show and the image of pure LF entertainment. She sells the crowd a product and they love it. Meanwhile, she saves herself from a beating at the end of the night.

Les Misérables

The prostitutes singing "Lovely Ladies" is another example of Level 3–The Lie. The music is rhythmic, bouncy, and fun, lightly giving the feeling of a Slavic dance, complete with a polka-sounding bass and xylophone. The feel is much like "It's A Hard Knock Life" in *Annie*. The only difference is, the ladies can't sing about their woes the same way that the kids do. If they do, they don't attract their customers, and as a result, they starve. The lie becomes necessary. What else can they do to survive but to sing a lie? Society has painted them into a corner – the red light district. They do this or die of starvation. They do this in desperation to feed their children. They do this at the cost of perhaps even their sanity. The point is either they pull themselves up by their garter belts and show the perspective customers that they would be a good lay or they sob through their real feelings and put off the customers. Of course, the men think that the ladies love to sell their bodies to them. Sadly, that still is prevalent today. But it's just an act – a lie – to keep their heads above water, a morsel of food on their table.

Think about it this way though. The name of the show is *The Miserables*. If the writers of this show wrote only Level 1–Tell It Like It Is songs we all would be so depressed by the end of the first act that we would be driving ourselves off a cliff at intermission. In some way, the writers had to find other kinds of music and emotions that offer contrast to being miserable, and the Level 3–The Lie is a strong way to do that.

Sweeney Todd

In the song "Pirelli's Miracle Elixir," Tobias (N) is trying to sell this "miracle hair-growing elixir" to the crowd. As were many elixirs at that time, this product is worthless. But poor Tobias has to sell it, and build it up to such height that once Pirelli (LF) comes out, people will not only watch and listen to him, but also buy the fake medicine. Tobias is a boy with absolutely no power in this show – he is N. He's scrappy, and claws and scrapes in any way he can to stay alive. He will literally say anything or do anything for a morsel of food. Not to mention the fact that he would easily get beaten if he didn't do what he was told. So, Tobias lies. He knows it and we know it. The music is upbeat, catchy, with accents hit at odd times. The music is Kurt Weill-esque and carnival-like in a dark way, almost like an old, rhythmic, honky-tonk circus coming to town. It feels LF, like Tobias is in total control, but he of course is not. He's only playing to the audience to sell them enough elixir to keep himself alive and unbeaten.

In all three cases, these characters sing lies: loud, rhythmic, persuasive, and powerful songs that we all tap our feet to and enjoy. Unfortunately for them, it is all a very sad, victim-oriented front that fills their hearts with desperation, powerlessness, hopelessness, and fear.

Level 4–The Struggle

Level 4–The Struggle is exactly what you will experience and go through when analysing a character and their music that is under this category! It's a struggle – literally and figuratively. This level deals with a character who is struggling between being N and LF. These characters are aware of their truth, but struggle with their pure truth. These are characters that have an unfulfilled need and who are yearning for something, yet they are still trying to take action to alleviate their problem. They are characters that perhaps have a lot of LF qualities in their personality, yet when push comes to shove they have a need that has not yet been fulfilled. These are characters that may actually try to take control of the situation, try to negotiate the problem that they have, or try to solve the problem by thinking through it and being aware of the situation and its outcomes. The important part about this level, however, is that these characters sing through this process, but ultimately FAIL in what they were trying to accomplish. In other words, after the song is done, and the day is done, their need is still unresolved.

This makes analysing Level 4–The Struggle very difficult and confusing. But it ultimately creates some amazingly complex and wonderful characters! These characters in some way walk, talk, and sing like LF characters, but they are not LF. The songs of Level 4–The Struggle are generally powerful and rhythmic – even with tour de force! You follow them in a song like this in the same way as you would follow a LF character. They can be persuasive in nature. But the bottom line is: you are still rooting for them and they can't quite achieve what they need or desire to achieve.

The Sound of Music – *the movie*

Maria's "I Have Confidence" is a perfect example of this kind of Level 4–The Struggle. In this song, she knows she has self-doubt and so she struggles with it, trying to overcome her worries. She knows she must pursue this new governess job with confidence. Throughout the entire song, she is bolstering herself up, giving herself the needed jolt to succeed. But, in the end, when she arrives at the gate of the Trapp family mansion the music suddenly stops in its tracks. Maria is blown away by the size of the mansion, thus exposing the real trepidation she has with her new assignment. She knows she must have confidence, but in the end, she still has her self-doubts and is asking for help. The song is miraculous! It is one of the most powerful LF characteristic songs around. It constantly builds in stature, like a growth arc, is rhythmic, fast, driving in momentum and energy. Maria gets more and more energized. The keys continuously modulate to increase excitement. But in the end, even though she gets to the door and knocks, and presents herself in the best way she can, she still is, deep down inside, uncertain of herself. Thus, the struggle. Thus, her lack of success in taking care of her problem. After all is said and done, she is still N.

My Fair Lady

Another Level 4–The Struggle song is "I've Grown Accustomed to Her Face." This is where Henry Higgins, who is now becoming N during this part of the show, is struggling between missing Eliza desperately and resenting her, thus wanting to throw her out with the trash. In his aggressive moments in the song, reprising the music of "I'm an Ordinary Man," the music is wonderfully attacking, articulate, loud, and pattered to send his point home – the same characteristics as his LF music earlier in the show. But then, he immediately goes back to specific, special moments of Eliza and him, where he is saddened at her departure and is realizing that her absence is hurting him deeply. In the end, he wallows in his newfound N energy, not being able to logically and pragmatically erase her from his memory. He's trying to navigate this new sense of yearning and unfulfillment. Again, we will cover this unique ground plan of characters that switch from LF to N or N to LF much later. Don't assume that this happens much at all in your analysis work of musicals!

Show Boat

"Why Do I Love You" is this happy-go-lucky, celebratory, testament-of-love song between Ravenal and Nola. The music is a sweet, lilting, early 1900s song in cut time, with a tempo of 70. This song may not sound like the huge, raucous-sounding LF song that we tend to expect as a LF song, but it is clearly a positive song. It feels like a wonderful day at the fair! LF, right? Nope. Ravenal and Nola are at the fair with Captain Andy and Parthy. They are trying so hard to show the parents that they are indeed happily married, and that Ravenal's "business" is doing marvellously. His gambling addiction, however, is getting the best of him, and he doesn't know when to quit. The couple are hiding the fact that they are struggling to be happy. Through this song they are trying to convince themselves how happy they are, even though deep down inside their hearts it is becoming increasingly difficult to find that joy. Their needs are not resolved, as we find out in the next scene when Ravenal permanently leaves Nola because of his incapability to support his family with his gambling life.

Could this song be an N Level 3–The Lie song? After all, Nola and Ravenal are lying about their situation, aren't they? I believe not. I feel that they are truly trying to convince themselves that things are okay, and that life will only get better. They are being truthful in what they are singing – they do truly love each other and this love is the only foundation they feel they need to build upon in order to build a perfect life together. However, at this moment they are struggling to believe that this will happen – and of course, it doesn't in the next scene. It gets worse. Much worse.

Level 5–Protest Too Much

The Level 5–Protest Too Much song is exactly what we have talked about in the lyric Need energy chapter earlier in the book. It's a song in which the character is unaware of her/his own pure truth and therefore, believes in the lie that she/he is singing. So many times we as humans are clueless as to what we really want or feel, which is why we all need a therapist at some point in our lives. We are in this sphere of major self-denial. For example, when a loved one dies, there are people who never allow themselves to grieve. They deny that they are even affected by the death, so they live on as if nothing happened, subconsciously avoiding all the pain and loss. It's not a healthy thing. As I would always say after going to a funeral, "I don't worry about the individual who is devastated by the death of a loved one – I feel they're doing great. They are going through the needed, painful work of grieving. It's the one at the funeral who says they are just fine and appear as if nothing is wrong, that I truly worry about."

Characters who sing these Protest Too Much songs are unaware of their own insecurities. They have subconsciously talked themselves into believing the opposite – and I use "subconsciously" very purposely here because it is important to point out that these characters are not lying. They are singing what they believe to be true, even though we know it isn't.

As always, the music will be the ally of the character who is singing. Music will always truthfully reflect the emotion of the character at that moment in time. When N characters sing Level 5–Protest Too Much songs, the music will reflect that position that the characters are believing in, because the character feels she/he is speaking the truth. This is why Need energy Level 5–Protest Too Much songs sound and feel like Life Force numbers. They are boisterous, over-compensating, rhythmic to a fault, and in-your-face. The character is desperately trying to prove that they have the world by the tail and that they are fine. It is the audience who is the wiser – knowing that the wool can't be pulled over their eyes. Audiences are smart that way.

Kiss Me Kate

Let's look at Kate's song "I Hate Men" again as the Level 5–Protest Too Much song that it is, and this time include the music analysis. When strictly just analysing the title, "I Hate Men," we already know that no woman (or man for that matter …) can totally and so completely hate one-half of the population of the world. Kate is truly feeling and believing at that moment that she hates all men. But she really doesn't. She's just mad as hell at Fred Graham for being so unfeeling as to give her a bunch of flowers that has a love note attached addressed to Lois, her cast friend. She is rightfully hurt and angry, but frankly, she is actually still in love with the freeloader Fred. The music in "I Hate Men" reflects her state of mind at this very moment. The slams of brass after every line of "*I hate men*" accentuate that powerful belief that Kate does indeed hate men. You can just see her slamming down a mug hard on a table to make her point. Then the song goes into a wonderfully rhythmic patter that sends this feeling of powerful LF energy to the piece. She's loud, brassy, stating her credo with tremendous belief and purpose. But all the while we're snickering and saying to ourselves, "Yeah, right, Lilli, get over it. Just get off stage, kick Fred in the groin, and then make out with him til the cows come home!"

Camelot

It is the same with Lancelot's song, "C'est Moi." This too, is a Level 5–Protest Too Much song. The song sounds LF with its first notes played, beginning with trumpets blaring a fanfare to the entrance of Lancelot. How can that NOT feel like LF? It's a royal welcome and introduction. Immediately we think that Lancelot is of a more important, higher class. As the song rolls on, the rhythmic and adventurous musical characteristics, complete with slams and articulations, reflects his outside belief that he is a knight of human perfection. Through the music, you feel the tromping of the horse, the blaring of attack, and the majestic royal presence. It is loud, brassy, rhythmic, articulate, and full of presence. Yes, Lancelot is the best knight in the country. Yes, he is fearless with the enemy and will sacrifice himself for the king. Yes, Lancelot is the epitome of male strength and physical agility. But his Achilles heel is love, and that love manifests itself in Gueneviere. He becomes butter in their relationship. In "C'est Moi," he fully believes that he is the best to lead the knights of the roundtable. But when you look deep inside Lancelot he is totally insecure in uncontrolled love. Perfection is an ideal, and is unattainable in human form – even Lancelot. Lancelot is pulling the wool over his own eyes in this song – perhaps as a cover to a once hurtful dumping by a young woman early in his life?

Spring Awakening

"Don't Do Sadness" is a more contemporary example of a Level 5–Protest Too Much song. Immediately when you hear the introduction of the song, with the syncopated, 3/3/2 accents highly articulated in the cello's bowing, you feel the intensity and rhythmic emotional impact of a characteristically driven LF piece. Moritz, however, is a N character who has been thrown out of the house by his imperialistic father because he failed his final examination (a test, of course, that the teachers made sure Moritz would fail …). Moritz leaves carrying a pistol. He sings metaphorically about being like the butterfly or the wind, passing by without really feeling – just enjoying the moments. He, too, like the butterfly or the wind, doesn't feel sadness – or so he says … He is, of course, devastated by the fact that his father threw him out and even more so that his mother didn't support him by helping him financially to run to America to get away. He is so overwhelmed by all of these feelings of rebellion, dejection, inadequacy, loss of love and parental support that he truly feels nothing – no sadness in his situation. He wants *"no part of it,"* and *"doesn't need it in his life."* This is what he believes at that moment, and we know that this is totally opposite what he is truly feeling inside – a huge sense of loss and sadness. The music grows from a string quartet accompanying him in the verse to a climactic rock ensemble of electric guitar, bass, piano, and a rock drum beat on the refrains. It totally sounds LF, but it is N, a Level 5–Protest Too Much song.

Need energy music summary

Once we have analysed a musical through its dramatic question, song assignments, lyrics, and energies it is then that we take a look at the music from a deep analysis standpoint. Once you begin and you're looking at a N character song, always first start by looking at Level 1–Tell It Like It Is. After all, that is the most used of the five levels of songs. If it doesn't sound like your Basic Need Energy Music Characteristics song, then start going around the circle to see where it does fit. It's at this point that you must look deeply into the character's lyrics to understand what she/he is going through and why, considering their emotions and motivations.

8

The Life Force Energy Music Circle of Truth

The Life Force Energy Music Circle of Truth also consists of five different "character mindset" levels for a Life Force character. Like the Need Energy Music Circle of Truth, under each level is a description of how the characters perceive and act upon their pure truth. You will notice that the names of the first four levels of the five levels are the same as the Need Energy Music Circle of Truth, however they are now from the perspective of Life Force characters. As with the Need Energy Circle, all LF levels are equal in their own way. What the levels do describe is where LF characters stand in regard to their own pure truth. You will notice one difference right away in that for every LF level, the LF characters *are fully aware* of their pure truth. This is a characteristic of all LF character personalities. They are the central driving force of the show. They give the N characters a direction to follow in order to find resolution. Of course the LF characters will be aware of their own truth – they have to, or they wouldn't be LF characters. LF characters are in control and they know where they are going. Therefore, with this in mind, their music will reflect that direction. The big difference here, versus the Need energy music, is that LF characters control how they will choose to sing their music. It is that Life Force choice that decides whether the LF music *sounds like the traditional, basic LF song or sounds like its **N opposite***.

Level 1–Tell It Like It Is

This level in Life Force is also the most predominant of all five levels in the LF Circle. This is where LF characters are aware of their own pure truth and sing as that central driving force of the musical. LF characters are there to give advice, persuade, direct, suggest, and in any other way, offer resolution possibilities to the N character's problems. LF characters are acutely aware of

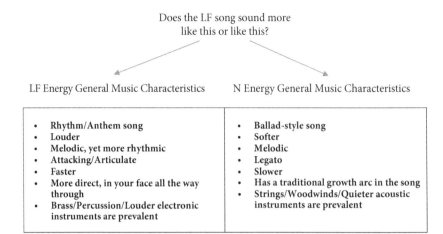

Figure 10 Does the LF Song Sound More Like This or Like This?

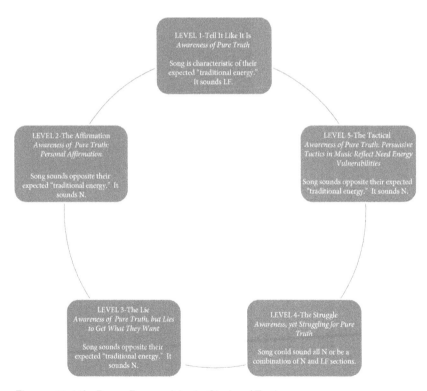

Figure 11 Life Force Energy Music Circle of Truth.

the situation and therefore sing their truth, defining who they are, where they are going, and what their belief system is. They are in essence "telling it like it is" to the N characters and/or to the audience. They offer that possibility of solution to whatever the problem is in the musical and its N characters.

So how does the music reflect this state of character?

Level 1–Tell It Like It Is follows the Basic Life Force Energy Music Characteristics – it's a rhythmic song or anthem, louder, faster, melodic in nature yet with rhythm, more direct and in-your-face, more articulate and attacking, and the instrumentation leads towards louder, bolder instruments like the brass and percussion. Again, it won't necessarily have all of these qualities, but it will have a lot of them. Keep in mind that we are looking at the music in broad brushstrokes. But, by looking at these broader characteristics, we again can utilize this information to help us focus, analyse, and justify the energies of our characters.

The Wiz

The Wiz sings "So You Wanted to Meet the Wizard": a very strong and bold example of a Life Force entrance song. The song musically starts with the fanfare of blaring trumpets playing in their high range, the percussion accentuating the beat through loud drum strokes and cymbals. It forces you immediately to take attention and watch this man. It is fast, rhythmic in its syncopations, attacking, and yet still has a wonderful melodic line. The Wiz is magical, powerful, controlling, charismatic, and he has all the answers to the N characters' problems. He makes this very clear in the song by blowing up things, dressing boldly, and daring the N characters to make a move. The Wiz is very honest about who he is and what he can do – the perfect blend of power and awe in a Level 1–Tell It Like It Is song.

Oklahoma!

"Oh What a Beautiful Morning" is another strong Life Force Level 1 song sung by Curly. It doesn't have the flashiness of "So You Wanted to Meet the Wizard," but it is still powerful in its own way – in Curly's simplicity. He is marking his truthful state of being at that moment and is truly expecting the day to be perfect. Not that he is so infatuated with the weather, but he is embracing the day for what it will be – the day he asks Laurey to go to the box social with him and she, of course, answering yes. Musically, he is singing this song full-voiced, confident, wonderfully melodic, letting the music and lyrics soar to the heights of his love for Laurey – as high as an elephant! The music may not have a rapidly moving tempo, but within its moderate movement is the bold, full, and unapologetic simplicity that is prevalent in Oklahoma countryside. It's a direct statement of his passion and love.

Kinky Boots

Lola sings "The Sex is in the Heel" to Charlie and the rest of the employees after they have made the first prototype of a kinky boot – much to the dismay of Lola. She knows what works in a boot, both in the practicality and the sexuality of the style. The only way she can *persuade them* to get on board and do the right thing is by blowing them away with a song! "The Sex is in the Heel" starts with Lola singing along with a strong, syncopated, short and attacking funk beat played by the bass, with the synthesizer and drums playing at counterpoint. By the time the song revs up into the chorus singing and the band rocking, one can't help but join in to the beat and the fun. This is a perfect example of a song in which the LF energy is truthful and believes in what she is singing about. And that belief is, in order for the factory to survive, they must make a boot with sexy heels. The music follows traditional LF music characteristics, therefore is a Level 1–Tell It Like It Is song.

Levels 2–5

The rest of the levels, 2 to 5, are Life Force songs that sound like the Basic *Need* Energy Music Characteristics. What? Not this again! How can a LF character have N sounding music characteristics? If a character is the central driving force of a show, attractive to be with, persuasive, and powerful, how could this type of character possibly sing songs that sound like Need songs? Won't that take away from their power?

On the contrary.

There is incredible power in silence. Think about how effective it is when a parent just quietly, fully, and under control, says "No" to the demands of a child. Or, think about when an evil person whispers horrible words into the ear of his/her victim. Some of the most effective and powerful national and international agreements are made under the power of a silent, listening mediator. Power doesn't always have to be boisterously in your face – look at

Ghandi or Mother Theresa. What decides *the kind* of power that one uses in a situation is often what decides whether that person truly succeeds or not. It's the wise, aware, skilful, and responsive craftsperson who can manoeuvre through the muck of conflict and need. They will be the ones that will indeed succeed in the end. Besides, a contrast of different sounding LF songs is really effective for LF characters. Level 2–5 LF songs give LF characters a more diversified and nuanced arc to their roles.

The key to these next four levels is the fact that LF characters are *totally aware of the pure truth* and that they will do what is necessary to guide the N characters to their resolution.

Level 2–The Affirmation

This level allows LF characters to be human – that is, to show that they have a human side along with their "superhuman" Life Force energy. The Level 2–The Affirmation song gives LF characters the chance to open up and admit their personal affirmation. LF characters sing about who they really are, truthfully and purely. It can be sung as a secret to the audience, or it can be openly sung directly to other N characters. One must keep in mind that this is showing strength in LF characters, not weakness. There is pure truth and honesty in this when LF characters sing this type of song. They are basically just telling it like it is – no more, no less. The difference is they are singing a song where the music sounds like Basic Need Energy Music Characteristics.

When singing a song like this it is not necessary to be boisterous. It is more powerful and effective to sing it subtly and with complete clarity. This is why the music reflects this through the use of the Basic Need Energy Music Characteristics. It is a ballad, slow, legato, growing in intensity as the song progresses to the point of a huge climax at the end. The difference is that LF characters aren't looking for something or for resolution in their being. They are personally affirming their view on the world to themselves and others. They are showing them or teaching them something personally from their heart.

Les Misérables

A strong example of a Level 2–The Affirmation song for a LF character is Javert's song "Stars." Here is a man so infused in his own belief system that he must personally affirm it to the world. He is totally honest in giving his credo and, in turn, the music reflects that honesty. The music sounds like the epitome of a classic Level 1–Tell It Like It Is Need song. It begins quietly and smoothly with harp and acoustic guitar, and continues to grow in strength and power until at the climax, brass is blaring and cymbals are rolling. Javert will not be moved! He will live his credo or die with it. Oooo, and I guess he does … too bad for him.

Next To Normal

"He's Not Here," sung by Dan, LF, is probably the most poignant and gentle LF song of honesty that one could ever listen to, let alone one that has your heartstrings pulled massively. Diana has just entered with a birthday cake for Gabe – a son they lost sixteen years earlier. Dan tries to break the news to her gently, lovingly, that their son is not here, that he is dead. How does a person ever deal with someone who is suffering from mental illness and refuses to believe the reality of that statement? It's heart-wrenching for both of them. She hallucinates Gabe being there, Dan is trying to bring her to reality to heal. Dan is supported strictly by the flowing, docile phrase fragments of a piano, and a lone cello, reminding us of the pain and hollowness of the heart.

The Music Man

In the reprise "Till There Was You" Harold sings his love to Marian – a love he never recognized until that moment. As this scene begins, the town is chasing after Harold. Winthrop has run into Harold and Harold admits to him that he is a dirty rotten crook. Harold begins to assess his life, and then decides that he will face the people of the town. He then sings this reprise to Marian. Even then, however, **he is in control**. He is the central driving force. He is even more attractive to be with now that he is repenting. Even in his darkest moments, Harold is always larger than life, strong, and visionary. So the Level 2–The Affirmation song is perfect for Harold to sing at this point. He's actually opening his heart for the first time in his life, and that honesty requires a gentle, truthful, beautifully melodic, and slow ballad song to support his change. This LF song shows strength and integrity. It also, obviously, connects him to Marian with an eternal love.

Level 3–The Lie

The Level 3–The Lie Life Force song, like the Need song, is where LF characters are indeed aware of the pure truth of the situation, but lies about it. The difference is, LF characters are not only aware of the situation truth, but they are actually using this as a way to get what they want through deceit and dishonesty. This isn't about trying to help resolve the unfulfillment of the N characters. It's about getting what they want. No one is forcing them to lie. LF characters are choosing to lie to take control of a situation. They prey on the N character's vulnerabilities. So, one can surmise that this type of song is sung by an evil LF character – one that we wouldn't want to support at all. These anti-LF characters are misusing their power over others for their own self-centered benefit. These LF characters are bad people.

Sweeney Todd

A wonderful example of a Level 3–The Lie song is when Sweeney Todd (LF at this point) is trying to get Judge Turpin (LF) to get a shave once again at the end of the show. "Judge's Return" (A reprise of "Pretty Women") is a marvellously luscious song where Todd is again convincing Turpin that he needs a close shave in order for the judge to lure the fancy of Johanna. He is accompanied by strings and a solo oboe – simple, beautiful in melody, yet deadly. Todd knows full well that the judge isn't going to make it out of his barbershop alive this time around. That both of them sing this ballad in a duet makes it even more gripping. Because "Judge's Return" has the characteristics of a Need song, it again disarms the judge, and allows Todd access to the judge's neck. Todd is instilling a sense of buddy-buddy trust with Turpin, knowing that if he wins over Turpin's trust, the judge will then stay for the shave. This is a song of deception. How ironic that "Pretty Women" ends up being one of the most beautiful and melodic ballads in the musical, and ends up being the most deadly for Judge Turpin!

Jekyll and Hyde

Another example of a Level 3–The Lie song is Hyde's reprise of "Sympathy Tenderness." Here, Hyde (LF) has broken into Lucy's bedroom, frightening Lucy (N). He calms her through the reprisal singing of Lucy's previous Need song. Hyde is lying about being sympathetic and tender. The music disarms her. The music's minor key, with the piano sounding music box-like, makes for a comforting, settling, bedroom scene. It's soft and trustworthy, plus, it is a song that was a secret of hers. He uses this song and her own words, to manipulate her, to calm her, to have her trust in him. He, however, has only one goal in mind and one alone: to kill Lucy, and he unfortunately does. That big bad wolf …

The Phantom of the Opera

"The Mirror" is an example of a Level 3–The Lie, but in a different kind of format. With the soft tremolo of the lower strings and the muffled timpani roll in the background, we certainly know that this song is mysterious, magical, and evil. The Phantom, singing melodically with reverb, is deceiving Christine, through magic and hypnotism, by having her believe that he is really her father. The oboe comes in, offering a more haunting sense of the moment. This "*angel of music*" lies. He is just singing that to falsely create trust between Christine and himself. He knows what he is doing and he uses that knowledge of Christine's loss of her father to his advantage. His ballad-style, disarming music reflects that misuse of trust by being quiet, yet mysterious, as if it's coming from the grave. The Phantom is not the type of guy you want your daughter to date.

Level 4–The Struggle

Oh no, not another struggle! I'm afraid so, but this one is where LF characters are struggling between LF and N. LF characters are definitely aware, yet struggling with their pure truth. These characters have vulnerabilities and needs, but *they are not the focus of the dramatic question*, so therefore they are not Need songs. Yet, they sing about it, struggle with it, and then finally come to grips with it. The biggest difference is the end, when all is said and done, LF characters will be okay and will survive. They have what is needed inside of them to either shake it off or to do something about the issue. They aren't feeling like they are held hostage by it. They will have resolution in whatever they decide. It may not be what we as an audience are looking for, but it is done nonetheless.

This again makes analysing Level 4–The Struggle very difficult and confusing to analyse. LF characters in some way walk, talk, and sing like N characters, but still they are not. The songs of Level 4–The Struggle are generally ballad in nature with a tour de force climax at the end. You follow them in a song like this as you would a N character. They can be unsure, unsteady, and vulnerable in nature. But the bottom line is you know at the end that they are going to be alright, for they have a certain amount of LF moxie or chutzpa that will get them through their tough time. We know that when the going gets tough, these tough characters get going.

You will find that these types of songs make analysis very difficult and will drive you crazy. My point to you is, embrace the conflict and uncertainty. These characters are deeply complex in nature and a blast for actors to play when they have the opportunity! It forces you to really dig deep in your analysis to make sure you figure it out as correctly as possible. It allows for great theoretical discussions with your other workmates!

Les Misérables

The epitome of a song that can totally mess up one's mind as to whether it is Life Force or Need is the song "On My Own," sung by Eponine. In my humble opinion, and much to the chagrin of many of my students, Eponine is a LF character. Yes, she is in love with Marius and wants him to be with her, but she is feisty and strong, and takes care of herself quite well. She isn't even afraid of the revolution – she partakes in it. Eponine is a strong woman who has a healthy dose of allegiance for her country in her. She is even the first to volunteer to cross the barricade to help the revolutionary cause. Is she doing this as a suicide pact because of the loss of Marius in her life? I think not. In the song "On My Own," she expresses her struggle between dreaming of a time with Marius and then in reality not having him. She goes back and forth. But, in the end, she will continue to learn, and Marius's world will continue to turn without her.

Eponine is resolved in the fact that she will not get him for her own. It is hard for her, but reality must set in – she will not get him. So with this major struggle within her, we hear music that sounds like a typical Need song: a huge ballad, soft, legato, incredibly melodic, with a growth arc that climbs to the height of longing and climax. Soft strings, harp, and oboe begin the song and by the end of the song horns and trombones are blaring with full orchestra. Then, at the end, it drops back to the subtleness that it started with, and Eponine sings her realization. She *will* learn from this and she *will* continue to live out her life – on her own.

Does this mean that we don't care about Eponine because she isn't a N character? Heavens no. She is all the more complex because of her frailties. God knows, we all have them. But what defines us is also how we deal with these frustrations. She moves on, fights for her country, and dies for it. What could be more purposeful and heroic in one's life?

Jekyll and Hyde

Emma's "Once Upon a Dream" is another Level 4–The Struggle song. Emma sees how Jekyll is more and more becoming distance and distraught. She sings her love to him and tries to get him to trust her with his supposed secrets. The song is a ballad, beautifully melodic, and legato. It starts with harp, strings, and some woodwinds, then grows to a climax with the addition of glockenspiel. Then, it ebbs, fading down to just strings again for the preparation of Emma's final decision. Emma does not become distraught to the point of never being able to recover. She tells Poole that she is pretty much done with Jekyll unless he asks for her. She will be strong and fine whether he returns to her or not. In the end, she has made the tough-love decision.

Les Misérables

"Javert's Suicide," with Javert singing, is another prime example of a character who has a major struggle in his life. The man is a very strong LF character: an authority figure who has major power over his subjects, powerful in physique, and a huge, clear credo of what is right and what is wrong. He will always believe that Valjean is a criminal and he will never move from that stance, no matter what Valjean says or does in society. But at the end of the show, when Valjean has the chance to finally kill Javert, he does not, and spares his life. This becomes a defining moment for Javert, where suddenly his world of consistency that he has been so comforted with, is thrown upside down. Life no longer is black and white. He is faced with this unwanted paradigm.

The song is masterful in having Javert go through all of his conflicting emotions with conflicting styles of music. In the first section, he is holding tightly onto his credo and belief system. The music sounds LF in its power and momentum. The strings go into agitated tremolo and the brass plays with accented blaring marking Javert's insistence to his credo. Cymbals, timpani, and tom tom accents make his point in frantic flare and tempo, finally ending with Javert's ultimatum that it is either him or Valjean.

But ...

The brass holds as long as it can, and finally fades to softer strings, and Javert must face his demons – is his credo flawed? Suddenly, the music goes into the style of a N song: a powerful, desperate ballad that grows and grows, all during his questioning, to a climactic, brass-blaring peak when Javert asks the question of whether Valjean's crimes should *"be reprieved?"*

His struggle continues, and we're hearing him slowly fade to the reality that his world is changing. The N strings continue to dominate and Javert continues to doubt. But at the moment of final decision, he pulls up his bootstraps and knows what he must do to maintain that credo: commit suicide.

The strings again go into agitated tremolo. The brass accents each piercing point. The man will live and die his credo, and therefore live and die as a LF character. He is making the decision to kill himself rather than change. Fascinatingly enough, with true LF flair, his final lyric word, *"on,"* ends with cymbals rolling and brass blaring at double forte, proclaiming the profound dissonance in both orchestral musical harmony as well as in his life. There's a reason why people love this song so much, and actors love to sing it! What a great LF Level 4–The Struggle song!

Level 5–The Tactical

Unlike the Need Level 5–Protest Too Much song, the Life Force Level 5–The Tactical song is one where LF characters are aware of their pure truth, and they aren't afraid to use their powers of persuasion to help the N characters. These LF character songs are aware of and use tactics to their advantage, and also to the advantage of the N characters. Right away, I'm sure that this sounds manipulative and negative, but I assure you it doesn't have to be. There are good and bad LF characters that use this level to achieve the success they are looking for. When used negatively, you then have the evil characters who manipulate N characters by ensuring their trust with them, even though the evil characters are out there trying to take advantage of them. They aren't concerned at all about the N characters' well-being. The good LF characters are trying to help the N characters by opening up, being honest, and basically getting down to their level. LF characters will use this tactic level to try to disarm any fear from the N characters and to develop trust with them. To do this, LF characters sing music that the N characters can relate to. The N characters will not consider this LF tactic song as a threat but as a comfort. Of course, used abusively, the Level 5–The Tactical song could be a terrible thing for the N characters, and could be leading them into danger. At that point, it could also then turn into a Level 3–The Lie song if the LF character starts lying.

The Level 5–The Tactical again sounds like a Basic Need Energy Music Characteristic song. The music tends to be non-threatening, soft, gentle, and tender. It comes off as being a very honest and approachable song that N characters will react favourably to. Just as in life when someone in need is having a difficult time and the friend, mentor, or lover comes over to console and comfort him/her, so too does The Tactical Life Force song.

The Fantasticks

El Gallo's song "Try To Remember" is a nice example. El Gallo is trying tactically to lull the audience into a time in their lives when things were good, warm, and golden. He lulls us into this mellow and amber dream by requesting us to follow him. It's a wonderfully gentle, flowing, legato, piece of persuasion, and we of course, do want to join him in his story. He sings this beautifully simple and honest ballad with soft, gentle, harp, pizzicato string bass, and a melodious, ever-flowing piano accompaniment. After this song, we are his for the entire evening, no matter what he has up his sleeves.

Light in the Piazza

"Let's Walk" is sung by Margaret Johnson and Signor Naccarelli. Here, both Margaret and Naccarelli are LF characters – parents who control the destiny of their children. When Naccarelli has said no to the marriage of Fabrizio and Clara, Margaret suggests a walk. The two parents start to walk through the evening, while Margaret starts singing this non-threatening song. Through this non-threatening exchange of music and honest conversation, they both can come to the understanding that it is for the best that their children marry. The song is tender and gentle, and very honest. It is a heart to heart song. If Margaret uses one of her LF belt numbers, Signor Naccarelli will immediately taken the defensive and they will not find concensus. Just mix Italy, love, and a tender song and suddenly you have a great tactic to make change. And the result of this song is the ultimate resolution to the N characters' problems.

Sweeney Todd

Judge Turpin is an anti-LF. He's a very icky man. He's old, wicked, devious, unlawful, and has no conscience. He is also infatuated with Sweeney Todd's daughter and feels that she should be his property as spousal slave. In "Johanna" he's in a quandary though – he doesn't understand why Johanna would not be thrilled with him. Duh.

Beadle then takes over and uses a tactic of gentleness in order to change the Judge's mind about how he approaches her. His soft approach on "Ladies in Their Sensitivities" gently sways the position of the Judge, not to use force on her, but to use tactics of romance and sensitivity. The light, lilting ballad offers a feeling of heart to heart between Beadle and the Judge. But the underlying truth is that Beadle is fearful of him – the Judge has ultimate power – and Beadle certainly does not want to upset him and thus lose his privileges. So, he uses the tactic of soft, gentle, "truth" to get the Judge to go to the barber. Obviously, the Judge feels that his marrying Johanna will solve all of her problems and needs – the anti-solution.

Now, this is not to say that any other level song is tactic-less. Absolutely not. Characters must always use tactics to get what they are fighting for. If they don't use tactics, we would have pretty boring theatre. So what is the difference between a LF Level 5–The Tactical song and a Level 2–The Affirmation song where the actor is still using tactics? That's actually a tough question to answer and more goes by "feel" versus anything else. Generally, the Level 5–The Tactical song's sole purpose is to persuade the other character(s) to "go this way, versus that way." The LF characters can use this type of music to help the N characters find direction or perhaps even resolution in their unfulfillment. They can also use it to help try to change the minds of other LF characters who may have skin in the game with the N characters, and could actually help those N folk get closer to resolution.

An example of a LF Level 2–The Affirmation that could be considered a Level 5–The Tactical, but shouldn't be, would be "Bui Doi" from Miss Saigon. This is an amazing ballad song, with the traditional climactic arc at the end of the song. John (and his chorus of organizers) are wanting folks to be aware of, and take action for, all of the children who were born by Vietnamese women and fathered by US military men. Absolutely, by the end of the song, we all are convinced that these children should be taken care of. But this is not a Level 5–The Tactical song. This song is an anthem, a credo, sung by LF characters who are trying to change ignorant American views, not just trying to change one person's mind.

Music analysis summary

Can you listen to the music of a song without the lyrics and be able to dictate whether the piece is LF or N? The answer to this is that you could make some logical assumptions and educated guesses, but in the end, your answer would be no. You couldn't be sure until you read or listen to the lyrics that go along with it. There are too many intangibles that exist with the music – specifically the unpredictable emotions of human beings – to be able to dictate such an analysis. If I were to compose some music that was loud, agitated, and rhythmic yet melodic, would you be able to tell whether I composed it to describe a LF character who was revengefully angry or a N character who was at wit's end, devastatingly hurt? Probably not.

You really must analyse the lyrics in all of the songs first and then analyse the music in each song to see which level the music fits under. This will give you a much more clear direction as to where the character is going within the music and the lyric. The music and lyrics are partners who are so intricately entwined emotionally that we must analyse them both individually and together.

9

The Ground Plan

The ground plan of a musical is a short form key or map that shows the overall energy exchange and positioning of energy in a specific musical. I liken it to looking at the form of a piece of music. If the song is a basic verse/refrain type of song, then you would label it as AB form. Looking at an AB form gives you an overview of the type of song that it is. It can help you in your learning as well as in your organizational process of interpretation of the song. The ground plan of a musical is not really "form" in the music sense of the term, however, its overall view can give you a track to follow and a map to staying on that correct track. In essence, it's a visual key that suggests the design of the musical machine.

The ground plan deals with how the energies merge together and from which directions they come from. It can show the energy exchange relationship between the LF and N characters. It can also show the directional pathways of the energies and from where they came. It can show whether the LF energy is pushing N energy away or pulling N energy closer. It can show N energy choosing a LF. Whatever ground plan the musical is, it is designed by using the LF and N symbols, plus the use of arrows. The arrows show what direction the energies come from and which energy tends to be the grounded one.

The Fantasticks

The Fantasticks is a simply designed ground plan show. That's what makes it so brilliant and germane to this day. El Gallo is LF – big, bold, attractive to be with, charismatic, and the central driving force to the show. Matt and Louisa are N because both are yearning for adventure and love, and are unfulfilled where they are. Hucklebee and Bellamy are N characters because they want the best for their kids, yet they have no idea as to how to bring them up correctly as parents. They look to El Gallo for help. Since the Mute and the old actors Henry and Mortimer work alongside El Gallo and contribute to the magical theatrics of their world, they too are LF.

We start in the world of the two neighbouring homes of Hucklebee and Matt, and Louisa and Bellamy. El Gallo enters to help the fathers with their problem. An outsider LF character enters the world of the N community. The ground plan is:

LF→N

Brigadoon

Tommy is engaged to be married, but he's not sure he wants to be. He's uncertain and yearning for something more. He is N. He goes on a hunting trip to Scotland with his friend Jeff to get away and think. Suddenly in the mist, the small village of Brigadoon appears – a magical place that shows up only one day every hundred years. The people of the town are incredibly happy, safe, and fulfilled, and Tommy soon falls in love with one of the villagers, Fiona. She and the rest of the village are LF.

Tommy enters the world of Brigadoon and finds love and contentment. An outside N character enters the world of the LF community. The ground plan is:

N→LF

Jesus Christ Superstar

This show was written through the eyes of Judas. Judas isn't a settled man. He is rebellious in nature, taking on Jesus Christ at every turn. Judas has fear for himself, as well as Jesus Christ and the rest of the disciples. He's afraid they all will eventually be killed by the authorities if they continue in the direction that they are heading. Judas is lost, fearful, and misguided. He is N. Jesus Christ, being the Son of God, and a leader to the people is LF. On the other side, Pilate, Caiaphas, and the priests are anti-LF – full of power and authority.

Judas is caught between the two groups of people, struggling to decide which faction he should join and pledge allegiance to: Christ and his followers, or Caiaphas and the priests. A Need character is choosing between two LF communities. The ground plan is:

LF←N→LF

We call this The Choice ground plan.

Just how many ground plans are there? I get asked this a lot, and my answer does not resonate well with the ones who ask. There are a *minimum* of fourteen ground plans.

I would never try to limit the amount. First and foremost, I have never even come close to analysing the sheer wealth of musicals, so how can I say this for sure? Secondly, the world of musicals change constantly, and new, creative composers and librettists will always be trying out new ideas. They will break the "rules" of theatre in new ways, therefore creating new ground plans that we have never even thought of before.

What is interesting is how many musicals have the same ground plans. Below are some of the musicals that I have analysed through the years and their respective ground plans. All of us can use these as a base foundation to work from. What you can do now is analyse all of these shows to figure out why the ground plans are such!

Known ground plans

LF→N

This ground plan is where a LF character(s) enter into the world of N character(s). Examples: *The Music Man, Beauty and the Beast (Disney), Peter Pan, The Fantasticks.*

N→LF

This is where N character(s) enter into the world of LF character(s). Examples: *Brigadoon, Cats, Company, A Chorus Line, South Pacific, Titanic.*

LF←N→LF ("The Choice")

This is where the N character must make a choice between two LF characters/communities. Examples: *The Phantom of the Opera, Oklahoma!, Evita, Cabaret, JC Superstar, Next To Normal.*

LF→N←LF

This is where two separate LF characters/communities are influencing the N characters from two different perspectives. Examples: *Les Misérables, Rent, Hamilton.*

N→LF←N

This is where two separate N characters are brought/pulled together by LF character(s). Examples: *Showboat, Kiss Me Kate, Pajama Game.*

N←LF→N

This is where LF character(s) try to keep separate the N characters. Examples: *Light in the Piazza, Miss Saigon.*

N↔LF ("The Reversal")

This is where a N character and LF character at the beginning of the show end up reversing their energy (they become the opposite energy) by the end of the show. Examples: *My Fair Lady, Gypsy, Last Five Years, Sweeney Todd.*

The next three ground plans are ones where the LF is actually on a different plane. The N characters embrace that LF energy through their dreams, their faith, or their inner-most gut feelings.

"The Untouchable"

This is where the LF is only experienced in theatrical imagery (dreamland). In reality, only N characters are present. (Thus the tragedy …) Example: *West Side Story.*

Figure 12 The Untouchable.

"The Ethereal"

This is where the N characters actually have the LF energy entering them from an outside dimensional plane, but it is ethereal in nature. The LF is where the N characters are singing from within their deep-seated faith/

belief system. Even though the faith is within them, they are always looking out towards somewhere for their strength. That strength is sent to them from "up above." Example: *Fiddler on the Roof.*

Figure 13 The Ethereal.

"The Womb"

This is where the N characters actually have the LF energy entering them from within themselves, but it is ethereal in nature. The LF is where the N characters are singing from within their deeply suppressed feelings that have been forcibly controlled by an outside environmental faction: powerful social norms or mores. These N characters are in an oppressive environment, yet they all have the LF inside of them, allowing it to pop out and be who they instinctually really are for a certain duration of time. Example: *Spring Awakening.*

Figure 14 The Womb.

N→LF→LF→

"N Picaresque"

This is where N character(s) go from one LF character(s) to another LF character(s), and then to another LF character(s), until the N finally gets resolved. It is jumping from adventure to adventure in finding their resolution. Examples: *The Wiz, Pippin, The Wizard of Oz.*

LF→N→N→

"LF Picaresque"

This is where the LF character(s) go from one N character(s) to another N character(s), and then to another N character(s), until all of the Ns are finally resolved. It is jumping from adventure to adventure solving all the N characters' problems. Example: *Hello Dolly.*

[N→LF][LF←N→LF] ("Piggybacking")

(This is *Jekyll & Hyde*'s ground plan, used as an example – the other shows listed below have different piggybacking ground plans.)

This is where there are a combination of ground plans within one show, however only one ground plan is being used until the completion of that section of the show. Then, the next ground plan starts anew, piggybacking on the last ground plan. Each piggybacking section ends with a GM. Examples: *Jekyll & Hyde, Funny Girl, Sunday in the Park with George, Into the Woods.*

N/LF↔N/LF

This is a ground plan where both lead characters are both LF and N, and the energies of their needs match up with the other character's LF energy. Don't get caught into thinking that this happens often. It does not. I have only found one. Example: *The King and I*.

Sometimes shows are dealing with communities, sometimes they are dealing only with specific characters, and so the ground plans will not necessarily reflect that. All of these ground plans are dependent on the analysis of all of the lyrics and the music in the musical. In order to truly understand all of these ground plans you do need to go through the analysis work systematically – one step at a time. The next chapter will take you through that process.

10

The Analytical Process

Now that we understand what all of the terminologies and energies are, we now can begin the process of analysing a musical. It is very tough to do this at the beginning, but once you've done a few musicals, the process begins to make sense, and the analysis of the musical becomes a bit easier. My biggest words of advice are to never try to cut corners. Follow the process step by step every time you take on another musical. Don't feel rushed to get to the answers right away – take your time. It is also very helpful to do this as a group project. I'm big on collaboration, and to hear the interpretations and ideas from others is always helpful and beneficial, as long as they understand the concepts covered in this book. It also makes it a lot more fun – especially when the arguing and fights begin. In some of my classes in the past, I was playing referee, making sure the students didn't kill each other! Just remember, arguing allows for all interpretations to germinate, and it shows that we are all passionate about what we are reading. Don't be afraid to be passionate in your views – this is the utmost compliment to the creators of the show – you're showing your love and care of their characters!

As an example to work through the entire process, we will use the musical *The Music Man*. Structurally, it is an easier musical to analyse, with straightforward characters, a consistent community, and the music examples are fairly standard in origin. *The Music Man* did receive the Tony Award for Best Musical in 1957, winning over the masterpiece *West Side Story*. You will receive *West Side Story*'s more complex analysis in a later chapter.

The ten-step analytical process

1. Read the script and listen to the score for a first time

When you are reading the script, listen to the music at the same time. In other words, when you come up to a song in your reading, follow the lyrics as you are also listening to the score. Remember, music is an emotional boost, springboarding from a build-up of emotions in the script. It's a natural progression, and you need to feel that progression as you are reading. It's too easy for folks to just skim through lyrics and not listen to the music right away. To do this is to totally lose the potential for the identification of energies. Remember the Cardinal Rule of Energies: **it's the music and the lyrics.** It is the songs that the audience remembers, and thus defines the energies of the characters. How can you possibly do that if you aren't listening to the music at the same time as reading the lyrics? Don't forget that music is a universal communicator – it bridges the differences in languages, customs, and preconceptions. It is also the truthful emotion of that character at that moment.

As you are reading the script and listening to the score for the first time, try not to think about the analysis of the show too much. Allow yourself to enjoy the musical. Allow yourself to be pulled into its web. Feel with the characters, experience the moments with them. Allow yourself to be carried away into their world. However, try to make yourself aware enough so that you can occasionally ask yourself some basic questions. Try to be aware of why you continue to want to turn to the next page of the script. Try to be aware of whom you are rooting for and what you want them to achieve. Also, try to be aware of when you feel the musical is really beginning to take off – the engines starting. If it will help you, take minimal notes so you don't forget.

Try to avoid analysing character energies the first time you read through it. Sometimes when you do that too early on, it doesn't allow you the flexibility to accept changes, or different interpretations. It also prevents you from totally immersing yourself in the show – which then doesn't allow you to totally feel through each character. It needs to be experiential – you need to live through those characters and feel what they are feeling. Reading from a purely analytical side will prevent you from doing this. Remember that musicals are an art form to be *experienced* – they aren't purposely written just to be analysed! Don't rob yourself of that first artful, emotional experience.

2. Read the script and listen to the score for a second time

This next reading of the script and listening to the score should be more from the focus of analysis. Really start thinking about the dramatic question and who you are rooting for in the musical. Start noticing main characters and their songs. Start getting a feel for the types of songs they are, how they are used, and the power in which they are given. Take note as to how many songs each character sings, or how many songs a community of characters sing. Figure out the important relationships – the ones you really care about. Start dismissing other more analytically insignificant characters. Start looking for clues in the lyrics that perhaps give enlightenment to the kind of energy they are portraying.

Never ignore the stage directions. This is especially true when it comes to dances. Remember that dances definitely focus on the characters of importance and personifies/magnifies the energies of those characters. A dance segment description may only take one tiny paragraph in the script, but when performed, may take five minutes in length to dance. Five minutes of music and dance is an incredible amount of time to distinguish and focus character energy. It becomes *memorable*. Also, many times stage directions have music that is underscoring the dramatic action of the stage directions, and because of that it will have a huge impact on the direction of the story or the defining of character energy.

3. Create the dramatic question

This is the most important thing to do and get right in the analytical process. Don't glance over this important step. Really ponder what you wanted to find out in the story, who you were rooting for, and what you wanted as an ending. Don't forget the subtext in the show. Is there an overall bigger theme that the musical is covering besides the basic plotline? The stronger your dramatic question is, the better your chances will be in correctly analysing the musical.

I have found in my classes that sometimes students really have trouble getting everything they feel is important included into one short and simple dramatic question. To help them, sometimes I have them write down a list of things that they feel are important to include in the dramatic question, and then, when they are all listed, we try to find and cut out the similarities and redundancies. It's an arduous and tedious process to develop that clean, simplistic dramatic question, but when done right, the rest of the analysis falls much more easily into place.

I happen to be a "visual." I like to see things in front of me so that I can do my assessing through not only my own internal thinking, but also seeing it

> Dramatic Question: *"Will Marian find her true love in Harold Hill, and will the people of River City grow to find new excitement in their boring lives?"*

Figure 15 *The Music Man:* The Dramatic Question.

textually on the page. So, this next step is with a nod to all of those "visuals" out there in the world. Once you feel you have the dramatic question, get a clean sheet of paper, set it long ways, and write the title of the musical at the very top of the diagram. Draw a box outlining the parameter of the page. Then, inside the box, write the dramatic question at the very top. This then becomes your reminder, referral, and mantra through the rest of the process. I will be using this diagram format for the analysis of all musicals. Use it – it really is helpful.

4. List all analytically important characters

Now don't get me wrong. I firmly believe every character, no matter how small their role, is an important and integral part to the show. When I state to list all *analytically important* characters, I am talking about the characters that need to be considered for the overall analysis of character energy. They need to be characters that sing and/or dance a lot. Many times, if a character only sings one song in a show, that song is designed for one specific reason, and that's not necessarily to identify oneself as an energy. Sometimes the song is in there to break the mood of a show, or to add a certain levity that's missing in the show. Generally, if a character sings only one song, you probably don't have to worry about them in the analysis. However, if they have only one solo song, but they also sing in a chorus or a community a lot, then perhaps you want to include them in the same energy as the chorus. Likewise, if they only have one solo song, but have a major acting role, it may be worth including them in the analysis. Again, refer to the dramatic question for help and guidance.

When you look at *The Music Man*, you're dealing with a bunch of people who only have one or two songs. Figure 16 is the start of a list of the characters.

I believe everyone can understand listing Harold and Marian. They have plenty of songs throughout the show and they also are a part of the dramatic question. You probably have questions, however, as to why I am listing the School Board, and the Ladies separately, considering that they are a part

Figure 16 *The Music Man*: List of Characters.

of the community. The issue is that both groups sing a large number of songs and they frankly are given more focus in the show than the rest of the townspeople. Now, it may be that in the end, you will just include them into the townspeople, and that is okay, but for analytical reasons and for their sheer numbers of songs, we'll separate them for now. The same can be said for Winthrop and Mrs Paroo. We'll see how it pans out in the end. Either way you analyse it, it will end up working out the same way.

You may question why we don't include Charlie Cowell and the Travelling Salesman in the list. The fact is, they only sing in the first number ("Rock Island"), and that is mainly to introduce Harold. After that song, you never hear from them again, except for Charlie, and even then, when Charlie comes back into town much later in the show he never sings. So, they get the axe.

In regard to the kids in the show – Tommy and Zaneeta especially – they really don't sing without the townspeople, as in "Shipoopi" or "The Wells Fargo Wagon." We can consider them townspeople for analytical reasons.

5. List all the songs under the characters' names in performance order

You will notice in this next step that I've added a few new things (Figure 17). First of all, the songs are numbered in performance order. Secondly, I put the title of the song underneath the first character(s) who start the song. Even if, for example, the chorus may sing a line first, and then it becomes a solo song for one character for the rest of the piece, I still would put the title under the chorus. It has nothing to do with the importance of any group – it only has to do with who sings first. Thirdly, the arrows just show who else is singing in the song. The direction of the arrows is strictly just showing that it came out of the characters who sang first in the song. Finally, I only list the songs, reprises, and dances, while I ignore orchestral interlude music that is listed in the piano and conductor scores.

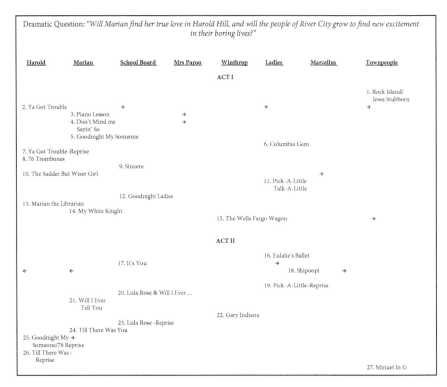

Figure 17 *The Music Man*: List of Songs.

Once you start looking at a diagram like this visually, you begin to notice right away what characters have the most focus in the show. Harold has nine songs, and Marian has eight. Both have more than any other group, and this is normal for leads in a show. Where we find an incredible amount of songs is when we look at the School Board, the Ladies, and the townspeople. If you combine all of the School Board, Winthrop, Ladies, and townspeople songs together, they total fifteen songs – a huge number. They are indeed an integral part of the musical and can't be ignored. With this in mind, it seems that our diagram has supported our dramatic question really well.

6. Lyrically analyse all of the songs

This is the tricky and most difficult part of analysis. It is the meat and potatoes of your work. You must really start dissecting each and every song that a character sings and then start comparing your findings with the characteristics of LF energy and N energy. This is where the real grunt work begins. Sometimes, you'll be able to look at a song and the character, and immediately know what energy they are. Then, just going through the rest of the songs from that character is just to make sure it stays consistent. Those analysis examples are heaven sent!

It's when you get a character that you have no idea what their energy is, or the character has conflicting songs that then confuses you. This is when you really need to bear down and get to the heart of the lyric and the character. Many times you even need to go through lyrics line by line. It's hard work, however, when you do this, you will be much more apt to get the analysis right. Be patient, be diligent, and don't give up. You will reap the benefits in the end. Most importantly, always justify your decisions using the **Need Energy and LF Energy Lyric Circles**.

Finally, do not try to analyse the music at the same time as you do your lyrical analysis! It will only make your analysis more difficult to figure out. Remember, the music depends on the energy of the characters, and what truths the characters are knowingly or unknowingly singing at that moment.

Life Force Energy Lyric Circle

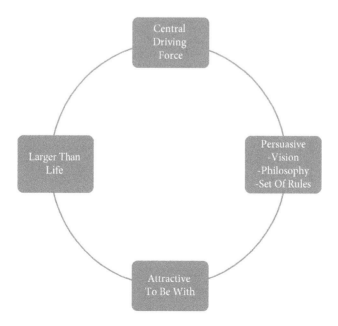

Need Energy Lyric Circle

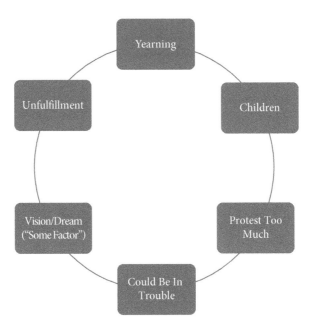

Figure 18 Need Energy and LF Energy Lyric Circles.

Once all of the lyrical analysis is done for the entire show, it is at that point that we then can go into the music analysis.

Marian

Let's arbitrarily start with Marian, since she is listed first in the dramatic question. The process in figuring out Marian starts with the basic question that is a part of the dramatic question: Who are we rooting for in this show? I think we could honestly say that we are rooting for Marian. We want her to find the love of her life, and we want the community to respect her. We truly want her to be happy, and there seems to be this overall cloud of discontentment with her. She maintains that she is fine, but this could easily be protesting too much. Our gut instinct would tell us that she is N energy, but now we need to prove it, and the only way to do that is to go through every song she sings lyrically, following the Need Energy Lyric Circle.

"The Piano Lesson/If You Don't Mind My Saying So"

We find out in this song that Marian is frustrated with the people of River City. The Ladies of River City ignore her advice and counsel. There is this fight between being book smart and down-to-earth real, and Mrs Paroo sees that. She believes Marian's standards are too high to find a man and that she should consider giving Harold a try. Marian belligerently disagrees. So with this song, we know that Marian would like to have a man in her life, but her standards are very high.

This points to Marian being N energy – having a **yearning**, being **unfulfilled**, but we must be careful at this point, because there are some very strong women out there and she could conceivably survive without a man in her life. She's the anomaly of a woman in River City, Iowa: educated, intelligent, and independent. In that case, she could be LF. Therefore, the verdict is still out as to whether she is LF or N. We need to look to her second song.

"Goodnight, My Someone"

SOME. Ok, there is a clue – the "**Some Factor**." Who is she singing goodnight to? She is singing to **some**one. Her love. How is she doing this? She's singing, wishing on a star. She is **unfulfilled** when she is truly comfortable enough to open up her heart privately to the world. She has this deep-seated **wish/ vision/dream** to be loved by a man, wherever and whoever he is. She **dreams** of the time that he will come into her life. This solidifies our theory that Marian is N.

Now, we need to confirm that she is N energy.

"My White Knight"

She is looking for that one man who will be modest, plain, gentle, and honest. A man who reads and takes an interest in art, and above all, an interest in them as a couple. She's a romantic. She will walk with this man, and she will love him "*til I die.*" This song takes us through the first act, so with this amount of information, at this point we could safely confirm that she is N energy.

Following the N energy lyric circle characteristics, Marian is **yearning** for a man/companionship, she is romantically **unfulfilled**, and she is **dreaming** of that perfect **some**one. She is showing us the emotional side of the story. We are rooting for Marian. Yes, she is a very strong woman, and one would think that on the surface, she would survive without a man. Nevertheless, in her private moments, when she is singing, her songs definitely contradict that theory. She and Harold are the roots and focus of the plot. This woman is N energy.

We must, however, continue on to make sure that there isn't some type of major change in the musical – a change which would then make her shift her energy. This is rare in show analysis, but it does happen at times.

"Shipoopi" (what kind of a word is that anyway?)

Marcellus sings this song and calls the dance. The Shipoopi is a dance that Harold had learned in the city and so the townspeople want Harold to teach it to them. Marian does not join in the dance until Harold takes Marian as his partner. Harold is teaching her how to dance, not the other way around. Marian is not in control – Harold is. She is at the mercy of what Harold does, and when she does join, she begins to truly enjoy it. Suddenly, Marian's eyes are opened to a possibility that Harold isn't as bad a fella as she may have thought. Could he be a potential resolution to her deep-seated need?

Suddenly the dance aspect of this number is very important in drawing those two people together. Harold and Marian must gradually show chemistry through their reactions and their dance by the time the song ends.

"Will I Ever Tell You"

Marian is now stating her love. She's **dreaming** of a love song. That pretty much sums it up. She's in love with Harold.

"Till There Was You"

It is at this point that she confesses to Harold that she has no high expectations of their relationship, but she is still grateful to him and for what he has done. She is trying to find resolution in this fact, but we know that deep down Marian wants Harold to stay with her forever. At this point, we don't know what he will do. She then starts to sing, professing that she never noticed bells ringing or birds singing until he came into her life.

She is definitely the emotional, loving side of the show. And yes, even though she is a strong woman on the outside by giving Harold the incriminating page of evidence that proved him a fraud, inside she is an unfulfilled school girl waiting for her first kiss. She sacrificed her love and feelings for Harold's well-being, knowing it would kill her inside. Marian is N energy throughout the entire show.

Harold

Harold is a very complex individual. Throughout most of the show he is a con-artist salesman wanting to take advantage of poor folk. What makes him so complex though is the fact that we still really like him, even though he is a criminal. That is great writing! What is also so bizarre about Harold is that we are also rooting for him, right? We aren't rooting for him to con the community and then leave town, though. We are rooting instead for him to change and turn into a decent human being. Will he be okay if he doesn't change? Absolutely. He's lived that way his entire career, and there is nothing that would point to him not continuing that way. We have no worries about him. Because of this insight, we have a clue to his energy – LF. But it is way too early to determine this. We must follow the energy circles through each of his songs.

"Ya Got Trouble"

In this song, Harold is trying to sell the town a barrel of goods, plain and simple. He is creating hyperbole in the notion that there is trouble in the town due to the billiard parlor. Harold claims that it will destroy the moral fabric of their boys. Is this true? No. Do the townspeople listen and start to buy into what he's saying? Absolutely. Here is a man who creates a fictional stir in town so that he can sell goods. And boy, he's good at it.

He succeeds because he is so damn **attractive to be with** – so charismatic, energetic, and good looking. He is the **central driving force** in this song, corralling people together at the town square to listen to what he has to say. He is certainly **larger than life** considering that he has no fear in gathering strangers in a strange town to listen to his lies. That takes real guts! He's a leader, for sure, even though his motives suck.

Finally, by the end of the song, he has the entire town singing about their troubles (of which they don't have) and looking to him as a messenger of God. Harold has the incredible capacity to sway audiences towards his specific goals. He is a master of **persuasion**. He actually gets them to sing in perfect harmony and believe in what he is pitching. How appropriate that this "Messenger of God" gets them to sing in unity, in a high-energy, gospel-like revival song!

There would be no doubt that Harold is LF. But then again, we need to confirm our theory, so we must continue on our analysis path.

"Seventy-Six Trombones"

What do you do when you instil this notion of trouble in the town? Well, of course, you offer them the perfect solution to the problem! After reminding the town of their troubles, he then gives them a solution – a boy's band. This resolution seems possible! He gives his **persuasive vision** of what this boy's band could do: how they would look, how the band would keep them out of trouble, and how they would help the town of

River City. In listening to him, the townspeople dream right along with him. What **persuasion**! By this time, it becomes pretty obvious that Harold is LF. It also places the townspeople clearly towards the N energy side, considering that they are being swayed and swindled, but we will look at them later.

"The Sadder But Wiser Girl"

This is where we learn what kind of a girl Harold likes – one with no attachments. He knows exactly what he needs and *he gets it*. He is setting down his **set of rules** as to the kind of girl that will fit his criteria. He's a one-night-stand kind of guy – no sailor-knots tied on him. Interestingly enough, he also is increasing the distance between himself and Marian in this song. We now have an even bigger obstacle between what we want to see happen with Harold and Marian.

Marcellus was a former partner/con artist with Harold, but has now reformed himself and is living a happy, fulfilled life with a nice girl, Ethel. Marcellus has settled down and has given up that type of criminal life. He has chosen this life and is happy about it. He is fulfilled and complete. Marcellus also understands and is quiet about Harold's life of con. He doesn't sing, but he dances in agreement with Harold. Marcellus is leaning towards being LF.

"Marian the Librarian"

This song is all about manipulation and **persuasion**. Harold is trying to take advantage of Marian and get her to go out with him. He's using every persuasive technique in the book. He is trying to woo her through talking sweet nothings. Harold also uses dance moves, and he even uses threats of library disruption. Despite her willpower, Marian is faltering, slowly giving in to his charm. Marian is the strongest and most intelligent person in River City, and yet Harold's power can still even sway her a bit. Harold is definitely LF.

"Shipoopi"

Harold is in control. He is teaching everyone else how to dance the Shipoopi – a big city phenomenon. He also uses this power of being **larger than life** and **attractive to be with** to coerce Marian to dance with him. We can't forget that he has an agenda – to get her in bed with him. He is still solidly LF. Marcellus already knows the Shipoopi through his work and experience with Harold. He knows the moves and calls the song. Thus, Marcellus is also LF.

An interesting fact is that the same song can be LF to one singer but N to another. In this song, Marian and the townsfolk all sing and dance at the end of the song. They are caught in the LF whirlwind of Harold. However, they are still N energy folks, and for them, this is a N song. It is all about who is in control and who is following blindly.

"Goodnight My Someone/Seventy-Six Trombones Reprise"

This is where Harold's conscience finally starts to get the better of him. During the last verse of the reprise, the two characters, Marian and Harold, switch their songs. This does not mean that they are switching energies. Marian is simply starting to find resolution and Harold is starting to acknowledge a change within him.

"Till There Was You Reprise"

As Harold talks with Winthrop and admits that he *is* a dirty rotten crook, he begins to assess his life, and at that moment, decides that he will face the people of the town. Even then, *he is in control*. He is the central driving force. He is even more **attractive to be with** now that he is repenting. Even in his darkest and most vulnerable moments, Harold is always **larger than life**, strong, and **vision**ary.

Finally, closing in on the end of the show, Harold still will accept whatever consequences happen to him. It may not be pleasant, but he will survive. He just changes his values. Therefore, Harold is LF through the entire show. You could bet your bottom dollar that if the show continued, Harold would end up being mayor!

And do remember, Marian does not change from N to LF. Her need is just resolved with Harold deciding to stay.

The people of River City

People in communities are of all shapes, colours, and sizes. How can an entire town be LF or N? It really all depends on how the town is designed. You have to have a great, over-arching vision for what you want that community to be, and then in some way, stay consistent in its vision through the lyrics and music. If it is a LF community, you have to make sure that the community is self-assured, has a belief or higher moral that unifies them, or that they are at least settled, happy, and fulfilled in its living circumstance. N communities have to have an over-arching unfulfillment, yearning, or trouble that they all are experiencing. It may not be the main focus of the story plotline, but it definitely is in support of it. So, as we look at the community of River City, and especially its subcultures, we must keep in mind that they can be different within each subculture even though they all have the over-arching, unified fulfillment or need.

School Board members

The School Board members hate each other. They never get along. How can you be an effective School Board and not get along? I'd say that they are in **trouble**. Once Harold comes into town, it is their job and duty to acquire the necessary credentials from him, proving that he is legitimate. However, every time they are about to get the credentials from Harold (who, of course, hasn't any credentials), Harold gets them off track by mesmerizing them into singing another song. Even though they hate each other, once they start singing, they are happy as clams and forget about why they came up to Harold in the first place. Suddenly, the quartet is singing a love song to Lida Rose!

Harold's salesmanship on the School Board is almost magical in its power. He first introduces them into singing. Then, as the School Board continues to sing each song, we recognize that not only are they singing love songs to other women, but they are also personifying that love between themselves. Their troubles are gone – Harold has guided them to be BFFs! The School Board is N.

The Ladies

It is the same with the Ladies and Harold. The Ladies are small town hicks who gossip incessantly and have no sense of artistry or finesse. As with "Pick-A-Little, Talk-A-Little," they are mostly interested in hen-pecking gossip – a troublesome and self-destroying social behaviour. They have this insatiable need to gossip because it makes them feel self-important and vital in life, when deep down inside, they are totally insecure and bored. They are **unfulfilled**.

Harold showers them with kindness and compliments, and in doing so, they start to become assets to the community. Their gossiping eventually stops and they perform artistic dances! The Ladies are N.

Winthrop

He's a small, young boy – a **child**. He's honest, cute, and powerless. He has a lisp that he is self-conscious about. He depends on the adults around him to take care of him and keep him safe. He learns a song from Harold about a great city to dream about – Gary, Indiana. Winthrop learns to **dream** big and can actually feel confident singing the song because there are hardly any "s" sounds in the lyrics. This is all due to Harold. **Children** are almost always N. In this case, Winthrop is no exception.

Mrs Paroo

She mainly is a townsperson, but she also desperately wants the best for her daughter, Marian. Mrs Paroo loves her dearly and until Marian is settled, Mrs Paroo will be unsettled. She will **not be fulfilled** until her daughter is well taken care of. She also has no problem speaking her mind when it comes to Marian's love life. "If You Don't Mind My Saying So" definitely expresses Mrs Paroo's frustration with her daughter's finickiness and high expectations. Where will Marian ever find a man-combination of Paul Bunyan, Noah Webster, and Saint Patrick? Mrs Paroo may be a strong-headed, Irish woman, but she can't solve this problem without Harold's help. She is N.

Townspeople

First, let's address all the salesmen in the song "Rock Island," even though we've pretty much ignored the song and the group. All of these salesmen on the train are complaining about this one salesman, Harold Hill, who is giving all of them a bad name. Harold swindles towns out of their money by selling them the idea that they need a boy's band. He then leaves before towns realize it and before the boys learn to play. The song is a wonderful lament – the salesman are complaining that their reputations are getting destroyed because of this one guy. They have big **troubles**, so they are N.

Everyone in town is being manipulated by Harold and they don't know it. Even the leader of the town, Mayor Shinn, gets caught in Harold's salesmanship hypnosis. He may pop out of it sooner than others, but he certainly is not in control of the situation, even if he is the mayor. Harold is conning the town without them even knowing it. Why are they so susceptible? The author, Meredith Willson, certainly isn't just saying that all Iowa folks are gullible, stupid hics? The town must have something missing in their lives, and "Iowa Stubborn" is the answer to that question. In the song, they are singing of their boring, woeful life. They are **yearning** for excitement and change, and they have no idea as to how to find it. They certainly do know what is wrong with all of them, for they list it in droves in their song.

In "Trouble," they are manipulated into believing that there is **trouble** in River City, even if there really isn't.

"The Wells Fargo Wagon" is coming to bring their instruments, and when it arrives, Harold is the first there to deliver Winthrop his trumpet. That wagon represents their solution to their **yearning** and **troubles**. Each of them is hoping that the wagon has "*something special*" for them.

"Shipoopi" is a song where Harold teaches them all how to dance The Shipoopi. They are having more fun than they have had in years! Harold is their answer to their doldrums in life. Everyone is changed when Harold is around! The townspeople are N energy. River City is a community of N.

Interestingly enough, listing all of the subsections of townspeople, we find out that they all ended up being N characters anyway. So, you can't lose either way you do it – separately like we did, or doing all the townspeople together as one large group. The outcome will still be the same.

A note here. This is where analysis really comes in handy for a director or a choreographer. Looking at "Iowa Stubborn," for example, in the script it just says the townspeople sing it. But would you include Marcellus in the group in this song? I wouldn't. He's LF and it wouldn't make sense. He doesn't share the same values. Likewise, I wouldn't include Marian, because even though she is N, she isn't the same Iowa person as the rest of the town. She's "ostracized" from them because of her intelligence and impatience with the community.

LF	N	N	N	N	N	LF	N
Harold	Marian	School Board	Mrs Paroo	Winthrop	Ladies	Marcellus	Townpeople
				ACT I			
							1. Rock Island/ Iowa Stubborn
2. Ya Got Trouble	→				→		→
		3. Piano Lesson	→				
		4. Don't Mind me Sayin' So	→				
		5. Goodnight My Someone					
					6. Columbia Gem		
7. Ya Got Trouble-Reprise							
8. 76 Trombones							
		9. Sincere					
10. The Sadder But Wiser Girl						→	
					11. Pick-A-Little Talk-A-Little		
		12. Goodnight Ladies					
13. Marian the Librarian							
	14. My White Knight						
				15. The Wells Fargo Wagon			→
				ACT II			
					16. Eulalie's Ballet →		
		17. It's You					
←	←				18. Shipoopi →		
					19. Pick-A-Little-Reprise		
		20. Lida Rose & Will I Ever…					
	21. Will I Ever Tell You						
				22. Gary Indiana			
		23. Lida Rose-Reprise					
		24. Till There Was You					
25. Goodnight My → Someone/76 Reprise							
26. Till There Was-Reprise							
							27. Minuet In G

Dramatic Question: *"Will Marian find her true love in Harold Hill, and will the people of River City grow to find new excitement in their boring lives?"*

Figure 19 *The Music Man*: List of Character Energies.

7. Musically analyse all the songs

We are now at the point where we have a solid analysis map of all of the characters. Now, we need to find out what kind of N and LF energy songs the characters are singing. We will use our lyric analysis work as the basis for our music analysis. This process is the same in that we will just go down the list of songs for each character in order. Keep in mind that songs that are sung by multiple groups can have different energies for the same song, so it would be the responsibility of the actors to portray/interpret those songs with their energy and motivations in mind. Above all, they must keep in mind that the music will always speak the truth to that character.

The process of song level identification is as follows:

1   Identify what main character(s) sing the song and notice her/his/their assigned energy.
2   Does this song sound like it has the traditional LF or N energy music characteristics?
3   If your LF character is singing a song that sounds like LF, then it is a Level 1–Tell It Like It Is LF song. If your N character is singing a song that sounds like N, then it is a Level 1–Tell It Like It Is N song. Your work is done for that song.
4   If your LF character song sounds like N, or if your N character song sounds LF, then you must go through the rest of the levels of the Music Circle of Truth for N or LF.
5   Start at Level 2, and slowly analyse each level to see which one fits that specific song.

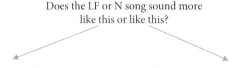

Does the LF or N song sound more
like this or like this?

LF Energy General Music Characteristics	N Energy General Music Characteristics
• Rhythm/Anthem song • Louder • Melodic, yet more rhythmic • Attacking/Articulate • Faster • More direct, in your face all the way through • Brass/Percussion/Louder electronic instruments are prevalent	• Ballad-style song • Softer • Melodic • Legato • Slower • Has a traditional growth arc in the song • Strings/Woodwinds/Quieter acoustic instruments are prevalent

Figure 20 Does the LF or N Song Sound More Like This or Like This?

Life ForceEnergy Music Circle of Truth

Need Energy Music Circle of Truth

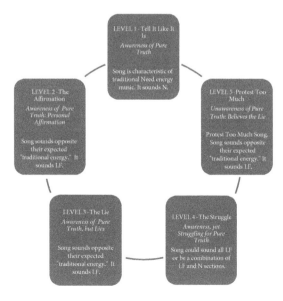

Figure 21 Life Force and Need Energy Music Circle of Truths.

Marian – N

"The Piano Lesson/If You Don't Mind My Saying So"

The music doesn't sound like a "Need song," but we do know because of the argument that Marian is unfulfilled about not having a man. Both Marian and Mrs Paroo are affirming what they believe to be true in a rhythmic and argumentative way, so the music is reflecting this. They are fighting, and how many fights are quiet? The song bounces through with a strong, snare-brushed beat, with woodwinds and strings taking the majority of the song. This song sounds LF, so it is a N Level 2–The Affirmation.

"Goodnight, My Someone"

Marian is opening her heart to the stars in a very gentle, honest, and musical ballad way. It starts with just piano, and then grows in strength with strings accompaniment. The song continues to grow in the B section with the tempo increasing and adding of woodwinds. It has a nice growth arc. It sounds like a typical ballad, and it is. This song sounds N, so it is a N Level 1–Tell It Like It Is.

"My White Knight"

Marian again is passionate about who she wants in a man. She's very honest, open-hearted, and very descriptive and detailed in what kind of man she wants. The song is wordy, but the melody still grows, with string and woodwind accompaniment. After the B section, the song climaxes nicely at the end with Marian singing a nice, full high note to finish the piece. This song sounds N, so it is a N Level 1–Tell It Like It Is.

"Will I Ever Tell You"

Marian is singing about her love for Harold. Again, she is honest, quiet, and in solitude. The music reflects this romantic moment in the style of the old, 1940s and early 1950s love ballad, complete with strings, pizzicato bass, and brushed snare keeping the beat. This song sounds N, so it is a N Level 1–Tell It Like It Is.

"Till There Was You"

This time Marian is singing in front of Harold. She declares her love for him in a typical ballad-style piece. Opening with strictly strings and harp, the music is lush in romantic ebb and flow. The velvet melody soars and grows in strength until it peaks with fullness and strength at the end. No question here – this song sounds like the perfect N song, so it is a N Level 1–Tell It Like It Is.

"Goodnight My Someone/Seventy-Six Trombones Reprise"

Marian is now singing in support of her decision to allow Harold to escape from River City. She now is gaining some of Harold's confidence and strength, and she reflects that power musically by switching songs at the end and reprising "Seventy-Six Trombones." She, however, isn't resolved as of yet. This song sounds N at the beginning and so it starts as a N Level 1–Tell It Like It Is, but then changes to a N Level 2–The Affirmation when they switch tunes.

Harold – LF

"Ya Got Trouble"

Harold's first LF song "Trouble" is a booming, snappy, and very persuasive piece of music. Harold is giving them the old one-two sales pitch with eye-popping energy in his music. It's a 1950s rap! The patter is fast, followed and accentuated with loud, surprising slams from the brass and percussion instruments. It's rhythmic, accented, articulated, fast, and growing in arc. It's all done to make Harold the point of attention. This song sounds LF, so it is a LF Level 1–Tell It Like It Is.

"Seventy-Six Trombones"

Harold has created this vision and dream in the minds of the River City people. He has mesmerized them. Now to climax his point and fulfil their dream, he brings out the blaring brass, which is a huge attention-getter. The song is full, and big – it's a marching band! This is Harold's final point to his sales pitch and he ends it with a musical exclamation point. The song is wonderfully melodic, huge, and splashy, with the brass and percussion leading the way. This definitely sounds LF, so it is a LF Level 1–Tell It Like It Is.

This is probably a good place to ask the question: "Since Harold is a scam artist salesman, wouldn't everything that he sings about be a lie or at least The Tactical in nature?" First of all, the way Harold is set up, he really isn't evil. We do have a sense of decency in the man, even though he's gone down the wrong path. Secondly, there are a couple of scenes which justify the fact that he truly believes in the dream of a boy's band:

1   When he makes sure he gives Winthrop his trumpet first. That's a sign that he really does care for the kid.

2 He imagines himself on the footbridge conducting a band with a twig.

3 He even states to Winthrop at the end of the show that he always believes there's a band. He's being truthful at that moment.

If we truly believed that Harold was there to be evil and hurt the town of River City, the show would not work.

Finally and most importantly, Harold's song "Trouble" (or any other number for that matter) is not a Level 3–The Lie song or Level 5–The Tactical for the simple reason that they sound LF. Any LF song that sounds LF is a Level 1–Tell It Like It Is song, and Harold is in fact, telling it like it is. Yes, he is scamming them, but he's doing it by finding a weakness in the community that will then be filled by the introduction of a boy's band. The boy's band will, *and does*, solve their needs.

"The Sadder But Wiser Girl"

Harold is singing his credo and philosophy with this bouncy song rendition about his view on relationships with women. Interestingly, it starts with the soft percussive sounds of pizzicato strings and a splash of woodwinds, but then the percussion takes over with a nice beat and slams of brass, drums, and xylophone. The interludes are loaded with Dixieland band jazz blues music that continues to give Harold the driving force that he needs to send his point home. It's very rhythmic and articulated. It sounds LF, so it is a LF Level 1–Tell It Like It Is.

"Marian the Librarian"

Harold is persuading Marian to join him in a meeting of the women's guild. The song has a bit of bounce, but also very much following the rules of Marian's library – being very quiet. The music has this suppressed rhythmic tempo that just wants to explode out. It's hard not to tap your foot and get caught up in the momentum of the piece. Even though it's quiet, LF music characteristics still rears its energetic head into the song. The dance interlude reflects this not-quite-suppressed and controlled energy. Again too, Willson's use of slams with the percussion and brass to accentuate a point, all the more reminds us of Harold's LF being. This sounds LF, so it is a LF Level 1–Tell It Like It Is.

Harold is definitely pushing hard to get Marian to join him. One might think that he's using every tactic in the book to sway her. He woos her, tells her that he loves her, tries to get her to feel sorry for him, and even threatens her with noise. If this isn't a Level 5–The Tactical song, what is? One simple point: the LF song has to sound like N in order for it to be Level 5, and that just isn't the case. He's honestly working his salesman magic on her.

"Shipoopi"
This is a song and dance from "the big city" that Harold and Marcellus share with the town. The music is fast, patter-like, powerful, bouncy, catchy, high energy, and the dance reflects this as well. It's almost a high-octane square dance. It climaxes to a large choral finale. The townspeople are again caught up in the central driving force energy of Harold and Marcellus. It sounds LF, so the song is LF Level 1–Tell It Like It Is.

"Goodnight My Someone/Seventy-Six Trombones Reprise"
Harold eventually switches songs with Marian and sings the slow "Goodnight My Someone" ballad. This was a N song for Marian early on in the show. As soon as Harold switches to that song, he is just being honest in his realization that he loves Marian. He's not unfulfilled without her, he just realizes that he may want to change his life to be with her. Therefore, the music reflects this honesty with no bells and whistles – just down-to-earth, slow, beautifully melodic music. At first, it sounds LF, so at the beginning it is a LF Level 1– Tell It Like It Is. However, when they switch songs, his song sounds N, so it becomes a LF Level 2–The Affirmation.

"Till There Was You Reprise"
Marian sings this as a Need song earlier in the show, but now it transforms into a Life Force song for Harold. He accepts his fate, his love, and becomes open-hearted and honest for once in his life. He is truly being himself to Marian. He affirms his love to her, and is willing to change his life for her, thus the ballad-style song. It sounds N, so it is a LF Level 2–The Affirmation.

The people of River City
The School Board members – N
All of their barbershop quartet numbers are N Level 1–Tell It Like It Is. They all have a sense of old time, melancholy ballads with lyrics that are more folk tunes than musical tunes with a lyrical purpose. However, in the "Lida Rose" duet with Marian, or "Goodnight Ladies," where they pick up the tempo in both pieces, there is rhythmic power to the songs. There, they become Level 2–The Affirmation.

As a side note, Meredith Willson was brilliant in this. How could you possibly show musically a more close-knit, tightly interwoven piece of music than barbershop music? What better way to metaphorically show musically how a bunch of bickering, fuddy-duddy, old codgers who hate each other can finally get along together? When we hear them sing, we can't even decipher individual parts – their blend and harmonies are that close together.

The Ladies – N

"Columbia Gem" "Columbia Gem" is a N Level 2–The Affirmation song. It is LF in quality because of its anthem-like, patriotic power. The women are affirming their need for importance and recognition.

"Pick-A-Little, Talk-A-Little" "Pick-A-Little" sounds LF due to the hen-pecking sound and rhythmic bounce of the piece. The bright tempo, in tandem with fast-paced 16th note patterns, add a crazy, if not frantic, feel to the song. The instrumentation may be quiet, but the pushing of the railroad beat with the brushed snare keeps the piece going high octane. This song sounds LF, so it is a LF Level 2–The Affirmation song.

"Eulalie's Ballet" This song is a simple N Level 1–Tell It Like It Is. They are dancing their hearts out with little success to a slow, emotionally moving piano piece. The music almost kills them, making them the weak, unflexible, unartistic, and desperate-for-attention group that they are.

Winthrop – N

"Gary Indiana" Winthrop declares his dream of seeing "the big city." Harold taught this song to him – a LF energy, bouncy, kid's number – so it becomes a dream song for Winthrop. It's a place he wants to go visit and epitomizes it as the place to be. Marian joins in to build the number, as well as a splash of brass and volume at the end. It sounds LF, so it is a N Level 2–The Affirmation song.

Townspeople – N

"Iowa Stubborn" This song is listing their woes – all that is awful about the Iowa folks. This type of lament song, listing their troubles with each other, is

pretty comic. Thus, it requires that upbeat feel in the music. Its humour is in the fact that their way of living *is* unexciting, mundane, and boring. Because of their unabashed honesty and anthem-like belief, the song mirrors the people, clip clopping their way through life like an old horse. It sounds LF, so it is a N Level 2–The Affirmation.

"Ya Got Trouble" "Trouble" is a gospel revival song full of LF belief and power, but they are being mesmerized by Harold. He is taking them for a ride that is never going to happen. They are so naïve and sheltered that they don't even know what is hitting them. The song is powerful, high energy, and full of emotion. The townspeople are so hungry for excitement that this salesman seems like a dream come true for them. This is a huge LF sounding song, therefore it is a N Level 2–The Affirmation.

"The Wells Fargo Wagon" This song is a real LF bouncer, with incredible anticipation and movement, but the anticipation is the Harold Hill band instruments that offer hope in a life that has always seemed void of excitement. They are desperately wishing for the arrival of these instruments so that their lives will change for the better. The upbeat, clip-clopping beat of the horse and wagon, accompanied by the offbeat of pizzicato strings stirs a sense of anticipation immediately. By the climax of the piece, the chorus is singing double forte to the crash of cymbals and the brass blaring fanfare for the arrival of Winthrop's trumpet. This too, sounds LF, so it is a N Level 2–The Affirmation.

"Shipoopi" By now, you finally get the idea – the townspeople are always N Level 2–The Affirmation songs since it is Harold who is selling them the goods. He's giving them exactly what they want – fun and excitement in their boring lives. "Shipoopi" does the same. It is non-stop, fast, high-energy singing and dancing song that sounds LF. Of course, Harold and Marcellus, the LF energy in the show, taught them the dance. Every song is *affirming and satisfying* the holes in their lives. It also is making them think that these dreams that Harold brings to them are the answer to their prayers.

You'll notice in the Figure 22 that I use abbreviations for the music levels. **LF1** would be Life Force Level 1–Tell It Like It Is, for example. **N2** would be Need Level 2–The Affirmation, and so on.

Dramatic Question: *"Will Marian find her true love in Harold Hill, and will the people of River City grow to find new excitement in their boring lives?"*

LF Harold	N Marian	N School Board	N Mrs Paroo	N Winthrop	N Ladies	LF Marcellus	N Townpeople
				ACT I			
							1. Rock Island/ Iowa Stubborn **N2**
2. Ya Got Trouble **LF1**	→**N2**				→**N2**		→**N2**
	3. Piano Lesson **N2**		→				
	4. Don't Mind Me **N2** Sayin' So		→				
	5. Goodnight My Someone **N1**						
					6. Columbia Gem **N2**		
7. Ya Got Trouble-Reprise **LF1**							
8. 76 Trombones **LF1**							
		9. Sincere **N1**					
10. The Sadder But Wiser Girl **LF1**						→	
					11. Pick-A-Little **N2** Talk-A-Little		
		12. Goodnight Ladies **N1**					
13. Marian the Librarian **LF1**							
	14. My White Knight **N1**						
				15. The Wells Fargo Wagon **N2**			→
				ACT II			
					16. Eulalie's Ballet **N1**		
					→		
←**LF1**	←**N2**	17. It's You **N1**					
						18. Shipoopi **LF1**	→**N2**
					19. Pick-A-Little-Reprise **N2**		
		20. Lida Rose & Will I Ever **N1**					
	21. Will I Ever Tell You **N1**						
					22. Gary Indiana **N2**		
		23. Lida Rose -Reprise **N1**					
	24. Till There Was You **N1**						
25. Goodnight My → **N2/1** Someone/76 Reprise **LF1/2**							
26. Till There Was- Reprise **LF2**							
							27. Minuet In G

Figure 22 *The Music Man*: List of Music Truths.

8. Figure out the Alignment energy

The first thing we must always consider before deciding upon the A is to make sure that at least one LF and one N song have been sung. In *The Music Man*, there doesn't seem to be a problem here since "Rock Island/Iowa Stubborn" and "Trouble" are introduced right away. We, however, still aren't quite sure where the show is going at that point. "If You Don't Mind My Sayin' So" starts us questioning about Marian's needs, but it's not until she sings "Goodnight My Someone" that we finally get it. The light bulb goes on when we hear Marian's deep-seated yearning for a man and her unfulfillment in life because of that absence. We also then realize that Harold could be her answer. At this point, we know where the show is going and what the dramatic question is. Depending on the show, this happens around the twenty-minute mark.

Another interesting thing about the Alignment is the way Meredith Willson brilliantly interweaves Marian and Harold melodically. Some may have noticed that the melody line of "Goodnight My Someone" is the same melody as "Seventy-Six Trombones," only augmented in length. What a great way for Willson to subconsciously implant that melodic seed in our minds early on in the show. Of course we want Marian and Harold to get together – it's musical destiny!

9. Figure out the Growth Moment energy

When reading the show, the GM could potentially happen in two different spots, and so we have to figure out the correct one. The first spot is the "Till There Was You Reprise," sung by Harold. This song does answer and offer resolution to Marian's need. Harold has changed/reformed and fallen in love with Marian. He is also willing to stay in River City to accept the consequences of his unlawful actions. The problem with this being the GM is the fact that the townspeople of River City are still not resolved. They are angry and revengeful. They want to tar and feather Harold because they have lost their money and there is no boy's band. This unanswered problem is more than just a coda issue. The townspeople of River City are truly a big part of this story, and we want them resolved too. Once Marian slaps the townspeople across the pate to make them realize what Harold Hill had really done for their town, and then finally, when all the boys play their instruments – albeit terribly – the town is finally resolved. The GM is "Minuet in G."

10. Figure out the ground plan of the musical

The way this musical is set up, the entire town of River City is N. They are a community of N. Harold, who is LF, is not from that community. He enters their world to offer them a new look on life. The overall ground plan of this show is a LF character going into a N community:

$$LF \rightarrow N$$

Harold infiltrated their community world to get something from them, and in the meantime affected their lives permanently.

The final finished *The Music Man* diagram is shown in Figure 23.

Dramatic Question: *"Will Marian find her true love in Harold Hill, and will the people of River City grow to find new excitement in their boring lives?"*

LF Harold	N Marian	N School Board	N Mrs Paroo	N Winthrop	N Ladies	LF Marcellus	N Townpeople
				ACT I			
							1. Rock Island/ Iowa Stubborn **N2**
2. Ya Got Trouble **LF1**	→**N2**				→**N2**		→**N2**
	3. Piano Lesson **N2**		→				
	4. Don't Mind Me **N2** Sayin' So		→				
	5. Goodnight My Someone **N1**						
					6. Columbia Gem **N2**		
7. Ya Got Trouble-Reprise **LF1**							
8. 76 Trombones **LF1**							
		9. Sincere **N1**					
10. The Sadder But Wiser Girl **LF1**					→ 11. Pick-A-Little **N2** Talk-A-Little		
		12. Goodnight Ladies **N1**					
13. Marian the Librarian **LF1**							
	14. My White Knight **N1**						
				15. The Wells Fargo Wagon **N2**			→
				ACT II			
					16. Eulalie's Ballet **N1** →		
		17. It's You **N1**					
←**LF1**	←**N2**					18. Shipoopi **LF1**	→**N2**
					19. Pick-A-Little-Reprise **N2**		
		20. Lida Rose & Will I Ever **N1**					
	21. Will I Ever Tell You **N1**						
				22. Gary Indiana **N2**			
		23. Lida Rose-Reprise **N1**					
	24. Till There Was You **N1**						
25. Goodnight My → **N2/1** Someone/76 Reprise **LF1/2**							
26. Till There Was- Reprise **LF2**							
							27. Minuet In G

A: Goodnight My Someone
GM: Minuet in G
Ground Plan: **LF→N**

Figure 23 *The Music Man*: Final.

Summary

You've now made it through the entire process of analysing a musical step by step. As long as you follow this process, chances are you will succeed in your task. What I noticed through the years in my classes, is that they really had trouble with the first two or three musical analysis processes, but eventually, it became easier and easier for them to the point that they could start doing some things in their heads. Bravo!

Now, as you go through the next ten chapters, just follow the process and all will be good with the world!

11

1927 – The Birth of the Musical

Show Boat

A sign of the times

People didn't know what to make of *Show Boat*. Is it a Follies show? Is it a mixture of Vaudeville with song and dance sketches? Are they really trying to be serious in comic entertainment? Considering the original *New York Times* review in which the unknown *Times* critic said *"'Show Boat' is, with a few reservations in favour of some of the earlier 'Follies' and possibly 'Sally,' just about the best musical piece ever to arrive under Mr. Ziegfeld's silken Gonfalon,"*[1] you can consider this interesting fact: we are never completely ready with great change when it happens, we aren't quite sure how to embrace great change when it happens, and that generally speaking, we'll always prefer and lean towards the comfortable. Ahhhh, the pitfalls of being art innovators.

Credits

Music by Jerome Kern
Lyrics and Book by Oscar Hammerstein II
Based on the book *Show Boat* by Edna Ferber
Dialogue directed by Zeke Colvan
Dances arranged by Sammy Lee
Produced by Florenz Ziegfeld

History at a glance

Show Boat innovatively broke the mould and created the musical play that we still recognize today. *Show Boat* actually had songs that related to and furthered the plot. It was the integration of these two mediums – the book and the music – that opened people's eyes to new possibilities for musical theatre. It proved that musical theatre could deal with not only comic entertainment but also with serious issues: racial oppression, bigotry, and miscegenation. This was an amazing feat considering its year, 1927. *Show Boat* also gave its characters a strong growth arc within the show, allowing Magnolia especially, to grow and change as the show progressed. And one cannot ignore the fact that this show really opened up possibilities into the musical theatre future by having a mixture of races – Black and white – in one cast, sharing lead roles as well as supporting ones.

THE ANALYSIS
Create the dramatic question

Show Boat is a unique type of show. Unlike its successor musicals of the 1930s, *Show Boat* doesn't deal with fairy tales and lightly sugared "boy meets girl" scenarios. It is a musical that focuses head on with the reality of the times. Therefore, the dramatic question needs to look a bit more deeply into the relationship of Magnolia and Ravenal. It doesn't feel right to just ask "Will Magnolia and Ravenal get together and live happily ever after?" This show has a growth arc for these characters, and in some way, we should address that in the dramatic question.

List all analytically important characters

We need to address four different character concerns in this show. The first is Captain Andy since he doesn't sing all that much in the show, yet he's an

> Dramatic Question: *"Will Nola and Ravenal finally mature and grow enough to have a nurturing and lasting relationship?*

Figure 24 *Show Boat:* The Dramatic Question.

integral part of the show. In this case, I would include him since the chorus sings about him in "Cotton Blossom," and Captain Andy patters some of his lines with music underscoring, especially when he's playing his role as barker to the crowds. He also is involved in the large chorus numbers of the Finales, in which he is an instigator and ally to what the chorus is singing – the wedding in Act I and happy ending of Act II. Frankly, he could sing along with them with no problem. He is a key element in this show and should be listed.

Parthy is a challenge. Both Captain Andy and Parthy are tour de force characters, but Parthy isn't given songs to sing. Part of this is because her belief system runs totally against everyone else on the boat. Even at the end of Act I, when everyone is waving off Nola and Ravenal to the church, Parthy has fainted. She was against the wedding. Parthy is mainly a protaganist in the show – no character can get away with anything until they've gone through her. If she would have been given a lot of songs to sing, it truly would have changed the entire map of the show. Captain Andy and crew would have lost too much power. Interestingly, the Paper Mill Playhouse's 1989 performance of *Show Boat* had Parthy singing in "Why Do I Love You," which would then give her the needed song to justify her analysis, but this is a rewritten version of the original script. Because she doesn't sing in the original production, we'll keep her off the character analysis list.

Steve doesn't sing or dance, and then leaves with Julie in the middle of Act I. He is never heard of again, so he's off the list.

The large ensemble numbers are hugely important, yet so many different ensemble groups sing them: from stevedores and white and Black communities, to audiences and fairgrounds people. How can we possibly differentiate between all of them? We don't. List them as the Chorus. They have many big numbers, but they are usually setting the scene and plot – the various role diversity really doesn't matter in the show. That's not to say that you wouldn't be able to list them all separately, but you would find out in the end that they are all in the show for the same purpose, therefore sharing the same energy anyway.

Dramatic Question: *"Will Nola and Ravenal finally mature and grow to have a nurturing and lasting relationship?*

Nola   Ravenal   Queenie   Joe   Captain   Ellie   Frank   Julie   Chorus

---

Figure 25 *Show Boat*: List of Characters.

List all of the songs under the character's name

					Dramatic Question: *"Will Nola and Ravenal finally grow to have a nurturing and lasting relationship?"*			
Nola	**Ravenal**	**Queenie**	**Joe**	**Captain**	**Ellie**	**Frank**	**Julie**	**Chorus**
					ACT I			
				←				1. Cotton Blossom
←	2. Where's the Mate? 3. Make Believe							
←			4. Ol' Man River				5. Can't Help Lovin' Dat Man	→
			←	←				→
					6. Life Upon the Wicked Stage			→
		7. Ballyhoo & Dance						→
					8. Dance	→		
9. You Are Love →								
←	←	←	←	←				10. Finale
					ACT II			
								11. At the Fair →
12. Why Do I Love You? →								12. In Dahomey
							13. Bill	
14. Can't Help Lovin' Dat Man-Reprise								
	15. Only Make Believe-Reprise							
					16. Goodbye My Lady Love →			
17. After the Ball								→
			18. Ol' Man River Reprise					
	19. You Are Love Reprise							
20. Finale →	→	→	→	→	→		→	→

Figure 26 *Show Boat*: List of Songs.

Lyrically analyse all of the songs

Nola

Nola is naïve, sheltered, very young, and inexperienced with the ways of the world. Her parents almost treat her as if she is a **child**. She falls in love with a stranger, Ravenal, at first sight. In "You Are Love," Nola sings about pretending and **dream**ing to be with him "*day after day.*" She can't live without him – she is **yearning** for him and **unfulfilled** without him. She is totally dedicated to him. She is N.

Ravenal

Ravenal is a drifter and a gambler. He has charisma and good looks, but he has a deep-seated feeling of **unfulfillment**, expressed in "Where's the

Mate For Me." He's longing for that "*harbor, somewhere*" to settle down with a woman. He falls in love with Nola, love at first sight. They are like two school children – always **yearning** to grab that extra moment to be with each other, even though Parthy has no liking to him at all. Because of his gambling addiction, he can't provide the steady, safe family life that Nola and Kim need in order to live normally. His gambling is an addiction – **trouble**. Ravenal is N.

Queenie

Queenie is a tour de force character who has no problem stating what she feels or what someone should do. She has a **larger than life** personality and the energy to support it. In "Ballyhoo," she is also **persuasive** in getting the Black community to line up and purchase tickets for the show! Queenie is definitely the **central driving force** within her marriage to Joe. Both she and Joe are well taken care of and happy on the Show Boat. They have stability. Queenie is LF.

Joe

Here is a man who does what he does when he wants to do it. He has a life **credo** that he follows and he never will steer away from it. His big **credo** song is "Ol' Man River," a song that teaches folks about life and the way it just "*keeps rollin' along*." Joe is **attractive to be with** because he's so easygoing and comfortable with who he is. He's a country, common sense type of philosopher. Joe is LF.

Captain Andy

Captain Andy is the **central driving force** of the entire show. He is the owner and Captain of the ship – he has power. He's also a parent to Nola. He's **attractive to be with** and **larger than life.** He works the entire show to make sure everyone is happy. He's boisterous, he directs the shows, and he narrates them for the audiences. He's **persuasive** by ballyhooing the townspeople, proclaiming it's a show not to be missed. He works to try to get Nola and Ravenal together – he's an ally to them. Captain Andy, as a parent, even rescues Nola when she is about to fall flat on her opening act at the Trocadero. Captain Andy is LF.

Ellie and Frank

Both of them are seasoned, vaudevillian actors who know the business. They have steady employment with the Show Boat. Their acts are high energy, singing and dancing, to entertain the audiences. They are **attractive to be with** because they are local "stars." They don't have a worry in the world, except for maybe Ellie wanting to get married to Frank, and Frank having cold feet about it. Even then, Ellie plays the good act about how life on the stage is wicked, but that's all in fun – she goes right on acting with Frank. Regardless, we don't worry about them – they are happy in life. Ellie and Frank are LF.

Julie

Julie is a more difficult character to analyse because her life changes so drastically through the run of the show. In Act I, she is a strong cast member of the Show Boat, happy and safe. She is a teacher and mentor to Nola, giving her piano lessons as well as sharing her life lessons. In "Can't Help Lovin' Dat Man of Mine," she sings her life credo about loving only one man "*til I die.*" She is a strong influence on Nola, **larger than life**. Julie is **attractive to be with**, being a star on the Show Boat. She seems to be LF. But once the authorities come in to accuse her of being of mixed blood, she has to leave the boat. We then don't hear from her again until the middle of Act II. It is then that we see she has become an alcoholic and alone, barely making it to rehearsal on time as a singer. Still, in spite of her unreliability, she pulls out a gorgeous song rendition of "Bill" to keep the staff of the Trocadero at bay, and to keep her job at the same time. But when Nola comes to the Trocadero in desperation to audition for a job, we see Julie heartbroken, watching over her. Julie then makes the decision to sacrifice her job to Nola by going on a drinking binge. The issue here is that we really *feel for* Julie. She's been dealt a tragic and unfair hand by simply being of a different race. Of course she would then be N, right? No. What we must remember is what Julie does at the end. She *sacrifices her job and livelihood for Nola.* That takes huge courage, love, and kindness, and it was her choice to do that. She was parenting Nola for one final time. Therefore, she maintains her LF energy in spite of the fact that her life is pretty much over. Julie is LF.

Chorus

We never worry about or think about the chorus at all within the context of the plotline. They sing many songs, but mainly to set scenes and to give the scenes a boost of energy. Their music is lively, happy, and full of life, as they are as characters. They are LF. The only group ensemble where you may have trouble analysing would be the Stevedores, considering they are heavy-working, dock labourers. Yet, they aren't there complaining and giving up. They keep working because of the vision/credo of "Ol' Man River," which gives them strength to continue on. They are LF. See Figure 27.

Musically analyse all of the songs

Most of the songs are fairly self-explanatory – they are either a LF or N Level 1–Tell It Like It Is or a LF or N Level 2–The Affirmation. I am assuming that those two song levels are easy to understand: they either sound LF or N when they are LF or N, or they sound the opposite of their natural LF or N sound characteristics. In *Show Boat*, there aren't very many surprises in the analysis.

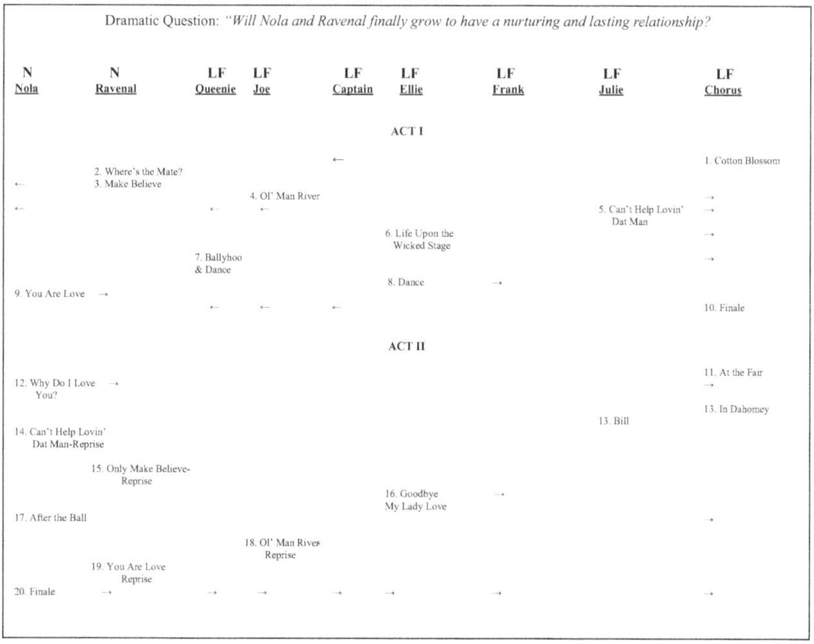

Figure 27 *Show Boat*: List of Character Energies.

Part of this is due to the nature of the musical from that period – they do tend to sing what they believe to be true. This was the culture of the time.

The only contrasting song level in *Show Boat* is "Why Do I Love You," which is a N Level 4–The Struggle song. As stated in the previous chapter, the two characters Nola and Ravenal, are trying to make themselves believe that everything is beautiful and perfect, even though underneath this cloak of happiness is a couple who is struggling to keep their marriage together. They are trying to act resolved by singing this strong, lilting, "life at the fair is awesome" LF sounding song, and yet they are not succeeding. They are struggling to survive and only masking it with a false sense of happiness and LF sounding characteristics. See Figure 28.

The Alignment energy

The Alignment energy in *Show Boat* is the song "Make Believe," where Ravenal and Nola fall in love at first sight, and then sing about it. We know of Ravenal's unfulfillment in the previous song, "Where's the Mate For Me," but we haven't even met Nola. It is during "Make Believe" that they both sing,

N Nola	N Ravenal	LF Queenie	LF Joe	LF Captain	LF Ellie	LF Frank	LF Julie	LF Chorus
								Dramatic Question: "Will Nola and Ravenal finally grow to have a nurturing and lasting relationship?
				ACT I				
				←				1. Cotton Blossom **LF1**
←	2. Where's the Mate? **N1**							
	3. Make Believe **N1**							
			4. Ol' Man River **LF2**					
← **N2**		←	←				5. Can't Help Lovin' Dat Man **LF1**	→
					6. Life Upon the Wicked Stage **LF1**			→
		7. Ballyhoo & Dance **LF1**						→
					8. Dance **LF1**	→		
9. You Are Love **N1** →								
		←	←	←				10. Finale **LF1**
				ACT II				
								11. At the Fair **LF1** → **LF1**
12. Why Do I Love You? **N4** →								13. In Dahomey **LF1**
							13. Bill **LF2**	
14. Can't Help Lovin' Dat Man-Reprise **N1**								
		15. Only Make Believe-Reprise **N1**						
					16. Goodbye My Lady Love **LF2**	→		
17. After the Ball **N1**								→
			18. Ol' Man River Reprise **LF2**					
	19. You Are Love Reprise							
20. Finale →	→	→	→	→'	→	→		→

Figure 28 *Show Boat*: List of Music Truths.

and we then know that both long for each other. It is at this point that we want them to get together. However, immediately at the end of the song, the local authorities request Ravenal to come down to the station. This creates distance. Suddenly, we begin to wonder about his history. Likewise, Nola has to go back inside or her mother will give her trouble. We realize there's some distance there also, wondering how a protective mother will accept a strange man in her daughter's life.

The Growth Moment energy

One could consider two places for the GM: "You Are Love Reprise" or the "Finale of Act II." At this point, one has to consider where the needs of the characters are actually resolved in song. When Ravenal comes back to the Show Boat at the urging of Captain Andy, Ravenal is unsure whether it was a good idea for him to come. He'd abandoned Nola so long ago, and Nola since then, had created a successful career for herself and her daughter, Kim. He starts to sing "You Are Love" alone and Nola overhears him. She responds to him with a verse herself. By the time the song is through, they are in a passionate embrace, and we know that all is good with them again. That is when their needs are resolved. "You Are Love Reprise" is the GM.

The Finale" immediately follows, bringing out the cast, and adding the exclamation point to Nola and Ravenal's resolution. "The Finale" is a Coda.

The ground plan of the musical

Nola is N. Ravenal is N. They are separated by many obstacles of which they must overcome. It is Captain Andy and the Show Boat that brings them together. It is Captain Andy who offers Ravenal and Nola the leading roles that Steve and Julie vacated. It is Captain Andy who helps Nola succeed in her opening at the Trocadero. And finally, it is Captain Andy who brings Ravenal back to the Show Boat at the end. The ground plan is:

$$\text{N} \rightarrow \text{LF} \leftarrow \text{N}$$

Nola   Ravenal

Show Boat Community

Figure 29 *Show Boat* Ground Plan.

Dramatic Question: *"Will Nola and Ravenal finally grow to have a nurturing and lasting relationship?"*

N Nola	N Ravenal	LF Queenie	LF Joe	LF Captain	LF Ellie	LF Frank	LF Julie	LF Chorus
				ACT I				
				←				1. Cotton Blossom LF1
	2. Where's the Mate? N1							
←	3. Make Believe N1							
← N2			4. Ol' Man River LF2					
		←	←				5. Can't Help Lovin' Dat Man LF1	→
					6. Life Upon the Wicked Stage LF1			→
		7. Ballyhoo & Dance LF1						→
					8. Dance LF1	→		
9. You Are Love N1 →								
		←	←	←				10. Finale LF1
				ACT II				
								11. At the Fair LF1 → LF1
12. Why Do I Love You? N4 →								
								13. In Dahomey LF1
							13. Bill LF2	
14. Can't Help Lovin' Dat Man-Reprise N1								
	15. Only Make Believe-Reprise N1							
					16. Goodbye My Lady Love LF2	→		
17. After the Ball N1								→
				18. Ol' Man River Reprise LF2				
	19. You Are Love Reprise							
20. Finale →	→	→	→	→	→	→		→

A: Make Believe
GM: You Are Love Reprise
Coda: Finale
Ground Plan: N → LF ← N

Figure 30 *Show Boat*: Final.

Note

1   Amusements, *The New York Times*, 28 December 1927.

12

1940s – The Beginning of the Golden Age

Oklahoma!

A sign of the times

Sometimes, as with *Oklahoma!*, reactions to a show are unanimously positive. People love it from the get-go and the show soars to both critical and financial heights. Despite initial scepticism on the state of the Theatre Guild, *New York Times* reviewer Lewis Nichols's first night notice offered a rebuttal, commenting that *"for years they have been saying the Theatre Guild is dead, words that obviously will have to be eaten with breakfast this morning … "*[1] In what became universally acclaimed notices, he goes on to say *"wonderful is the nearest adjective, for this excursion of the Guild combines a fresh and infectious gayety, a charm of manner, beautiful acting, singing and dancing, and a score by Richard Rodgers which doesn't do any harm either, since it is one of his best."*[2] Every artist and producer prays for this type of review. Yes, it did have new innovations, but the overall package of the show was simply good, wholesome entertainment, at a time when the nation really needed it.

Credits

Music by Richard Rodgers
Lyrics and Book by Oscar Hammerstein II
Based on the book *Green Grow the Lilacs*, by Lynn Riggs
Staged by Rouben Mamoulian
Choreographed by Agnes de Mille
Produced by the Theatre Guild

History at a glance

The United States of America had just entered the Second World War on 7 December 1941. After a year and a half of war, Americans were starting to feel the wears and tears of wartime news, worries, and death counts. *Oklahoma's* Broadway opening on 31 March 1943[3] proved to be the right musical at the right time. Immediately, both the public and the critics declared *Oklahoma!* a sensation, supported by rich combinations of brilliant, new forms in musical theatre and much needed Americana. Rodgers and Hammerstein's music and lyrics captivated audiences and Hammerstein's libretto started a generation of musicals that came to be determined and designed by the libretto rather than by the songs. Composers and lyricists began to base their musicals on novels, versus original librettos. Thanks to Agnes de Mille's choreography, *Oklahoma!* was the first musical where dance would further the plotline and dream ballets became the norm. *Oklahoma!* paved the way for cast leads to grow from two to as many as six actors. Finally, *Oklahoma!* was the first musical that created an original Broadway cast album.[4]

THE ANALYSIS
Create the dramatic question

Oklahoma! on the surface is a show that has very little plot. Like *Show Boat*, one could easily state the dramatic question to be, "Will Curly and Laurey get married and live happily ever after?" But again, looking deeper, this is more than just a show about simple boy meets girl, boy breaks up with girl, boy and girl get back together. Curly and Laurey like each other a lot (dare I say "love?"), but they get caught up in their own egos so much that each of them aren't willing to admit their fondness for the other. This locking of horns grows exponentially when in her stubbornness, Laurey accepts to go to the box social with her farmhand, Judd. Suddenly, we are watching a relationship triangle that grows into a death challenge at the finish line. We can't ignore the importance of Judd here. Without him there is no obstacle, thus no distance.

> Dramatic Question: *"Will Laurey finally reject Jud and accept a life of happy marriage with Curly?"*

Figure 31 *Oklahoma!*: The Dramatic Question.

List all analytically important characters

We can assume that Curly, Laurey, Judd, Ado Annie, and Will are included on the list. They all have songs and are integral parts of the story. But there are a few people that we should discuss also for consideration.

Ali is a wonderful character, a peddler, who tries to woo Ado Annie into bed with him at the nearest hotel. He really doesn't sing much – one song, "It's An Outrage" – but he does serve as an important obstacle between Will and Ado Annie. I would include him on the list, for the same reason that I didn't include Parthy on the *Show Boat's* list. If Parthy had sung just one song you wouldn't be able to ignore her, and she would have to be on the list. With Ali, you can't ignore him because he does sing that one song. Finally, Ali couldn't be considered part of the community because he's an outsider.

Aunt Eller is a wonderful character and she does sing some solo lines, but those are always with the townspeople, and she is a part of the town. Therefore, I would just consider her a lead townsperson, chorus member, like Ado Annie's father.

Which brings us to all the townspeople. We have some wonderful individual characters making up the community. They sing solos in "The Cowboys and the Farmers," and "Kansas City," but again, like Aunt Eller, they really belong together as a part of a community. The townsfolk play a huge role in this show – they sing a lot! If they had solo numbers like the School Board or the Ladies in *The Music Man*, then we should analyse them separately. But none of them do, so they are strictly a community of townspeople, therefore being listed as a chorus.

> Dramatic Question: *"Will Laurey finally reject Jud and accept a life of happy marriage with Curly?"*
>
> **Laurey   Curly   Jud   Annie   Will   Ali   Chorus**

Figure 32 *Oklahoma!*: List of Characters.

List all of the songs under the character's name

\multicolumn{8}{c}{Dramatic Question: *"Will Laurey finally reject Jud and accept a life of happy marriage with Curly?"*}
Laurey	**Curly**	**Jud**	**Annie**	**Will**	**Ali**	**Chorus**
				ACT I			
	1.Oh, What a Beautiful Morning						
2. Laurey's Entrance -Reprise							
	3. Surrey With the Fringe on Top						
				4. Kansas City		→	
	5. Surrey With the Fringe – Reprise						
			6. I Cain't Say No				
	←		7. Entrance Ensemble →			→	
8. Many a New Day						→	
					9. It's a Scandal!	→	
10. People Will Say We're in Love	→						
	11. Poor Jud is Daid →						
		12. Lonely Room					
13. Out of My Dreams-Reprise						→	
14. Dream Ballet	→	→				→	
				ACT II			
	←			←		16. The Farmer & Cowman	
			←	17. All or Nuthin'			
18. People Will Say We're in Love-Reprise	→						
←	19. Oklahoma					→	
20. Finale Ultimo	→		→	→		→	

Figure 33 *Oklahoma!*: List of Songs.

Lyrically analyse all of the songs

Laurey

Laurey is in love with Curly, but refuses to admit it. On the outside, she won't give him the time of day, but on the inside, she is so wanting him to profess his love to her. In "Many a New Day," she is **protesting too much** about her true feelings for Curly. She's trying to convince herself that there are other fish in the sea. But she doesn't want other fish. She is **yearning** for only Curly's love and she is **unfulfilled** without it. She *"longs to fly"* into Curly's arms in "Out of My Dreams." She is so unsure of what to do that she takes an elixir to help her find the answers she needs. In her elixir nightmare, she needs Curly to save her, as she needs him to save her from Judd after she fires him later in the show. She is N.

Curly

Curly is a strong, charming, smart, and respectful cowboy. He has charisma and is **attractive to be with**. Absolutely, he is the **central driving force** to this story. He opens the show with a major credo song, "Oh What a Beautiful Morning." He's optimistic and powerful. Curly is showing his creativeness of **persuasion** in "Surrey With the Fringe on Top" when he tries to woo Laurey to the Box Social with tall tales. He loves Laurey, but he too, caught in his own bullheadedness, won't be the first to admit it. There is no doubt that a 1940s, early Western, traditional boy and girl relationship occurs here in this musical. The man is definitely the one to care for the woman. Curly is LF.

Judd

Where Curly has the brains, Judd has the brawn. He's a strong farmhand who lives in a smokehouse on Aunt Eller and Laurey's property. He has a shaded past, and enjoys the darker, sexual side of women. He's powerful and shows signs of evil, but not enough through most of the show for us to thoroughly toss him away. He has "sexual needs" for a woman. He's the opposite of what Laurey is truly looking for in a man. However, like a tornado, Judd has an evil **attractiveness**. His sheer strength is a threat – **larger than life**. And, as in "Lonely Room," he is not planning on waiting for someone to help him. He's going to go outside and grab himself a bride. Judd is anti-LF.

Ado Annie

Ado Annie has realized over the past year that she has "blossomed" in certain womanly, physical ways, and so suddenly men are looking at her for a first time with desire in their eyes. Ado Annie likes that a lot. She actually likes it so much that she can't seem to stop herself from throwing herself at a man, even though she has given her heart to Will. She keeps two men, Will and the Peddler, dangling on a very troublesome and weak line. She's **yearning** for the touch and attention of any man, even though she has Will's commitment. She is N.

Will

Bless his heart. Will means well, but let's just put it nicely: if his brain were a V8 engine, his engine is only working on one piston. The only tool in his toolbox is an anvil. Clear enough? What makes him so **attractive to be with** though, is his honest-to-God truthfulness and dedication to Ado Annie. He loves her with all of his heart and he will move mountains for her. However, he will only tolerate so much, setting the ground rules with him and Annie: it's "*all er nothin'.*" He's also a talented cowboy, proving this by winning the $50 prize at the rodeo. He is LF.

Ali

Ali is **attractive to be with** because of his unique background and culture. At that time, anything or anyone from a different country was considered exotic, unique, and therefore was empowered just for the fact that they knew all about the world. Locals had no idea what it was like outside their small, tiny frame of reference. Ali also has the benefit of being a peddler, and so he is extremely good at selling items, and therefore very **persuasive.** He uses that persuasive talent to try to bed women at each stop and he resents it when that **credo** of his is under attack: "It's a Scandal! It's an Outrage!" He's not the best man for Ado Annie, but he *is* a man none-the-less. Ali is LF.

Chorus

Again in this show, the chorus takes on a very active role. The townspeople are made up of strong-valued, physically strong Western folk. They take pride in their heritage and also in the roles they play to contribute to the town. They are fit, hardworking cowboys and farmers, fighting to make the land profitable and livable. They have a very deep-seated moral constitution, which will then give them a stubbornness when it comes to change. The people in the town are happy, fulfilled, and truly enjoying the life they have chosen. In "The Farmer and the Cowmen," when push comes to shove, they know they need to support each other, and "*stick together.*" We don't worry about them at all. The Chorus is LF. See Figure 34.

Musically analyse all of the songs

You will notice that *Oklahoma!* has a few more other levels of songs in its repertoire. Besides the usual majority of LF levels 1 and 2, and N levels 1 and 2, we also have some interesting contrasts. The first is "Oh What a Beautiful

N Laurey	LF Curly	LF Jud	N Annie	LF Will	LF Ali	LF Chorus
			ACT I			
	1. Oh, What a Beautiful Morning					
2. Laurey's Entrance -Reprise						
	3. Surrey With the Fringe on Top					
				4. Kansas City		→
	5. Surrey With the Fringe – Reprise					
			6. I Cain't Say No			
	←		7. Entrance Ensemble →			→
8. Many a New Day						→
					9. It's a Scandal!	→
10. People Will Say We're in Love →						
	11. Poor Jud is Daid →					
		12. Lonely Room				
13. Out of My Dreams-Reprise						→
14. Dream Ballet →	→					→
			ACT II			
	←			←		16. The Farmer & Cowman
			←	17. All or Nuthin'		
18. People Will Say We're in Love-Reprise →						
←	19. Oklahoma					→
20. Finale Ultimo →	→		→	→		→

Figure 34 *Oklahoma!*: List of Character Energies.

Morning" that Curly first sings, but then we have Laurey sing a bit of it afterwards. This is interesting because Curly and Laurey are different energies. Curly first sings it as a LF Level 1–Tell It Like It Is song. It's his credo and strength in optimism. When Laurey sings it, the song not only subconsciously connects her with Curly in a symbiotic way, but it also takes the same song and switches it to N Level 2–The Affirmation. She sounds LF but is still N. You'll find this to be the case many times when a LF character sings a duet with a N character. It's the same song, but different levels depending on your energy. "People Will Say We're in Love" and "All Er Nothin'" are two good examples.

"Surrey With the Fringe on Top" is worth talking about. At the beginning and through two-thirds of the song, it sounds like a typical, persuasive LF1 song. However, the last verse is purposely written quietly and slower all the way to the end. It lasts close to two minutes. At that point, it could change and be a LF Level 5–The Tactical. He is definitely using his persuasive techniques in a very powerful way by mesmerizing her. It's a truthful, honest way that Curly wants to feel and wants her to feel for him. Is he lying? Absolutely. Could this be then at that point a LF Level 3–The Lie? I don't think so. He's playing the same position that Harold Hill played. They are lying, but deep inside, they are believing that it really *could be true*. Curly gets caught up in his own dream with Laurey for that moment, and it's not until Laurey wakes up to it that Curly does too, and then the fight begins again. The LF Level 3–The Lie is reserved for evil doers – not good, wholesome folk like Curly or even the loveable scam artist, Harold Hill. But the last two minutes of this song could be a change to LF Level 5–The Tactical.

Laurey sings "Many a New Day" with her woman ensemble, trying to persuade them that she could care less about Curly. She's mad at him and neither one of them are willing to budge an inch. So Laurey sings that there are other men out there that she can be happy with and the song sounds LF because of it. She's **Protesting Too Much**. She is not interested in another man deep inside, but she's not willing to even face that. She's convinced herself otherwise. The women ensemble is LF1 – they're singing all about it very matter of factly and believe in what Laurey is saying.

"Poor Jud is Daid" is a great example of a LF Level 5–The Tactical song. Curly is the brains of this piece and "poor" Jud is falling for Curly's shenanigans. Curly is using every tactic in the book to get Jud to think about killing himself. If we really thought that Curly would be successful in his attempts, we'd really lose a lot of respect for him. That's pretty unethical. Instead, it's more comic relief. Yes, at that moment in time, Curly is truly thinking that this is a good tactic to get Laurey back. Do we ever see it working out? Nah. Like this song and "Surrey With the Fringe on Top," sometimes Curly's ideas are creative to try to get what he wants, but they also are kind of dumb ideas because they will backfire on him.

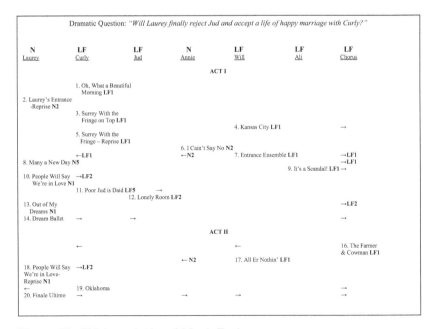

N Laurey	LF Curly	LF Jud	N Annie	LF Will	LF Ali	LF Chorus
	1. Oh, What a Beautiful Morning **LF1**					
2. Laurey's Entrance -Reprise **N2**						
	3. Surrey With the Fringe on Top **LF1**					
				4. Kansas City **LF1**		→
	5. Surrey With the Fringe – Reprise **LF1**					
			6. I Cain't Say No **N2**			
	←**LF1**		←**N2**	7. Entrance Ensemble **LF1**		→**LF1**
8. Many a New Day **N5**						→**LF1**
					9. It's a Scandal! **LF1** →	
10. People Will Say We're in Love **N1**	→**LF2**					
	11. Poor Jud is Daid **LF5**	→				
		12. Lonely Room **LF2**				
13. Out of My Dreams **N1**						→**LF2**
14. Dream Ballet	→	→				→

ACT II

N Laurey	LF Curly	LF Jud	N Annie	LF Will	LF Ali	LF Chorus
	←			←		16. The Farmer & Cowman **LF1**
			← **N2**	17. All Er Nothin' **LF1**		
18. People Will Say We're in Love- Reprise **N1**	→**LF2**					
←	19. Oklahoma					
20. Finale Ultimo	→		→	→		→

Dramatic Question: *"Will Laurey finally reject Jud and accept a life of happy marriage with Curly?"*

Figure 35 *Oklahoma!*: List of Music Truths.

"The Dream Ballet" is instrumental and long. If you're a choreographer, you really need to be aware of the given energies of each song used in the ballet, and then logically match that energy to the characters that will be dancing, while still telling the storyline of the dream. That will help you stay consistent with the ground plan of the show, and hopefully the vision of the director.

The Alignment energy

Many would assume that the Alignment of the show is after Laurey sings "Oh What a Beautiful Morning" during her first entrance. That makes sense – both Laurey and Curly have sung a song and established their energies to a point, and we know by that symbiotic merging that they should get together. There is one problem with that, however: there isn't any real obstacle getting in their way of getting together except for a stupid little spat. It's not until Jud's entrance that we get it. With Laurey using Jud as her tactic to get back at Curly, suddenly the obstacles, and therefore the distance of the show, grows exponentially. We also know that Jud is a part of the dramatic question, so it's important that he appear before we start to feel like we know where the show is going. Remember, the A energy does not have to be musical in nature. The A is Jud's entrance.

The Growth Moment energy

This is the one reason why *Oklahoma!* kind of drives me crazy. It's an extremely long show, and after awhile, it just gets annoying. You just want to grab Laurey and Curly, smack 'em across the pate, and say, "Get over it already, and just get married for crying out loud!" It's the growth moment and the storyline that get in the way. Where we feel that the Growth Moment actually happens, is the song "Oklahoma." It's a huge number, with big, boisterous energy, and Laurey and Curly finally get married. It's an awesome number with an awesome climax! What else is there that we want?! The resolution has happened, Curly and Laurey are together, Jud has lost, and Oklahoma becomes a state. Yahoooooo, we're done!

Not.

We then have to deal with the townspeople banging pots and pans outside the newlywed's window at night, Jud coming back, Jud and Curly fighting, Jud dying, and then all of the court shenanigans to finally get the married couple on the dang horse carriage, off to their honeymoon. After well over twenty minutes of this, we finally get the "Finale" and the long-awaited end to the show.

The GM is "Oklahoma." The rest of the show is a Coda. And a looooooooong, snoooooooooring Coda at that.

The ground plan of the musical

Laurey is having to choose between her stubbornness and Jud, or her love for Curly. At the same time, Ado Annie is having to choose between flings with men like Ali, or her beau Will. These are parallel energy storylines. Pretty cool. The LF community of townsfolk really aren't a consideration in this ground plan. This ground plan is called "The Choice."

Jud	Laurey	Curly
LF	← N →	LF
Ali	Ado Annie	Will

Figure 36 *Oklahoma!* Ground Plan.

Dramatic Question: *"Will Laurey finally reject Jud and accept a life of happy marriage with Curly?"*

N Laurey	LF Curly	LF Jud	N Annie	LF Will	LF Ali	LF Chorus
			ACT I			
	1. Oh, What a Beautiful Morning **LF1**					
2. Laurey's Entrance -Reprise **N2**						
	3. Surrey With the Fringe on Top **LF1**					
				4. Kansas City **LF1**		→
	5. Surrey With the Fringe – Reprise **LF1**					
			6. I Cain't Say No **N2**			
	←**LF1**		←**N2**	7. Entrance Ensemble **LF1**		→**LF1**
8. Many a New Day **N5**						→**LF1**
					9. It's a Scandal! **LF1**	→
10. People Will Say We're in Love **N1**	→**LF2**					
	11. Poor Jud is Daid **LF5**	→				
		12. Lonely Room **LF2**				
13. Out of My Dreams **N1**						→**LF2**
14. Dream Ballet	→	→				→
			ACT II			
	←			←		16. The Farmer & Cowman **LF1**
			←**N2**	17. All Er Nothin' **LF1**		
18. People Will Say We're in Love-Reprise **N1**	→**LF2**					
←	19. Oklahoma					→
20. Finale Ultimo	→		→	→		→

A: The entrance of Jud
GM: Oklahoma
Coda: Finale Ultimo
Ground Plan: LF ← N → LF "The Choice"

Figure 37 *Oklahoma!*: Final.

Notes

1   Nichols, *The New York Times*, 1 April 1943.
2   Ibid.
3   Stempel, *Showtime*, 300.
4   Ibid., 311.

13

1950s – The Late Golden Age
West Side Story

A sign of the times

Like *Show Boat, West Side Story* deals with some pretty dark issues, in an artistic genre that at the time was referred to as "Musical Comedy." Reactions to this show were mixed, depending on how open a person was to pushing the boundaries of this form of entertainment. How does one react to a work that is so brilliant, yet "ugly" in nature? *New York Times* reviewer Brook Atkinson saw it this way, "*But the author, composer and ballet designer are creative artists. Pooling imagination and virtuosity, they have written a profoundly moving show that is as ugly as the city jungles and also pathetic, tender and forgiving.*"[1] Part of the retribution from the nay-sayers was the fact that *West Side Story* was passed up for Musical of the Year by the much safer *The Music Man.*

Credits

Music by Leonard Bernstein
Lyrics by Stephen Sondheim
Libretto by Arthur Laurents
Inspired by *Romeo and Juliet* by William Shakespeare
Directed, Choreographed, and Conceived by Jerome Robbins
Produced by Robert E. Griffith and Harold S. Prince

History at a glance

By the 1950s, the Golden Age musical was well established. With the success of *Brigadoon* in 1947 and *South Pacific* in 1949, composer/lyricist teams like Lerner and Loewe and Rodgers and Hammerstein became household names. By reputation alone, these teams were able to write musical after musical with producer support, whether they flopped once or not. Productions were becoming more and more based on realism and solid literature. *West Side Story* took it a step further. The team wrote a show based on the Shakespearean tragedy – *Romeo and Juliet* – and reconceived it with a focus on the darker side of New York society. At a time when civil unrest was starting to birth, *West Side Story* was brave enough to open up the ugliness and discontent between the white and Puerto Rican races in the Upper West Side of Manhattan. For sure, it was a hard sell to producers, and at first they shied away from the ambitious project. Luckily, Hal Prince and Robert Griffith saw its potential and decided to support the project. And with that support, *West Side Story* then was able to change the course of musical theatre by showing audiences that an important darker subject, a complicated and operatic jazz score, and an innovative and extended choreographic presence can make for great and history-making theatre.

THE ANALYSIS
Create the dramatic question

We know what we want: Tony and Maria together. The challenge is that it is not just about love or stubbornness as in *Oklahoma!*. The obstacles in this show are so much greater and the stakes so much higher. We're dealing with two groups of people who literally hate each other because of their skin colour and background. Tony was a part of the Jets gang and Maria's brother Bernardo is a part of the Sharks gang. How can two kids who are in love change the deep-seated prejudice of race and immigration? That is the challenge in this piece. It's not just about whether Tony and Maria will get

Dramatic Question: *"Will Tony and Maria together break the barriers of gang prejudice and hate, and find that peaceful, accepting world that they so desperately long to be a part of?"*

Figure 38 *West Side Story:* The Dramatic Question.

together, but it's also dealing with where they can find a place that's safe and accepting of the love they share for each other.

List all analytically important characters

One of the challenges in this musical is the fact that it is so community oriented. Everyone in some way is related to one side or the other in the turf wars between the gangs. So then it becomes who is highlighted enough to warrant being listed separately versus just being a part of the group. Logically, when looking at all the songs and dances, we can narrow down that list to Maria, Tony, Riff, Bernardo, and Anita. The rest can just fall under the listing of Sharks or Jets.

One thing I would suggest you take note of right away is the absence of songs or dances from Doc and Officer Krupke. Also, take notice that there aren't any form of adults in this show that take any kind of major focus, let alone have any music. They have none. The show doesn't even have parents! The cast is represented by youth, and only youth. This will play an important role in your analysis later on.

Dramatic Question: *"Will Tony and Maria together break the barriers of gang prejudice and hate, and find that peaceful, accepting world that they so desperately long to be a part of?"*

Maria   Tony   Riff   Bernardo   Anita   Jets   Sharks

Figure 39 *West Side Story:* List of Characters.

List all of the songs under the character's name

	Dramatic Question: *"Will Tony and Maria together break the barriers of gang prejudice and hate, and find that peaceful, accepting world that they so desperately long to be a part of?"*						
Maria	**Tony**	**Riff**	**Bernardo**	**Anita**	**Jets**	**Sharks**
				ACT I			
		1. Prologue	→		→	→
		2. Jet Song			→	
	3. Something's Coming					
←	←	←	←	←	4. Dance at Gym	→
4A. Meeting Scene	→					
	5. Maria					
6. Balcony-Tonight	→					
			←	7. America		→
		8. Cool			→	
9. One Hand One Heart	→					
←	←	←	←	←	10. Tonight	→
	←	←	←		11. The Rumble	→
				ACT II		
12. I Feel Pretty						
13. Ballet Sequence- Reprise & Dance	→				→	→
					14. Gee Officer Krupke	
15. A Boy Like That/ I Have a Love			→			
				16. Taunting Scene	→	
17. Finale	→			→	→	→

Figure 40 *West Side Story:* List of Songs.

Lyrically analyse all of the songs

Maria

Maria is sheltered and protected by her brother Bernardo and his street-smart girlfriend, Anita. She is young, still in some ways a **child**, anxious to enter the world of the high school teenager. She goes to the high school dance and experiences love at first sight with Tony. She **yearns** for Tony and as the relationship grows, she is **unfulfilled** to the point that he will be the only one she sees herself with "*forever.*" She is also in **trouble** because not only is Tony of a different race, but he also used to be the leader of the Jets, while her brother Bernardo is the leader of the rival Sharks. She is N.

Tony

Tony is a boy that got smart. Originally, he was the leader of the Jets, and he thought that was all that he needed. It wasn't. He had **dreams**. He had decided to get a job at Doc's Drugstore. Yes, he is trying to pursue his dreams, but it has always been out of his reach – unattainable. In "Something's Coming," he always knew there was more to his life – **some**thing is coming (the **Some Factor**). He is **unfulfilled** until he finds out what that **some**thing is, and it ends up being Maria. He falls in love at first sight. He also must navigate the **trouble** that this brings, being white and a former Jets gang leader. Tony is N.

Riff and the Jets

This is where it really gets tricky, but if you look at the circumstances and facts, and combine them with his lyrics, it'll make sense. Riff is the leader of the Jets. He's tough, physically strong, street smart. Does this make him LF? I think not. First, he's in high school, not yet an adult. He leads his gang into **trouble** with the police constantly. And the biggest factor, which can go across the board to all of the Jet gang members: are they happy and satiated in life? Will they survive no matter the consequences? No, not really. They are constantly in rumbles – that is not a safe, survivor-able world. They know what they want – to rid their area of the Puerto Ricans. Why? It's due to prejudice, hate, fear of losing control, fear of losing power, and fear of losing self-worth. And why are they in a gang in the first place? They are **unfulfilled**, **yearning** to be a part of something that will give them self-esteem and safety, and they don't even know what that is and how to get it. In "Jet Song," they only know that they have each other and in order to be safe, they need to "*stick together*" to be "*well protected.*"

These kids are *desperate.* All that is important in their world at this point is their turf. And when another gang infiltrates their world – the only thing that they have in life of any consequence – they become *desperate*, fighting like trapped, cornered wild animals. They must assure each other to "*get cool, boy*" in order to survive.

Everything is against them – no support, understanding, they're in a rough, low socio-economic area. They're stuck. They don't see a future and they know it. So in "Gee, Officer Krupke," of course, they lament their lousy situation, but they won't show how it hurts them. Their lament is probably based in sad truth: that their mothers and fathers are "*junkies*" and "*drunks.*" They make fun of it just to survive. Riff and the Jets gang are N.

Bernardo and the Sharks

Everything that I wrote about Riff and the Jets can be copied and pasted underneath Bernardo and the Sharks. They are in the same terrible situation, with the same terrible problems. They are also together as a gang for the same reasons: to protect themselves from the other race who hates them, to protect their turf, to protect their self-esteem, and to protect the little power they have. It's all about hate, fear, and losing power, so if they are jumped by the Jets, they'll be *"ready to mix, tonight."* They are **desperate**, **unfulfilled**, and in **trouble.**

An added **yearning** for Bernardo and the Sharks was the need to escape Puerto Rico to live in the United States, to pursue the American dream. But being immigrants adds more pressure on them as a people due to the prejudice of Americans who feel they don't belong there. The built-in systemic racism makes it that much more difficult for them to acclimate and prosper. They will take that chance, though, because the world knows about that unforgettable American optimism – come to America, and you will find the answers to your economic hardships – washing machines and big, *"chromium steel"* cars. Bernardo and the Sharks are N.

Anita

Anita isn't insulated from this terrible world. She is certainly a part of Bernardo's and the Shark's world. She is also desperate and **unfulfilled**, desiring a safe home, preferably with Bernardo. She has the same **yearning** to live prosperously in America. She wants respect and dignity from the white Americans. She is also young, and as much as she tries to act like the street-smart adult, she is still a kid like the rest of them. She tries to teach Maria about the wickedness of Tony, and all whites by warning her to stay around *"her own kind,"* but those words ring hollow. Even following that she has lost her own love, leaving her desolate and broken.

We also cannot forget that before the song "A Boy Like That," she is sexually attacked, raped, by the Jets gang. She is a victim of abuse of the worst kind, and how can she ever trust that race again after that? Anita is N.

Wait! Where's the LF?

I really hate to do this to you, but this musical is one of those special anomaly shows. I have found three shows so far that deal in this unique field: *West Side Story*, *Fiddler on the Roof*, and *Spring Awakening*. They deal with one energy – the LF energy – that isn't necessarily assigned to a specific character or characters per se. These shows deal with the LF being on a different reality plane or dimension. The LF in these shows aren't directly flesh and blood in the character role sense. The LF exists, and is sung and danced by the characters on stage, but it's an energy that is more existential. The LF exists, but in a different form. Let's take a look at this from a different perspective.

West Side Story very deliberately avoided having adults sing in this show. Doc doesn't sing, the detective and officer Krupke don't sing, the teacher in the gym doesn't sing. And where are the parents of the kids? It's as if the kids are on their own with no protection or guidance at all. The fact of the matter is, if the adults would've sung, or even existed, then the show would have had to make them LF. They would've had the power, the control, and they would have then dictated the kids' destiny. This is not how the show was conceived and designed. Part of the tragedy in this show is that the end could have been avoided if adult supervision had existed.

So where is this LF energy floating around?

In *West Side Story*, the LF energy exists through theatrical imagery. This is when the N energy world of the kids "changes" into a safe place. There are four instances in this show.

1 Act I: When Maria is trying on her dress for the dance, she twirls in happiness and delight. When this happens, in the stage directions, ribbons stream down from above. It literally takes her into a dream of euphoria and safety. This world of safety, where dreams are answered, then becomes the magical transition to the next scene, which is at the high school dance. Yes, this is short, but it does introduce us to the conventionality of theatrical imagery, so that the following larger scenes are easily accepted by the audience.

2 "Dance at the Gym/Meeting Scene": It is the moment when Tony and Maria's eyes meet. Suddenly, the world of the high school disappears, leaving Tony and Maria alone to meet, dance, and fall in love in total seclusion and privacy. They have gone to a LF place of safety, possibility, and wonder. There isn't Riff coming into the picture to interrupt Tony by saying, "What the heck are you doing?!" Bernardo isn't there to pull Maria away and send her home, telling her that they don't dance with "those kind." This is an entirely new world of love, peace, and

possibilities. This world is a **central driving force**, very **attractive for them to be in**, and certainly **larger than life**. Powerful? Oh yeah. Prejudicial? Oh no. This is magical – and a magical world is LF.

3 "One Hand One Heart": Tony and Maria are in the Bridal Shop. Tony has just promised to Maria that he will stop the rumble that is scheduled to happen that night between the Jets and the Sharks. This cements a truth in Maria's mind that Tony is a good young man, and that perhaps the fighting will end between the two gangs. This trust becomes the bond that then allows them to go through with their wedding vows, under the magical world of dream again. Once the world of the Bridal Shop disappears, they again are well taken care of by the theatrical imagery of LF. No one can interrupt their vows. No one can take away that moment of love. No one is worried about safety or prejudice. It's the magical world of peace and ultimate safety.

4 "Somewhere Ballet Sequence": Tony has accidentally killed Bernardo, and flees the scene. He runs to Maria's apartment, and sneaks in by the fire escape. He tells Maria what happens and tries to calm her down. He wants them to escape from New York, to find a place of peace and acceptance for the two of them. They are in trouble, desperate, and there is no one to help them but themselves. It is that time again when the bedroom disappears and they do a ballet of love to the music of "Somewhere." Again, that magical world wraps its arms around them and takes care of them. They are safe for one final time. The last theatrical image.

Some of you are probably wondering if four instances of LF music is balanced enough to take on all of the N songs on the other side. That's a good question. But take note: just this last piece "Somewhere Ballet" lasts for seven and a half minutes. That is a lot of LF time. You can also probably guess that musically, there's probably going to be a lot of N Level 2–The Affirmation songs. These songs add a lot of necessary up-tune energy to the show.

Where LF isn't shown strongly or directly is in the script – perhaps only a paragraph or two of stage directions. This is why it is so important and imperative that you read all of the stage directions in the scripts closely. Sometimes a dance is only mentioned in one line of stage directions, yet the dance may take five minutes to perform, which then becomes a major memorable impact to the audience. To the impatient reader, they could easily skip over this.

Dramatic Question: *"Will Tony and Maria together break the barriers of gang prejudice and hate, and find that peaceful, accepting world that they so desperately long to be a part of?"*

N Maria	N Tony	N Riff	N Bernardo	N Anita	N Jets	N Sharks
				ACT I		
		1. Prologue	→		→	→
		2. Jet Song			→	
	3. Something's Coming					
LF 3A. Scene Change						
←	←	←	←	←	4. Dance at the Gym	→
LF 4A. Maria/ Meeting Scene	→					
	5. Maria					
6. Balcony-Tonight		→				
			←	7. America		→
		8. Cool			→	
LF 9. One Hand One Heart	→					
←	←	←	←	←	10. Tonight	→
←	←	←	←		11. The Rumble	→
				ACT II		
12. I Feel Pretty						
LF 13. Somewhere Ballet - Reprise & Dance	→		→	→		
					14. Gee Officer Krupke	
15. A Boy Like That I Have a Love				→		
				16. Taunting Scene	→	
17. Finale	→			→	→	→

Figure 41 *West Side Story*: List of Character Energies.

Musically analyse all of the songs

With the imbalance of actual N songs with LF songs, it was absolutely imperative that the bulk of the N songs have to be Levels 2–5. It is only logical. First and foremost, this musical is based on a Shakespearean tragedy, so it is going to be heavy on the emotional side already. To counteract that, Bernstein consciously or subconsciously had to compose a plethora of Need music that sounded LF, just to keep the energy up in the show. You can't have a huge amount of N Level 1 songs in a show – people would either fall asleep or be so darn depressed that they would leave the theatre and end it all. So in his brilliance, Bernstein wrote music that was high energy, upbeat, danceable, and syncopated for N characters – mainly for the two gangs. It made sense considering these N characters were tough, physical, desperate, frustrated, and angry. They were also, in general, pretty darn truthful – a perfect combination for N Level 2–The Affirmation songs. Right in tune with Bernstein's music was Sondheim's lyric work. He wrote wonderfully energy-balanced lyrics. When LF was needed, he wrote strong, aggressive, and macho gang lingo that gave the appearance of LF energy. "Cool" is a great example of a N song that really comes off as LF energy.

Ironically, the LF music in this show is not the typical LF Level 1–Tell It Like It Is music. Instead, it is LF Level 2–The Affirmation music. It parallels the truthful need for Tony and Maria to find that world of peace and acceptance. In essence, Tony and Maria are the N characters who receive all of the slower, beautiful, opera aria-type music. Bernstein keeps their music consistent, be it LF or N: "One Hand One Heart," "Somewhere," "Maria," and "I Have a Love."

The final song that you may have questions about is "Gee, Officer Krupke" – a N Level 2–The Affirmation lament. Why would this not be a manipulation/tactical Level 3–The Lie? They're trying to make excuses for their poor behaviour, listing example after example of all the things they have had to go through as a troubled kid. Aren't they just lying to us and to themselves? I think not. For them to sing about all of these different scenarios in such detail, some of them, if not all of them, had to have some

Figure 42 *West Side Story:* List of Music Truths.

of that negative experience to draw from. For sure, the scenarios have been grossly exaggerated, but for it to be funny it really does have to be believable. I totally believe that these kids have been through "the system," and that "the system" failed them terribly. Therefore, like Ado Annie's "I Cain't Say No," "Gee, Officer Krupke" is also a complaining song, a lament, N Level 2–The Affirmation.

The Alignment energy

The Alignment seems pretty self-explanatory. First of all, we know that we must have both LF and N songs introduced, so that in itself would take us to the gym's dance and Tony and Maria's meeting for the first time. Secondly, we see them gaze at each other for the first time, love at first sight, while the world surrounding them disappears. We know right at that moment that this is what the story is about, what their obstacles are, and how the gangs will affect that relationship. The A is the "Meeting Scene" at the dance in the gym.

The Growth Moment energy

With all of our hearts, we are rooting for Tony and Maria to get together, get on that bus with the money Doc loans Tony, and find a safe haven and new life for themselves. It all seems possible to us. But the 1950s late Golden Age musicals were introducing the notion of realism: in costumes, sets, and even the motivations of dance moves. But mostly, realism took over this notion of the "fairy tale" musical. Musical creative teams were trying to create art that mirrors actual life in many ways and *West Side Story* slaps us in the face with that reality. Tony gets shot at the end due to rumour and misunderstanding. He dies in Maria's arms. Maria uses the moment to threaten, criticize, accuse, and despise both gangs for their hand in Tony's death. Most importantly, she reaches them – teaches them the futility of it all. Both gangs then, unified, lift up Tony's dead body and respectfully march him out with Maria, as the music swells to the eerie playing of the theme "Somewhere" by hollow woodwinds. That is the moment that brings final resolution to all of the N characters' unfulfillment – the gangs learn to live together peacefully, and Tony and Maria, in a very dark way, have found their peace. This moment brings down the curtain, albeit slowly, for the end of the show. The GM is the "Finale."

This is an example of a Growth Moment that doesn't give the happy ending that people want, but does indeed resolve the dramatic question in a very powerful way. The Kleenex box industry celebrates this ending, while the audience smothers their faces in their tissues.

The ground plan of the musical

As I've said before, this show has a different planed design, with the LF being outside the usual dimension of realism and character. In showing that with the ground plan, different planed ground plans need to show that different dimension within it. The design for *West Side Story* is called *The Untouchable* ground plan. It's out there, somewhere, but we don't know where it is.

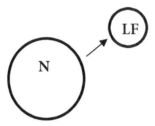

Figure 43 *West Side Story* Ground Plan.

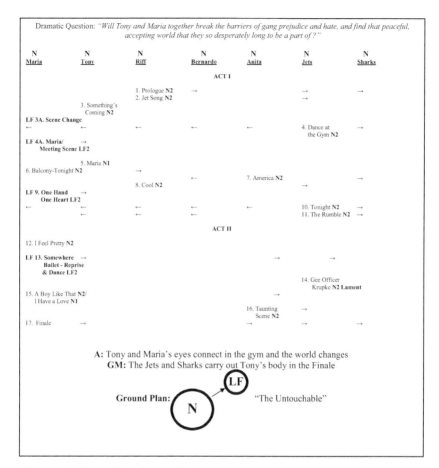

Figure 44 *West Side Story*: Final.

Note

1   Atkinson, *The New York Times*, 27 September 1957.

14

1960s – The Extravaganza Musical

Fiddler on the Roof

A sign of the times

One only has to look seven years into the future from *West Side Story* to *Fiddler on the Roof* to witness the ever-so-slow cultural movement and acceptance of serious drama in a Musical Comedy. As *New York Times* reviewer Howard Taubman stated, "*It has been prophesied that the Broadway musical theater would take up the mantle of meaningfulness worn so carelessly by the American drama in recent years. 'Fiddler on the Roof' does its bit to make good on this prophecy.*"[1] Who would ever have guessed that the Broadway musical world would take onto their veritable shoulders, a serious and even tragic Jewish drama that would push the limits of the audiences' comfort zone? *Fiddler* did, and won the Tony Award for Best Musical in 1965.

Credits

Music by Jerry Boch
Lyrics by Sheldon Harnick
Book by Joseph Stein
Based on Sholem Aleichem's stories
Staged and Choreographed by Jerome Robbins
Produced by Harold Prince

History at a glance

There's a reason why the 1960s was a decade to remember. From the civil rights movement for minority cultures to the peace movement due to the Vietnam War; from the women's liberation movement to the widening older and younger generation gap; from the eruption of rock and roll to the eruption of drug usage and experimentation; and from the assassinations of leaders to the placing of flowers in the shafts of guns; all of this affected everyone. All except perhaps the musical theatre scene. It's as if New York musical theatre was continuing the glory years of the Golden Age, insulated to the movement of the times. Within the theatre scene, the librettos became the stronghold of the musical and they ignored the continued national and global events as if they didn't exist. Production size of sets, costumes, orchestras, and casts got bigger and bigger, with nothing to help investors get their money back except through longer runs. Musicals were beginning to become hits or flops, period. One of the masterpieces of this period, a huge hit, was *Fiddler on the Roof*. Large in size, scope, and length, this musical did everything right in a decade that was unforgiving in its all or nothing standards. It also finally gave representation within its storyline to a once neglected religious faction – the Jewish culture. *Fiddler on the Roof* highlights the oppression of Jews under a Tsarist rule in the early 1900s.

THE ANALYSIS
Create the dramatic question

The bigger and more complex the show becomes, the more difficult it is to come up with an all-encapsulating dramatic question. In *Fiddler on the Roof*, a three-hour show, we are dealing with Tevye, his three daughters, their suitors, his wife, the poor village they live in, plus the issues of the slow disintegration of tradition whilst being under Tsarist rule and religious bigotry. Wow! I'm sure that there are many good dramatic questions out there for this show, but the following is what I came up with.

Dramatic Question: *"Will Tevye and the village of Anatevya survive the changing times of Jewish tradition and political oppression?"*

Figure 45 *Fiddler on the Roof*: The Dramatic Question.

List all analytically important characters

This is a tough one, again, because there is such depth and subplot in this massive show. My philosophy when I get into this type of predicament is to list more than I need to, and then I can always merge some of them together in ensembles later if necessary. There are three characters that I have included on the list that I do have questions about: Yente, the matchmaker. I'm including her because there is a song about her, and she does sing in "The Rumor." She could easily fall under the villagers of Anatevka, so if it does end up that her listing is unwarranted, I'll just place her back with the others. I feel the same way with Lazar, the butcher. He's instrumental in the song "To Life" with Tevye, but he could be shuffled to the villagers later.

This last one may surprise you. For the time being, I'm even going to include the Fiddler. The reason for this is that he seems to be a glue in the show, a magical being who shows up more than once, and plays music. He's pretty memorable. How does one ignore magic?

I did not include Chava's beau, Fyedka, since he does not sing.

Dramatic Question: *"Will Tevye and the village of Anatevya survive the changing times of Jewish tradition and political oppression?"*

<u>Tevye</u> <u>Golde</u> <u>Tzeitel</u> <u>Hodel</u> <u>Chava</u> <u>Motel</u> <u>Perchik</u> <u>Yente</u> <u>Lazar</u> <u>Anatevka</u> <u>Fiddler</u>

Figure 46 *Fiddler on the Roof*: List of Characters.

List all of the songs under the character's name

Dramatic Question: *"Will Tevye and the village of Anatevya survive the changing times of Jewish tradition and political oppression?"*										
Tevye	**Golde**	**Tzeitel**	**Hodel**	**Chava**	**Motel**	**Perchik**	**Yente**	**Lazar**	**Anatevka**	**Fiddler**
				ACT I						
										1. Prologue
2. Tradition	→	→	→	→	→		→	→	→	
		3. Matchmaker	→	→						
4. If I Were A Rich Man										
5. Sabbath Prayer	→	→	→	→	→		→	→		
6. To Life										
7. Tevye's Monologue										
		8. Miracles of Miracles			→					
9. Tevye's Dream	→						→	→	→	
10. Sunrise Sunset	→	→	→	→	→	→	→	→	→	
11. Wedding	→	→	→	→	→	→	→	→	→	
			12. Now I Have Everything			→				
13. Do You Love Me?	→									
							14. The Rumor		→	
			15. Far From The Home I Love							
16. Chavaleh Sequence				→						
							17. Tradition-Reprise			
←	←	←			←		←	←	18. Anatevka	
										19. Finale

Figure 47 *Fiddler on the Roof*: List of Songs.

Lyrically analyse all of the songs

Tevye

Tevye is a very hard-working, poor, boisterous, humble, short-tempered, deeply religious parent and farmer, who continues to support his family no matter how poorly off they are. He truly loves his family and what continues to get him through the tough times is his relationship with God. He is barely making enough to feed his family, his pull-horse is lame, and his daughters are constantly challenging him to make certain concessions in the dealings of their courtships and marriage. Each daughter asks a bit more of him. He doesn't know what to do – follow tradition or his love of his daughters. Where does he finally go for help each time? He talks to God. He asks for help and guidance, as in his singing of "If I Were a Rich Man," where he wonders and

dreams how it would rattle any plans of God if he were "*a rich man.*" He's constantly facing adversity and **trouble,** and he's **yearning** for answers and consolation. He and his family are an oppressed people by the Tsar. Tevye is N.

Golde

Golde is a mother who works extremely hard, like her husband Tevye. They have so little. They make do with what they have. As tradition has it, Tevye is the head of the household, and she must follow what he says. She too finds strength in her faith, but it wains with all the **troubles** and **plights** that they must always face. Even when asked a simple question of love by Tevye in "Do You Love Me," she still **laments** the struggles of fighting with him and starving with him. Her life has not been an easy one. Golde is N.

Tzeitel, Hodel, and Chava

When looking at the three daughters, they are all going through the same issues. The song that defines their life, and their energy, is "Matchmaker." They are all **children**, albeit of marrying age. They first think naively that the matchmaker is a great blessing – an exciting woman of good news for each of them. She's kind of like Mrs Santa Claus with a sack full of gorgeous, young men. They each will get the husband of their **dreams**. They are **yearning** for the matchmaker to find them a husband fast. They are **unfulfilled** without the right husband. But then the reality hits them that the pick of a husband could be disastrous, where any of them "*could get burned,*" and that they would be stuck with a loser husband for life. They have no power over the situation – it is the father who makes the call. They have to beg their father for their choices in husbands, totally ignoring traditions. Tzeitel, Hodel, and Chava are N.

Motel

A poor tailor. He's soft-spoken and sheepish. He is **yearning** for Tzeitel, **unfulfilled**. When he finally stands up to Tevye, reminding him that tailors deserve a happy life too, he does win over Tevye, and gets to marry Tzeitel. But the **troubles** and **hardships** continue. Their wedding is destroyed by the Tsarist authorities. They may be together, and happy together, but they are still oppressed. In the song "Miracle of Miracles," they even admit that it wasn't their doing that they could get together – it was due to the ongoing miracles of God. Motel is N.

Perchik

Perchik seems to be the most LF of any of the suitors. He's strong, smart, handsome, a teacher, and a revolutionary. He always thought he had everything, but it was "*only half true.*" The bottom line is that he doesn't have the power that he needs in order to marry Hodel and he realizes that without her, he is **incomplete** and **unfulfilled**. He still must go through Tevye – and Tevye makes the final decision. Once Perchik and Hodel do finally get together, Perchik must leave for Kiev, and there he becomes imprisoned. They are again **alone** and **unfulfilled**. Perchik never gets what he totally wants. He is N.

Yente

Yente is the matchmaker, and although she makes matches, she can't guarantee them. It's a job for her and a small paying job at that. She needs attention, to be listened to, and she's constantly **unfulfilled** in that need. She gossips to fill that void – just like the gossiping women in *The Music Man*. Only in this show, she doesn't sing "Pick-A-Little, Talk-A-Little." Instead, she sings "The Rumor." She is poor like most of the rest of the villagers in Anatevka. She even comically steals food from the people she visits. She's old and can't remember things. She's just trying to survive. Yente is N.

Lazar

Lazar has more wealth than most of the village of Anatevka. Yet, he is **unfulfilled**. He wants a match to replace his dead wife. He **yearns** for Tzeitel. Yet, he is shy and fearful about asking Tevye for his daughter's hand in marriage, since he is so much older. Lazar ends up not getting her in the end and therefore continues to be **unfulfilled**, in spite of his wealth. Lazar is N.

The villagers of Anatevka

Again in this show, the villagers take on a very active role. They are a people with a dedicated, deep-seated faith. They take pride in their heritage and their traditions – they live and die by them. And it is their Jewish faith that is their only stronghold in surviving the oppression that they are living in. They are very poor, most eat from hand to mouth. They are **yearning** for a better and more plentiful life. They are **unfulfilled**. They have no power over the Tsarist regime and are constantly reminded of their brutality and violence – **trouble**. Yet, they try to get by, barely, even when they must leave their village permanently. They are all N.

The Fiddler

The Fiddler is a very small role, but an important one. He is the metaphor for tradition and the unstableness of traditions' foundation if one starts to tinker with it. This fiddler is tradition, the power, the guidance, the wisdom, the faith, the credo, and philosophy. The Fiddler's music represents all of that and more. He is LF.

Wait! Not this again?

I'm afraid so, folks. This show again has a Life Force that is not within the usual plane. Unlike *West Side Story*, however, where the N characters are looking for their LF "somewhere out there," this time, the LF is known to them and coming from the outside – God. The LF is their Jewish faith and tradition. Their faith is the only thing that is keeping these poor people alive and sane. It is their comfort, their wisdom, their guidance, their stronghold, and their foundation. Without it, they would be lost.

So, if the LF is coming from God, how does it make itself known in the dynamics and design of the musical? This time, it is easier to see and hear than in *West Side Story*. It is through the faith-based music that they sing:

1 "Tradition"
2 "Sabbath Prayer"
3 "To Life"
4 "Tevye's Dream"
5 "Sunrise Sunset"
6 "The Wedding"

These songs and the rituals that go with them are their foundation and their grounding. It is their **central driving force** by way of their faith. It is **larger than life** – who is any larger than God? Its rituals and the comfort that comes along with them are **attractive to be with.** And certainly, the doctrine is very **persuasive**, with certain awful consequences if not abided by to the letter. My goodness, there is nothing more powerful than religious

Dramatic Question: *"Will Tevye and the village of Anatevya survive the changing times of Jewish tradition and political oppression?"*

N Tevye	N Golde	N Tzeitel	N Hodel	N Chava	N Motel	N Perchik	N Yente	N Lazar	N Anatevka	LF Fiddler
				ACT I						
										1. Prologue
2. Tradition	→	→	→	→	→		→	→	→	
		3. Matchmaker	→							
4. If I Were A Rich Man										
5. Sabbath Prayer	→		→	→	→		→	→	→	
6. To Life										
7. Tevye's Monologue										
		8. Miracles of Miracles			→					
9. Tevye's Dream	→						→	→	→	
10. Sunrise Sunset	→		→	→	→	→	→	→	→	
11. Wedding	→	→	→	→	→	→	→	→	→	
			12. Now I Have Everything			→				
13. Do You Love Me?	→									
								14. The Rumor	→	
			15. Far From The Home I Love							
16. Chavaleh Sequence				→						
								17. Tradition-Reprise		
←	←	←			←		←	←	←	18. Anatevka
										19. Finale

Figure 48 *Fiddler on the Roof.* List of Character Energies.

faith, and people of any faith will do whatever is necessary to keep it as it is and should be.

The Tsarist Regime and authorities could have been LF if they had sung, but they never do. They only have a few soldiers dance within the song "To Life," of which they are embracing that **credo** for that specific moment.

Musically analyse all of the songs

Once you finally have the lyric analysis set, the musical analysis is not very complicated. This musical uses LF and N Level 1 and Level 2 songs. They all either sound like their traditional Level 1–Tell It Like It Is songs, or they sound like the opposite, by being very truthful about it in Level 2–The Affirmation. It is interesting how the faith-based LF songs still have variety between sounding LF or sounding N. "Tradition," "To Life," "Tevye's Dream," and "The Wedding" are those full, celebratory, big-sounding LF numbers that one would expect. "Sabbath Prayer" and "Sunrise Sunset" are reflective,

N Tevye	N Golde	N Tzeitel	N Hodel	N Chava	N Motel	N Perchik	N Yente	N Lazar	N Anatevka	LF Fiddler
Dramatic Question: *"Will Tevye and the village of Anatevya survive the changing times of Jewish tradition and political oppression?"*										
				ACT I						
										1. Prologue LF1
2. Tradition LF1	→	→	→	→	→	→	→	→		
4. If I Were A Rich Man N1		3. Matchmaker N2	→	→						
5. Sabbath Prayer LF2	→	→		→		→		→	→	→
6. To Life LF1										
7. Tevye's Monologue N4										
9. Tevye's Dream LF1	→	8. Miracles of Miracles N2		→			→	→	→	
10. Sunrise Sunset LF2	→	→	→	→	→	→	→	→		
11. Wedding LF1	→	→	→	→	→	→	→	→		
13. Do You Love Me? N1	→		12. Now I Have Everything N1		→					
							14. The Rumor N2		→	
16. Chavaleh Sequence N1			15. Far From The Home I Love N1	→						
									17. Tradition-Reprise LF1	
←	←	←			←		←	←	18. Anatevka N1	
									19. Finale	

Figure 49 *Fiddler on the Roof*: List of Music Truths.

spiritual, heart-centred, reverent, and traditional. These songs need to sound like pieces of truthful affirmation and importance.

The only variant in the show is "Tevye's Monologue," which is a wonderful example of a Level 4–The Struggle song. He is struggling to decide whether he should follow the strict rules and doctrine of tradition or if he should follow the strong pulling of his heart to his daughter's well-being. Of course, he is talking with God about it, and as long as Tevye can justify the means through God, he'll go for it. The music goes back and forth, following the struggle of the decision.

The Alignment energy

It's a three-hour show, so the A better happen within that twenty minutes of beginning material if you ever want the audience to be on board for the duration of the show. The Fiddler plays at the beginning of the show, and then the song "Tradition" happens, which introduces the importance of their faith. That line has been drawn in the sand right away. It is then, when the song "Matchmaker" happens, that we witness the not-so-great affects of tradition. We have come to love Tevye's family and we want the best for them. We certainly do not want to see the daughters marry against their will and be woefully unhappy. This song shows the dilemma we'll be facing as the story progresses: tradition versus their happiness. "Matchmaker" is the A.

The Growth Moment energy

The "Chavaleh Sequence" definitely decides the fate of the third and final daughter who is at the age of marriage. But it is not a fate that finally gives resolution to the need of the family, let alone the need of the village. It increases the unanswered question to a higher level. The village is still under oppression and now Tevye, Golde, and Chava are miserable. No resolution as of yet. It is not until the very end, when the village is moving to new places all around the world that we see that there is hope for them all. And it is at that time, that Tevye even gives a bit of hope for Chava, by sending God's blessing. As they leave, he nods for the Fiddler to join them, letting us know that their traditions, and their faith, will accompany them and keep them safe on their journey. The Fiddler plays one last time and then follows them, again, like *West Side Story*, to the hollowing, hopeful sounds of woodwind accompaniment fading out to nothing. The GM is the "Finale."

The ground plan of the musical

West Side Story's ground plan had the LF outside of the N, being somewhere above and out of reach to the N. This time, with *Fiddler on the Roof*, the LF goes within each N character, and should be evident in some way in the ground plan. This is *The Ethereal* ground plan.

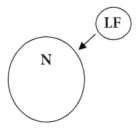

Figure 50 *Fiddler on the Roof* Ground Plan.

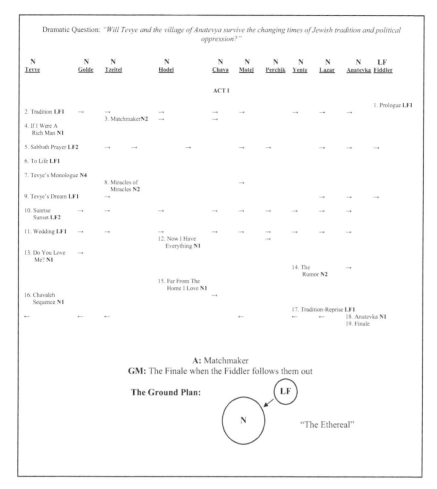

Figure 51 *Fiddler on the Roof:* Final.

Note

1   Taubman, *The New York Times*, 23 September 1964.

15

1970s – The Concept Musical

The Wiz

A sign of the times

Although the musical *The Wiz* had mixed reviews, there was no doubt that New York was witnessing a new phenomenon in musical theatre development. The power of suggestion became the prevalent attack in the Concept Musical shows of the 1970s. Walter Kerr of the *New York Times* put it this way, "*No elaborate shifting of scenery, no literal path'snalding from footlights into the far distance. Instead, four men with gleaming staves simply turned in from the wings, their yellow jackets unmistakably checked with paving blocks.*"[1] Broadway had witnessed the Yellow Brick Road literally taking life. Following the notion of Alfred Hitchcock, who always felt that the imagination of the audience is more powerful than anything he could do on film, the Broadway world suddenly embraced the power of imagination. As Kerr so pleasingly reacted later in his review, "*We were going for suggestion, discretion, a happy reticence, for a visual ingenuity …*"[2]

Credits

Music and Lyrics by Charlie Smalls
Book by William F. Brown
Adapted from the book *The Wonderful Wizard of Oz* by Frank Baum
Directed by Geoffrey Holder
Choreographed and musical numbers staged by George Faison
Produced by Ken Harper

History at a glance

Although Black American revues started as early as the 1920s and 1930s with *Chocolate Dandies* and *Shuffle Along*,[3] it has always been an uphill battle for the Black American culture to become mainstream. It still is. Yet we have witnessed tremendous success with such classic musical theatre productions like *Porgy and Bess*, and the all-Black cast of *Hello Dolly* in 1967. The 1970s welcomed in the musicals *Purlie* and *Raison*. But *The Wiz* was the musical that really embraced the contemporary African American soul. With its funky, high energy, and wonderfully melodic music by Charlie Smalls, the musical excited audiences for 1,672 performances on Broadway.[4] This was also at a time in Broadway history when the concept musical had taken hold: smaller production costs, smaller orchestras, and smaller casts, with books that didn't necessarily follow the traditional chronological time progressions that earlier musicals lived by. The concept musical was anti-extravaganza – look at *A Chorus Line* with an empty stage except for three mirrors! It was more minimalistic by nature. It was a lean, mean, musical machine that traded extravagance on the stage for streamlined storytelling and suggestive stage sets and costumes. Some look at this period as being cheap and not "up to Broadway standards." I totally disagree. I look at it as getting back to basics and letting the imagination of the audiences work again. It was a huge creative boom in the theatre world that allowed new ideas and formats to develop and form – *The Wiz* being one of them.

THE ANALYSIS
Create the dramatic question

This one is not so difficult since so many of us "older generation" folk lived through the yearly broadcasts on TV of the movie *The Wizard of Oz*. *The Wiz* follows the same format. Dorothy is whisked away from her home in Kansas and lands in the Land of Oz. In order for her to get back home, she traverses the Yellow Brick Road. She picks up the three friends along the way – the Scarecrow, the Tin Man, and the Lion who also need a brain, a

> Dramatic Question: *"Will Dorothy, the Scarecrow, the Tin Man, and the Lion survive and learn through their treacherous adventures to finally achieve their hopes: home, brains, heart, and courage?"*

Figure 52 *The Wiz*: The Dramatic Question.

heart, and courage respectively – and they together head to see The Wiz to solve their problems.

List all analytically important characters

There is no question that we must include Dorothy, Scarecrow, Tin Man, and Lion on the list. They all sing a lot and they are the ones we are rooting for. The big question is going to be how we deal with all of these other magical characters in the Land of Oz? This is one time where I did look at the list of songs right away to help guide me. I had an inkling that I could just list many of them under the "People of Oz." When looking at the list of songs and who sings what, it became evident very quickly that no one character stood out over all the others except for The Wiz, Glinda, and Evilene. Addaperle and her entourage do their thing with the one song and then they're pretty much done. I'm lumping them together with everyone else under the group "People of Oz."

Another question is what to do with Aunt Em. She sings her song at the beginning and then is not seen again until the very end of the show. Because she is not a part of the Land of Oz, it's important to list her separately. She will have her own individual energy line.

> Dramatic Question: *"Will Dorothy, the Scarecrow, the Tin Man, and the Lion survive and learn through their treacherous adventures to finally achieve their hopes: home, brains, heart, and courage?"*
>
> <u>Dorothy</u> <u>Scarecrow</u> <u>Tin Man</u> <u>Lion</u> <u>The Wiz</u> <u>Evilene</u> <u>Glinda</u> <u>People of Oz</u> <u>Em</u>

Figure 53 *The Wiz*: List of Characters.

List all of the songs under the character's name

Figure 54 *The Wiz*: List of Songs.

Dorothy	Scarecrow	Tin Man	Lion	The Wiz	Evilene	Glinda	People of Oz	Em
Dramatic Question: *"Will Dorothy, the Scarecrow, the Tin Man, and the Lion survive and learn through their treacherous adventures to finally achieve their hopes: home, brains, heart, and courage?"*								
				ACT I				
								1. Feeling We Once Had
							2. Tornado	
							3. He's the Wizard	
4. Soon As I Get Home								
	5. I Was Born On Day Before							
6. Ease On Down The Road	→							
		7. Slide Some Oil To Me						
8. Ease On Down The Road Repr 1	→	→						
			9. I'm A Mean Old Lion					
10. Ease On Down The Road Repr 2	→	→	→					
							11. Kalidah Battle	
12. Be A Lion			→					
			13. Lion's Dream				→	
							14. Emerald City Ballet	
				15. So You Wanted To Meet The Wizard				
	16. What I Would Do If I Could Feel							
				ACT II				
					17. Don't Nobody Bring Me No Bad News		→	
							18. Funky Monkeys	
							19. Everybody Rejoice	
←	←	←	←					
20. Who Do You Think You Are	→	→	→					
				21. Believe In Yourself				
				22. Y'all Got It				
						23. A Rested Body Is A Rested Mind	→	
						24. Believe In Yourself Repr 1		
25. Home								

Lyrically analyse all of the songs

Dorothy

Dorothy is home in Kansas, and she is not doing her share of work for Aunt Em. She's always "day**dream**ing," as if there's **some**thing more important to do. She's whisked away to Oz by a tornado. Dorothy is **yearning** to get back home, feeling as if she is "*drowning*," and full of "*fear*." In order to get back home, she can't do it alone – she must get help from The Wiz. She is constantly in **trouble** during her adventures. Dorothy is N.

Scarecrow, Tin Man, and Lion

All three of these characters are **yearning** for specific things that will finally **fulfil** them as complete beings: a brain, a heart, and courage respectively. Yes, during the show, each hint at signs and glimmers of strength and support to the others or to Dorothy, but their ultimate **unfulfillment** is not resolved until they see The Wiz for the answer. They too are in **trouble** during their adventures. We root for them like crazy! And will they make it? The Scarecrow responds with a hopeful "*somehow*," while The Tin Man **yearns** to get oiled up, and the Lion **protests too much** about being "*the king of the jungle*." All three of them are N.

The Wiz

The Wiz is the quintessential Life Force character. He's a **central driving force** – the foursome of Dorothy and gang are hell-bent on finding The Wiz so that he can solve their issues. The Wiz is **larger than life** – he's the Wizard! He's magical, knowing, mystical, powerful, everything that a being should be in order to take care of your problems. He's also **attractive to be with** – in a tornado type of way. He's charismatic, wears outlandish clothing, and blows up things on a whim. His magical powers burst forth in "So You Wanted to Meet the Wizard." The Wiz is LF.

Evilene

Evilene is a nasty, powerful witch/ruler. We're introduced to this magical, evil, and scary witch in the fun, rollicking, gospel-esque "Don't Nobody Bring Me No Bad News," where she sets down her all-important **set of rules** to her minions. She is the **central driving force** of the evil side of Oz. She's in charge, the leader of the Winkies. She's **larger than life**, and **attractive to be with** – in the same way as The Wiz, except that she is on the evil side. Evilene is anti-LF.

Glinda

Again, like The Wiz and Evilene, Glinda is magical and powerful too. She takes control of the situation after The Wiz accidentally flies off, making sure that Dorothy will be able to get home. She has the key – to believe in yourself and to click your heels three times. She is a **central driving force** character, **larger than life**, and **attractive to be with**. She also professes her "If You Believe" **credo** to Dorothy, accompanied by a clear **set of rules** that if followed, will get her home safely. Glinda is LF.

Aunt Em

She is Dorothy's guardian/parent. She is tough but she is loving and nurturing. In "The Feeling We Once Had," she has a heart-to-heart with Dorothy, knowing that at times they fight, but in the end, she "*still cares.*" She shows her love to Dorothy by providing for her, nourishing her, and guiding her with **sets of rules** that will help her grow to be a moral and kind adult. She is **larger than life**. She is LF.

People of Oz

The people of Oz are all shapes, sizes, and colours. Some are good, like the munchkins, Addaperle, or the citizens of Emerald City. Some are evil, like

Figure 55 *The Wiz*: List of Character Energies.

the Kalidahs, the funky monkeys, or the Winkies. What they all have in common, however, is the fact that they live in a enchanted world and are magical, colourful, or charismatic in some way. We don't worry about any of them – they control the journey of the foursome. Even when Evilene melts, and we find out that she had oppressed many of her citizens, within the context of the show, they still have had the power. All the Oz folks are a **central driving force**, **attractive to be with**, and **larger than life.** They are all fantastical. They are all LF.

Musically analyse all of the songs

The high-energy, rhythmic, pulsating, foot-tapping, syncopated funk music of *The Wiz* is extremely catchy and addictive. Even the slow-paced numbers have a pulse to them that raise the temperature of the production a couple

Dramatic Question: *"Will Dorothy, the Scarecrow, the Tin Man, and the Lion survive and learn through their treacherous adventures to finally achieve their hopes: home, brains, heart, and courage?"*

N Dorothy	N Scarecrow	N Tin Man	N Lion	LF The Wiz	LF Evilene	LF Glinda	LF People of Oz	LF Em
				ACT I				
								1. Feeling We Once Had **LF2**
							2. Tornado **LF1**	
							3. He's the Wizard **LF1**	
4. Soon As I Get Home **N1**								
	5. I Was Born On Day Before **N2**							
6. Ease On Down The Road **LF1**	→							
		7. Slide Some Oil To Me **N2**						
8. Ease On Down The Road Repr 1 **LF1**	→	→						
			9. I'm A Mean Old Lion **N5**					
10. Ease On Down The Road Repr 2 **LF1**	→	→	→					
							11. Kalidah Battle **LF1**	
12. Be A Lion **N1**								
			→ 13. Lion's Dream **LF1**					
				15. So You Wanted To Meet The Wizard **LF1**			14. Emerald City Ballet **LF1**	
		16. What I Would Do If I Could Feel **N1**						
				ACT II				
					17. Don't Nobody Bring Me No Bad News **LF1**	→		
							18. Funky Monkeys **LF1**	
							19. Everybody Rejoice **LF1**	
← 20. Who Do You Think You Are **N2**	← →	← →	← →					
				21. Believe In Yourself **LF2** 22. Y'all Got It **LF1**				
						23. A Rested Body Is A Rested Mind **LF2** →		
						24. Believe In Yourself Repr 1 **LF2**		
25. Home								

Figure 56 *The Wiz*: List of Music Truths.

of degrees. The music is its soul and the lyrics its backbone. There is nothing fancy or subtextual in this infrastructure. All of the songs are either basic LF or N, Level 1 or 2, except for one song – "I'm a Mean Old Lion."

"I'm a Mean Old Lion" is a great example of a **Protest Too Much** song. The poor lion, so embarrassed by his own fright and lack of courage, actually sings and acts as if he truly is this king of the jungle. In the song "I'm a Mean Old Lion," the Lion has entered, spouting off to look out and get out of here, because he is the number one, powerful and courageous beast. But we all know better. It's all a front to protect himself from humiliation in front of the others. This is why the lion is always a favourite of audiences – the poor king of the jungle is just a sweet pussycat that you just can't help but feel for. He is protesting too much, thus the song is N Level 5–Protest Too Much.

The Alignment energy

Very early on, the tornado swoops up Dorothy and delivers her to the Land of Oz. One would think then that we have a pretty good idea of her trouble and predicament. The problem is we can't assume this is the same Oz story that we all are familiar with. We have the LF song from the Tornado, and then Addaperle's helpful song, "He's the Wizard," from which we know that Dorothy has to go seek him for help. The issue is that we have not heard any character sing a N song. We have had characters sing to Dorothy, so we know that she is a focus; however, to cement the A, we need to have Dorothy herself sing. We finally get it when Dorothy sings "Soon As I Get Home." This is her desire, her want, her N. The A is "Soon As I Get Home."

The Growth Moment energy

Late in the show, we watch The Wiz solve the problems of the Scarecrow, Tin Man, and Lion. He is also planning on taking Dorothy with him on his balloon flight, however, ropes get undone and The Wiz whizzes away without her. With Dorothy being the main N character, she must have resolution in some way before the show ends. Glinda, the Good Witch of the North, sings "If You Believe," which gives Dorothy the solution to her quest, however, Dorothy hasn't done the clicking of her heels yet. Also, as the song states, Dorothy must "believe" before she clicks her heels. It is that stipulation that Dorothy must overcome before the magic takes her back home. The song "Home" is that thinking process that finally allows Dorothy to click her heels and arrive at home. The song masterfully builds up in intensity until it finally crescendos to a resolute ending of brass, percussion, and the clicking of Dorothy's heels. She's home. The song "Home" is the GM.

The ground plan of the musical

One would think that the ground plan for this show would be the simple N → LF. There is good logic behind this, and in many ways, one could justify and make a good argument for it. I cannot deny that. But there are a few things we need to consider in this show that makes it a bit more unique in its map. Yes, Dorothy, who is N, is entering the world of Oz, a LF land. But the threesome that she meets there – the Scarecrow, Tin Man, and Lion – are also N, and they live in this land of LF. That makes it more difficult to justify the simple N → LF concept.

Secondly, Dorothy is constantly moving from one adventure to the next. Each adventure is such a distinct new world. The Land of Oz is made up of such various and perilous counties, that each gives its own unique celebration as well as danger. And as Dorothy continues to go from "county to county," she meets and picks up her friends along the way, who then join in the next adventure. Likewise, other than Emerald City, they never go back to an area that they were at previously.

With this in mind, a more accurate ground plan is:

$$N \rightarrow LF \rightarrow LF \rightarrow$$

The name for this ground plan is N Picaresque. Who would've guessed that this show has the same Ground Plan as *Pippin*? It makes sense. *Pippin* is looking for the life that is right for him, and so he goes from adventure to adventure trying to find his niche: being a warrior, a king, a politician, an orgy object, and finally a farmer with Catherine. Pretty cool.

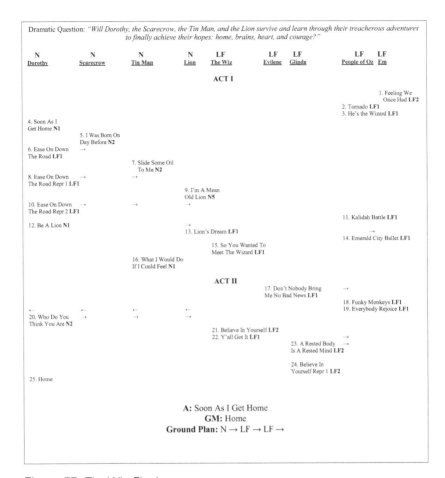

Figure 57 *The Wiz*: Final.

Notes

1   Kerr, *The New York Times*, 12 January 1975.
2   Ibid.
3   Flinn, *Musical!*, 309.
4   Gäntl, *The Musical*, 357.

16

Stephen Sondheim – The Through-Music Musical

Sweeney Todd: The Demon Barber of Fleet Street

A sign of the times

It's a whole 'nother animal. What else can you say about a musical that is actually more opera than musical, more Grand Guignol than musical comedy, and certainly more embedded in classical twentieth-century music than any other show written in musical theatre history? (Although I'm also in awe of Leonard Bernstein's score for *West Side Story*.) I mean, seriously? How does one review a musical about a Meat Pie shop with humans as the main course? And then include such a rich slate of characters and music? It is no wonder reviewers didn't know how to react to such a beast. As *The New York Times* reviewer Walter Kerr states rather blatantly, "*I am afraid that what 'Sweeney Todd' most wants to be is impressive. It succeeds in that … We are plainly in the hands of intelligent and talented people possessed of a complex, macabre, assiduously offbeat vision*."[1] And a beast it was.

Credits

Music and Lyrics by Stephen Sondheim
Libretto by Hugh Wheeler, based on a version of "Sweeney Todd" by Christopher Bond
Directed by Harold Prince
Produced by Richard Barr, Charles Woodward, Robert Fryer, Mary Lea Johnson, and Martin Richards

History at a glance

People are probably asking why I have an independent chapter for Stephen Sondheim, and not for any of the other "greats" in musical theatre history. It's basically because I feel that Sondheim's work tended to be the anomaly of the periods – it didn't follow the mainstream musical of the time. The shows that Sondheim wrote both music and lyrics for were never "extravaganzas" in the 1960s. *Company* certainly did fit into the Concept musical, however, *Sweeney Todd* was an entirely different beast altogether. It was the show that projected him into a period that I call the "Through-Music Musical." This period is a quasi-opera/musical that focuses much more on progressing the story through music versus the dialogue. *Jesus Christ Superstar* and *Tommy* started the rock opera kick. Other shows later followed suit: *Cats*, *Phantom of the Opera*, *Miss Saigon*, and *Les Misérables* to name a few, but they were more intentionally composed with "Musical Theatre Opera" and its grandiose production values in mind. In that respect Sondheim productions were always more minimalistic in nature. He followed the beat of a different drum. He took chances in storytelling structure, and was not afraid of visiting the darkest corners of humanity. This was certainly not the desire of the populist opinion – but yet he continued on, never giving up on his vision. Another major difference between Sondheim and the others, was his twentieth-century style of music composition that many people found unrelatable and unsingable. People were aghast that they couldn't exit the theatre humming one of his tunes. Yet now he is considered one of the most prolific and significant creators of musical theatre history, which is a major feat considering the obstacles he faced.

THE ANALYSIS
Create the dramatic question

This is definitely a musical about revenge. The first song, "The Ballad of Sweeney Todd," sung by the company who are all-knowing, immediately introduces us to the character of Sweeney Todd and his violent nature. In

Dramatic Question: *"Will Sweeney Todd get revenge by killing Judge Turpin?"*

Figure 58 *Sweeney Todd*: The Dramatic Question.

the song "No Place Like London," we begin to understand the wrath and injustice bestowed upon Sweeney when he was sent to prison for a crime he didn't commit. The Judge, who committed Sweeney to prison, wanted to rape Sweeney's wife, Lucy. He also stole Sweeney's daughter, making himself guardian of her after the sentencing. It's very clear that Sweeney wants revenge and we as an audience immediately feel for him, understanding his obsession for vengeance. For the rest of the show, we are wondering whether Sweeney will ever get it.

List all analytically important characters

This show is fairly self-explanatory with the listing of characters. They all sing quite a bit and are an integral part of the plotline. All incidental characters – i.e. Jonas Fogg – are not vital enough to warrant a listing. Those characters can be a part of the very vital chorus.

Dramatic Question: *"Will Sweeney Todd get revenge by killing Judge Turpin?"*

Sweeney   Mrs Lovett   Johanna   Anthony   Tobias   Judge   Beadle   Pirelli   Beggar W   Chorus

Figure 59 *Sweeney Todd*: List of Characters.

List all of the songs under the character's name

Dramatic Question: *"Will Sweeney Todd get revenge by killing Judge Turpin?"*									
Sweeney	**Mrs Lovett**	**Johanna** **Anthony**		**Tobias**	**Judge**	**Beadle**	**Pirelli**	**Beggar**	**Chorus**
			ACT I						
←									1. The Ballad of Sweeney Todd
←		2. No Place Like London						→	
3. The Barber & His Wife									
	4. The Worst Pies in London								
	5. Poor Thing								
6. My Friends	→								
					←	←			7. The Ballad of Sweeney Todd
		8. Green Finch and Linnet Bird							
		←	9. Ah, Miss!					→	
		10. Johanna I & II							
←	←			11. Pirelli's Miracle Elixir					→
				←		12. Entrance & Contest			
							←		13. The Ballad of Sweeney Todd
					14. Johanna				
	15. Wait						→		
							16. Pirelli's Death		
									17. The Ballad of Sweeney Todd
		←	18. Kiss Me Pt.1						
						19. Ladies in Their Sensitivities			
		←	←		←	20. Kiss Me Pt. 2			
					21. Pretty Woman I				
←					→				
22. Pretty Woman II	→	→							
23. Epiphany									
←	24. A Little Priest								
			ACT II						
				25. God That's Good!					
←	←		←				→		→
←			26. Johanna Act II Sequence						
←	27. By the Sea		→						→
28. Wigmaker/Ballad									→
←									29. The Letter
	←			30. Not While I'm Around					
	←			←		31. Parlor Songs			
									32. Fogg's Asylum
									33. City on Fire
		←							
←	34. Searching	→	→	→				→	→
35. Judge's Return					←				
36. Final Scene I	→								
37. Final Scene II	←	←	←	38. The Ballad of Sweeney Todd	→	→		←	→

Figure 60 *Sweeney Todd*: List of Songs.

Lyrically analyse all of the songs

Sweeney Todd

At the beginning of the show, Sweeney is mourning the loss of his wife, Lucy. He has lost his daughter Johanna and then found her under the clutches of the Judge. Sweeney's life was put into shambles by this evil, awful man.

Sweeney can only consider retribution for all of his losses. He is **yearning** for revenge. He will be **unfulfilled** in his life until his daughter is safe and taken care of. He is in **trouble** with the law – the Judge and Beadle. All the way through to "Pretty Woman," Sweeney is N.

Once Anthony interrupts the attempted murder of Judge Turpin by Sweeney in "Pretty Woman," Sweeney realizes he has lost his one chance for retribution. At this point, during "Epiphany," he slowly changes into a mad man, realizing that now "*all deserve to die*" and that the only thing he can do is to kill anybody in order to rid himself of his rage. Sweeney now has a **vision**, he becomes a **central driving force**, a **larger than life** murderer/psychopath. He becomes the mega-representation of Jack the Ripper. Sweeney has become LF.

Mrs Lovett

At the beginning of the show, Mrs Lovett is a content, very matter-of-fact woman, trying to scrape out a living in a lousy part of London. She owns a pie shop, in which she admittedly makes lousy meat pies, however, it's a living. She has accepted her fate. Mrs Lovett helps direct Sweeney with his need for revenge, first by saving his razor, and secondly by helping him get to Pirelli. Finally, in "A Little Priest," she comes up with the idea of the human meat pie. She's a **central driving force** in the show, guiding Sweeney. She has a **vision** for life and that vision is to live day to day to make enough money to eat. She is LF in the first act.

However, when we get to the second act, Mrs Lovett begins to change. She has fallen in love with Sweeney and suddenly has **dreams** of living together peacefully "*by the sea.*" She becomes a woman who will be **unfulfilled** until Sweeney accepts her as his mate – and this will not happen. After a while, she has trouble even taking care of Tobias, because she no longer can control Sweeney. Mrs Lovett becomes N in Act II.

Johanna

Johanna has been kidnapped and is imprisoned in one of the Judge's rooms. The Judge desires her. She is in **trouble.** She **yearns** for freedom, like the Linnet Bird caged outside at a kiosk. She **loves** and **yearns** for Anthony, and she needs him to save her. Johanna is N.

Anthony

Anthony is a strong sailor with integrity – he saves Sweeney. He falls in love with Johanna and does everything in his might to *"steal you, Johanna"* from the clutches of the evil Judge. He is **attractive to be with, larger than life**, and a **central driving force** in both Sweeney's and Johanna's lives. Anthony is LF.

Tobias

Tobias is a boy, a **child**, out on his own in a very violent and cruel world, without a mum or dad to take care of him. He is forced to lie and sell *"miracle elixir"* products to the public for the evil Pirelli, to avoid a beating. He's a slave. He's scraping to get by. He's **yearning** for a safe, comfortable place to live and eat. Tobias is N.

Judge Turpin and Beadle

Judge Turpin and Beadle have all the power. They're a judge and a public official who control the law, and use it to their evil advantage. They are **larger than life**, and are **central driving forces** for the evil side of the city. They can manipulate peoples' lives. The Judge kidnaps Johanna and wants to wed her, while Beadle plays to the Judge's evils by giving him *"sensitivity"* strategies. They are anti-LF.

Pirelli

Pirelli is charismatic, an expert salesman. He also has power by having money, a business, and "owning" Tobias. This *"barber of kings"* is egotistical, **larger than life** and **attractive to be with**. Pirelli is LF.

Beggar Woman

She was a woman who had everything beautiful in life and lost it all to a criminal judge. Now, this woman is mentally lost, has no money, is desperate with no place to go or live, and she is willing to *"split her muff"* to stay alive. She is N.

Chorus

Right from the start, in "The Ballad of Sweeney Todd" the chorus knows more than any one. They know how the story goes – they are like a Greek Chorus, commenting and narrating as the story continues. We never worry about them because they know the future and who are we to mess with that? They are a **central driving force** to this show. Note: this is why I believe that the 2007 movie really missed the boat and didn't work as well – that LF directional chorus was no longer there to guide the character, and us, along. The chorus is LF.

Dramatic Question: *"Will Sweeney Todd get revenge by killing Judge Turpin?"*

N→LF Sweeney	LF→N Mrs Lovett	N Johanna	LF Anthony	N Tobias	LF Judge	LF Beadle	LF Pirelli	N Beggar	LF Chorus
				ACT I					
←									1. The Ballad of Sweeney Todd
			2. No Place Like London					→	
3. The Barber & His Wife									
	4. The Worst Pies in London								
	5. Poor Thing								
6. My Friends	→								
					←	←			7. The Ballad of Sweeney Todd
		8. Green Finch and Linnet Bird							
		←	9. Ah, Miss!				→		
		10. Johanna I & II							
				11. Pirelli's Miracle Elixir					→
				←			12. Entrance & Contest		
←	←							←	13. The Ballad of Sweeney Todd
					14. Johanna				
	15. Wait								
							16. Pirelli's Death →		
									17. The Ballad of Sweeney Todd
		←	18. Kiss Me Pt.1						
						19. Ladies in Their Sensitivities			
		←	←		←	20. Kiss Me Pt. 2			
←			→		21. Pretty Woman I →				
22. Pretty Woman II									
23. Epiphany	→								
←	24. A Little Priest								
				ACT II					
←	←			25. God That's Good!				→	
←		←	26. Johanna Act II Sequence				→		
	27. By the Sea		→						
28. Wigmaker/Ballad									→
←									29. The Letter
	←			30. Not While I'm Around					
				←			31. Parlor Songs		
									32. Fogg's Asylum
									33. City on Fire
	34. Searching	←	→	→			→		→
← 35. Judge's Return		→		→	→			→	→
36. Final Scene I	→								
37. Final Scene II									
←	←	←	←	38. The Ballad of Sweeney Todd	→	→		→	→

Figure 61 *Sweeney Todd*: List of Character Energies.

Musically analyse all of the songs

Sweeney Todd, as well as most Sondheim musicals, is challenging when it comes to analysing the music. The main reason is the fact that because his musicals are Through-Music musicals, the songs in his shows tend to be longer and can flow from one section to another within the title of one song. It doesn't necessarily make it harder to analyse a song of his, but it can have multiple LF and N levels in the same song, depending on how hard and in-depth you want to go.

An example would be "Poor Thing." This song really has a unique ABA quality to it, with the A sections sounding like a N ballad, and the B section sounding like a LF song. Thus, I analysed it as a LF 2/1/2 song to differentiate between the sections.

Tobias singing "Pirelli's Miracle Elixir" is a good example of a N level 3–The Lie. He knows the elixir is a sham, yet he tries to sell it anyway, saying it's a miracle drug. He's doing this to survive. He knows that as long as he doesn't anger Pirelli, he will at least get fed once during the day. He also knows that if he doesn't do what Pirelli asks of him, Pirelli will beat/abuse him.

Likewise, the song "The Letter" sung by Sweeney is, for him, a LF Level 3–The Lie. He is tricking the Judge in the letter – not telling the truth – and Sweeney knows it. The song would not be a lie for the chorus ensemble, since they are reading it at face value. They are mere "reporters."

The songs "Searching" and "Finale 1" are LF Level 5–The Tactical for Sweeney. In "Searching" he's singing out to Tobias, trying to find the lad. He is using a kind tone to manipulate the boy into giving himself up, using a gentle, parental call. In "Finale 1," when Sweeney finds out that Mrs Lovett has lied to him about Lucy, Sweeney knows in his mind that he's going to kill Mrs Lovett. So he manipulates her with an enticing waltz-like dance to get her to let her guard down. The moment she does, he throws her in the oven. Yikes! See Figure 62.

The Alignment energy

Part of the challenge at the beginning of the show was to get a bunch of informational history out to the audience. We needed to find out about the travesty that happened with Benjamin Barker, his wife Lucy, and child Johanna. Without that information, we couldn't possibly feel sorry for

N→LF Sweeney	LF→N Mrs Lovett	N Johanna	LF Anthony	N Tobias	LF Judge	LF Beadle	LF Pirelli	N Beggar	LF Chorus
←N2				**ACT I**					1. The Ballad of Sweeney Todd LF1
←N1			2. No Place Like London LF1					→N1	
3. The Barber & His Wife N1									
	4. The Worst Pies in London LF1 5. Poor Thing LF2/1/2								
6. My Friends N1	→LF2								
					←LF1	←LF1			7. The Ballad of Sweeney Todd LF1
		8. Green Finch and Linnet Bird N1							
		←N1	9. Ah, Miss! LF2					→N1	
			10. Johanna I & II LF2						
←N2	←LF1			11. Pirelli's Miracle Elixir N3					→LF1
				←N2					
							12. Entrance & Contest LF1		
							←		13. The Ballad of Sweeney Todd LF1
					14. Johanna LF1				
	15. Wait LF2								→LF1
							16. Pirelli's Death LF1		
									17. The Ballad of Sweeney Todd LF1
		←N2	18. Kiss Me Pt.1 LF1						
					19. Ladies in Their Sensitivities LF2				
		←N2	←LF1		←LF1	20. Kiss Me Pt. 2 LF1			
←N1					21. Pretty Woman I LF2				
22. Pretty Woman II N1			→LF1		→LF2				
23. Epiphany LF1	→LF1								
←LF1	24. A Little Priest LF1								
				ACT II					
←LF1	←LF1			25. God That's Good! N2					→LF1
←LF2		←N1	26. Johanna Act II Sequence LF2					→N2	
←LF1	27. By the Sea N2								
28. Wigmaker/Ballad LF2			→LF2						→LF1
←LF3									29. The Letter LF2
	←N1			30. Not While I'm Around N1					
	←N2			←N2		31. Parlor Songs LF1			
		←N2							32. Fogg's Asylum 33. City on Fire LF1
←LF5	34. Searching N1	→N1	→LF2	→				→N1	→ LF1 → LF1
35. Judge's Return LF5					→LF2				→ LF1
36. Final Scene I LF5	→N2								
37. Final Scene II									
←	←	←	←	38. The Ballad of Sweeney Todd	→		→	→	→

Figure 62 *Sweeney Todd*: List of Music Truths.

Sweeney Todd – a potential vigilante who wants to kill a judge. Once we learn the story through "Poor Thing," we then see Sweeney's dilemma. But what will he do? We don't know this as of yet. It takes the song "My Friends" to answer that question. Suddenly, we understand how he will seek his revenge – through the use of his razor. The A is "My Friends."

The Growth Moment energy

The GM in this show is tragic, however, it's almost expected. Sweeney has gone mad. Once "Epiphany" is sung it becomes increasingly difficult to support and root for him. He has become a Jack the Ripper, with no conscience at all, and no moral compass to guide him. The GM is the "Judge's Return," when Sweeney finally gets revenge. His earlier need is now resolved, although now, because he's out of control and LF, it no longer feels like a "clean" retribution for the audience. It has gotten way out of hand. Also, it is way too late for Sweeney. He's a lost, murderous soul. But the dramatic question is finally answered at the "Judge's Return," so it is the GM.

The last three songs, then, "Finale 1," "Finale 2," and the "Ballad of Sweeney Todd," are there as a Coda to the show. They neatly tie everything together, albeit in a murderous rage and traumatized mental illness. Thank heaven they had the final chorus of "The Ballad of Sweeney Todd" to separate us a bit from all of the barbarousness preceding it. It was pretty gory and haunting.

The ground plan of the musical

The ground plan of this show is an energy reversal show. Sweeney Todd begins as N, seeking revenge for the travesty that the Judge created in Sweeney's life. At "Epiphany," Sweeney switches to LF for the rest of the show. Likewise, Mrs Lovett starts off as LF, helping guide Sweeney to achieve his revenge, but then switches to N at "By The Sea" when she finds she's truly in love with him and losing him. This show's ground plan is "The Reversal":

$$N \leftrightarrow LF$$

How bizarre is the fact that *Sweeney Todd* and *My Fair Lady* have the same ground plan? It's a good thing Eliza didn't have access to an oven during "Just You Wait." She may have then "cooked Higgin's goose."

Dramatic Question: *"Will Sweeney Todd get revenge by killing Judge Turpin?"*									
N→LF Sweeney	LF→N Mrs Lovett	N Johanna	LF Anthony	N Tobias	LF Judge	LF Beadle	LF Pirelli	N Beggar	LF Chorus
ACT I									
←N2									1. The Ballad of Sweeney Todd LF1
←N1			2. No Place Like London LF1					→N1	
3. The Barber & His Wife N1									
	4. The Worst Pies in London LF1								
	5. Poor Thing LF2/1/2								
6. My Friends N1	→LF2								
					←LF1	←LF1			7. The Ballad of Sweeney Todd LF1
		8. Green Finch and Linnet Bird N1							
		←N1	9. Ah, Miss! LF2					→N1	
			10. Johanna I & II LF2						
←N2	←LF1			11. Pirelli's Miracle Elixir N3					→LF1
				←N2					
						12. Entrance & Contest LF1			
							←		13. The Ballad of Sweeney Todd LF1
	15. Wait LF2				14. Johanna LF1				
								→LF1	
							16. Pirelli's Death LF1		
									17. The Ballad of Sweeney Todd LF1
		←N2	18. Kiss Me Pt.1 LF1						
						19. Ladies in Their Sensitivities LF2			
		←N2	←LF1		←LF1	20. Kiss Me Pt. 2 LF1			
←N1									
22. Pretty Woman II N1			→LF1		21. Pretty Woman I LF2				
23. Epiphany LF1	→LF1				→LF2				
←LF1	24. A Little Priest LF1								
ACT II									
←LF1	←LF1			25. God That's Good! N2					→LF1
←LF2		←N1	26. Johanna Act II Sequence LF2					→N2	
←LF1	27. By the Sea N2								
28. Wigmaker/Ballad LF2			→LF2						→LF1
←LF3									29. The Letter LF2
		←N1							
				30. Not While I'm Around N1					
	←N2								
				←N2					
							31. Parlor Songs LF1		
									32. Fogg's Asylum
		←N2							33. City on Fire LF1
←LF5	34. Searching N1	→N1	→LF2					→N1	→LF1
35. Judge's Return LF5					→LF2				→LF1
36. Final Scene I LF5 →N2									
37. Final Scene II									
←	←	←	←	38. The Ballad of Sweeney Todd	→	→		→	→

A: My Friends
GM: Judge's Return
Ground Plan: N ↔ LF "The Reversal"

Figure 63 *Sweeney Todd*: Final.

Note

1   Kerr, *The New York Times*, 11 March 1979.

17

1980s – The Spectacle Musical

The Phantom of the Opera

A sign of the times

We have all heard about the infamous battle between Andrew Lloyd Webber and *The New York Times* theatre reviewer Frank Rich. Mr Rich didn't give the expected "carte blanche glowing review" of *The Phantom of the Opera*, much to Mr Lloyd Webber's dismay. Rich's writing was more of a side-handed affirmation of frivolous futility: "*Only a terminal prig would let the avalanche of preopening publicity poison his enjoyment of this show, which usually wants nothing more than to shower the audience with fantasy and fun, and which often succeeds, at any price.*"[1] Whether you agree or disagree with the review, one must admit that there is something in this musical that now continues to bring in audiences for generations. There is something for everyone in this show, and frankly, can't that be enough?

Credits

Music by Andrew Lloyd Webber
Lyrics by Charles Hart
Book by Richard Stilgoe and Andrew Lloyd Webber
From the novel *Le Fantome de L'Opera* by Gaston Leroux
Directed by Harold Prince
Musical Staging and Choreography by Gillian Lynne
Produced by Cameron Mackintosh and The Really Useful Theatre Company Ltd

History at a glance

Historically, the musical *Cats* changed everything. Period. Suddenly, with *Cats'* mega-success – caught up in its non-stop energy and its absolutely dazzling costumes and technology – every other musical felt the unspoken need to "one better" the last. When New York was redefining the audience impact on their economy, they also at the same time redefined what an audience expected from Broadway's technology department. Thanks to the theatrical British Invasion of Cameron Mackintosh, *The Phantom of the Opera's* spectacle gimmicks were plentiful – from a gondola romantically cruising past lit torches to the iconic chandelier falling from the heavens. Thankfully, this grandiose production was also supported by the rich, luscious music of Andrew Lloyd Webber, and a storyline based from a classic novel. The show opened on Broadway at the Majestic Theatre on 26 January 1988 and had continuously run for over thirty years until the historic Covid-19 pandemic of 2020 appeared, which shut all of Broadway down for the year. This show defined a new reality – theatre now has become big business to a potentially infinitely revolving door of theatre tourists.

THE ANALYSIS
Create the dramatic question

This show is a classic example of triangular love – the Phantom, Raoul, and Christine – and the musical never deviates from that premise. In spite of the fact that an entire opera company is held hostage by this maniacal man of the shadows, we really are only interested in Christine's well-being. When stripped down to the basic foundation, we are wanting to find out whether Raoul will save Christine or the Phantom will keep her.

> Dramatic Question: *"Will the Phantom or Raoul win the heart of Christine?"*

Figure 64 *The Phantom of the Opera*: The Dramatic Question.

List all analytically important characters

Everyone would agree that the Phantom, Christine, and Raoul should be listed separately. All three of them are in the dramatic question and all three have a tremendous amount of music that they sing, including solo songs. So, the big question comes in as to whether we include Firman, Andre, Piangi, Carlotta, Giry, and Meg individually or as just a part of the Opera Company. I have seen this show twice on Broadway and have seen the film many times, and still, to this day, I can't keep the company characters straight. That tells me something. That tells me that their map in this show is treated more as community energy versus individual energy. Therefore, I choose to include all of these characters as part of the Opera Company. You could, however, list all of these characters in the chart, and you would find them ending up being all of the same energy anyway – no harm done.

There is no real scientific way to decide whether one should include individual characters as energy analysis material or to combine them as a group or community. In *The Music Man*, you certainly could combine all of the River City characters as townspeople and still come up with the same energy plot. It is all a matter of how you choose to interpret focus and how that lends itself to the dramatic question. Personally, I tend to feel and care more for the individuals in River City versus all of the individuals in the Opera Company. That is my own bias. It does not mean that my interpretation is right and yours is wrong. I tend to lean one way or another just by how the characters affect me. My gut tells me to focus more on the Beggar Woman in *Sweeney Todd* than with Firman and Andre, or the egotist Pirelli than with the self-indulgent Carlotta. It is just a different interpretation that gets you to the same point at the end of the process, as long as you follow your dramatic question diligently.

Dramatic Question: *"Will the Phantom or Raoul win the heart of Christine?"*
Phantom   Christine   Raoul   Opera Company

Figure 65 *The Phantom of the Opera*: List of Characters.

List all of the songs under the character's name

Dramatic Question: *"Will the Phantom or Raoul win the heart of Christine?*			
Phantom	**Christine**	**Raoul**	**Opera Company**
		ACT I	
	←		
			1. Dress Reh of Hannibal
	2. Think of Me	→	→
3. Angel of Music	→		→
	4. Little Lotte/The Mirror	→	
5. The Phantom of the Opera	→		
6. The Music of the Night			
	7. I Remember		
8. I Remember/ Stranger Than You Dreamt			
			9. Magical Lasso
←		←	10. Notes
		←	11. Prima Donna
			12. Poor Fool
	←	13. Why Have You Brought	
	14. Raoul I've Been There	→	
	←	14. All I Ask of You	
15. All I Ask of You – Reprise			
		ACT II	
	←	←	15. Masquerade
16. Why So Silent			
17. Notes/Twisted	→	→	→
	18. A Music Call	→	→
	19. Phantom of the Opera-Reprise		
	20. Wishing You Were Somehow		
21. Christine Wandering	→	→	
22. Before the Premiere		→	
			→ 23. Don Juan Triumphant
24. The Point of No Return	→		
25. Down Once More		→	→
26. The Phantom's Lair	→	→	→

Figure 66 *The Phantom of the Opera*: List of Songs.

Lyrically analyse all of the songs

The Phantom

Throughout the years in my class, students have always argued about the energy of the Phantom. Many, if not most, early on believe that he is N. There are a few good reasons for this. First and foremost, we do *feel for him*. This is due to the fact that according to our present moral standards, the Phantom had an unjust and awful life of which he had no control. Like the Hunchback of Notre Dame, in this time people who were disfigured were scarred by the terrible treatment of society. They were scorned, abandoned, mocked, put into freak shows, publicly displayed and humiliated, and given no hope for survival. They were tossed away like garbage. How can you not feel for someone like that? But, as I always remind the class much to their dismay, this guy also kills innocent people. It's not as if he is a saint. Raoul is right – the

Phantom is a madman – and you can't just let a guy like that do what he pleases. Just because he has had a bad life doesn't *totally* justify killing, does it? We can justify Sweeney Todd's obsession to kill the Judge in the first act, because it was set more as a Grand Guignol horror/tragedy. However, when Sweeney goes on a murder spree in Act II, the justification to support him dwindles and we begin to explore the ugliness of human obsession.

Secondly, disfigured, cruelly treated people deserve love also, right? We would like to see the Phantom have love. In some ways, we would like Christine to understand the Phantom – his hurts and desires. But, again, I had to remind my classes of the realities of the situation. The Phantom is using his powers *against* Christine. He is forcing her into his lair by hypnosis and magic. He is basically *raping* her mentally. He is the same kind of person as a creep nowadays who puts drugs into a woman's drink, and then takes advantage of her. This is not the type of man I want to feel for. I don't want to root for him. I don't want to like him.

A final note: please don't get me wrong. We should and *we have to* care for the Phantom. If we don't care for him, the show loses the entire triangular power struggle. At a certain psychological level, we must believe and desire Christine to choose the Phantom, as kind of a Mother Theresa saviour. We have to care for him, otherwise it just becomes a show about the good guy against the bad guy – a shallow, formulaic alternative. The interest of the show lies in this darker psychological experience of actually caring for a criminal madman, and that if Christine chose him, she would guide him to a kinder, gentler life. That is what gives the show its emotion and heart. So, as an actor, it is necessary that he finds the genuine goodness of the Phantom along with staying true to what he is energy-wise. He must be that central driving force, attractive to be with (in a tornado kind of way), persuasive, and larger than life, LF. In other words, he can't play a "helpless" Phantom.

There is no doubt that he is the **central driving force** of the show, he is **attractive to be with** like an erupting volcano, he is **persuasive** in a very magical and evil way, and he is **larger than life** in his magic and powers to get "*inside your mind.*" The Phantom is LF.

Christine

Christine is the meek, kind, and modest understudy to a diva and is suddenly thrown into the limelight. Automatically we are rooting for her as the underdog. She is hypnotized by the Phantom, being tricked into thinking the Phantom is her dead father – she's being mentally raped. She is a victim. Christine is in **trouble** and is **yearning** for her father, "*wishing somehow*" that he would come back. She falls in love with Raoul – she is **yearning** for him. She is powerless to the Phantom's magic. Christine is N.

Raoul

He is a business man of wealth and title – **attractive to be with**. He never fears the Phantom and accuses him of being a madman rather than a ghost. He takes charge to face this dilemma head on versus falling to the Phantom's demands. He is a **central driving force** and **larger than life**, a real leader. Raoul is gutsy, confident, and calm in "All I Ask of You" and makes sure that "*nothing will harm*" Christine. He is definitely LF.

The Opera Company

Carlotta

She must have constant primping so that her fragile ego and insecurities don't shatter. She seems to be LF in her demands, but she is out of control. She would wilt and die without the fame – she **yearns** for attention. She is also a victim of the Phantom. She is N.

Firman and Andre

They are the epitome of "Yes Men." They will do anything in their power – which isn't much when it comes right down to it – to make sure the show goes on. When adversity hits, they are beside themselves – they become wallflowers. They are depending on Raoul for the answers. They are both N.

The rest of the Opera Company

Their work, their art, their ways of expression, their entire livelihood is dependent on the running of shows. If they close, they are unemployed. If they don't do what the Phantom requires, they will die. In essence, they are powerless in their world, **yearning** for continued employment, and they are in **trouble** due to the Phantom. They are a N community.

Dramatic Question: *"Will the Phantom or Raoul win the heart of Christine?"*			
LF Phantom	**N** Christine	**LF** Raoul	**N** Opera Company
		ACT I	
	←		1. Dress Reh of Hannibal
	2. Think of Me	→	→
3. Angel of Music	→		→
5. The Phantom of the Opera	4. Little Lotte/The Mirror	→	
6. The Music of the Night	→		
	7. I Remember		
8. I Remember/ Stranger Than You Dreamt			
			9. Magical Lasso
←		←	10. Notes
		←	11. Prima Donna
			12. Poor Fool
	←	13. Why Have You Brought	
	14. Raoul I've Been There	→	
	←	14. All I Ask of You	
15. All I Ask of You – Reprise			
		ACT II	
	←	←	15. Masquerade
16. Why So Silent			
17. Notes/Twisted			
	18. A Music Call	→	→
	→	→	→
	19. Phantom of the Opera-Reprise		
	20. Wishing You Were Somehow		
21. Christine Wandering	→	→	
22. Before the Premiere		→	
			→
			23. Don Juan Triumphant
24. The Point of No Return	→	→	→
25. Down Once More		↙	→
26. The Phantom's Lair	→	→	→

Figure 67 *The Phantom of the Opera*: List of Character Energies.

Musically analyse all of the songs

The analysis for Christine, Raoul, and the Opera Company are basic LF and N level 1 and 2 all the way through. We need this to be the case because we have to have that truthful grounding in the show – especially coming from Raoul. The Phantom is evil. He is so incredibly deceitful and untrustworthy that we must have someone truthful and sincere to counteract him. We need Raoul to be our moral compass. Raoul only sings two LF Level 5–The Tactical songs, "Twisted" and "A Music Call," and that is when he is trying to persuade everyone else to follow his plan to catch the Phantom.

You'll notice that the Phantom is all over the board with music levels. The only music level he doesn't use is the Level 4–The Struggle, and that is because he is very set in his ways when it comes to his vision, credo, and desires. No one will change his mind. He uses his perverted ways of persuasion through lies and evil tactical manipulation, thus the Level 3s and 5s respectively.

LF Phantom	N Christine	LF Raoul	N Opera Company
Dramatic Question: *"Will the Phantom or Raoul win the heart of Christine?"*			
ACT I			
	←N2		1. Dress Reh of Hannibal **N2**
	2. Think of Me **N1**		→**N1**
3. Angel of Music **LF3**	→**N1**	→**LF2**	→**N1**
	4. Little Lotte/The Mirror **N1**	→**LF2**	
5. The Phantom of the Opera **LF1**	→**N2**		
6. The Music of the Night **LF5**			
	7. I Remember **N1**		
8. I Remember/ **LF1** Stranger Than You Dreamt **LF2**			
			9. Magical Lasso **N1**
←—**LF5**		←—**LF1**	10. Notes **N2**
		←—**LF2**	11. Prima Donna **N1**
			12. Poor Fool **N2**
	←—N2	13. Why Have You Brought **LF1**	
	14. Raoul I've Been There **N1**	→**LF2**	
	←—N1	14. All I Ask of You **LF2**	
15. All I Ask of You – Reprise **LF2**	→**N1**	→**LF2**	
ACT II			
	←—N1	←—**LF1**	15. Masquerade **N2**
16. Why So Silent **LF1**			
17. Notes/Twisted **LF5**	→**N1**	→5/1	→**N2**
	18. A Music Call **N1**	→**LF5**	→**N2**
	19. Phantom of the Opera-Reprise **N1**		
	20. Wishing You Were Somehow **N1**		
21. Christine Wandering **LF5**	→**N1**	→**LF2**	
22. Before the Premiere **LF1**		→**LF1**	
			23. Don Juan Triumphant **N2**
24. The Point of No Return **LF5**	→**N1**		
25. Down Once More **LF1/2**		→**LF1**	→**N2**
26. The Phantom's Lair	→	→	→

Figure 68 *The Phantom of the Opera*: List of Music Truths.

The Alignment energy

The alignment takes a bit longer in this show due to the fact that the Phantom doesn't show up for quite awhile. We experience his aggressive antics like the stage set falling, and we're told about him being "the ghost" of the opera house, but he doesn't show up until "The Mirror" ("Angel of Music"), which is well into thirty minutes of the show. By that time, we know that Christine is N, through her song "Think of Me" and her rise from a backseat, company dancer to the front-seat, leading star. We also have been introduced to Raoul through the song "Think of Me," and from that connection we know that they could get together. But it is not until the Phantom enters the picture that we have a real sense of where the show is going. Once he appears in the mirror and takes Christine away, we then understand the triangle, the dramatic question, and the incredible distance that is laid out for us. *"Will the Phantom or Raoul win the heart of Christine?"* And we are patient enough to wait a long thirty minutes for the Phantom to appear. After all, he is the title of the show.

The Growth Moment energy

Who will Christine choose? We finally find this out in the climactic song, "The Phantom's Lair." The Phantom has dragged Christine into his lair clad in a white wedding dress. Raoul had followed them, but is then caught and suspended in mid-air, hanging by the neck to a rope. The Phantom then demands that Christine make her choice: to marry him and save Raoul, or to choose Raoul and his death. At this point, Christine then walks to the Phantom and "kisses him long and full on the lips." It is at that moment that the Phantom realizes that he has gone too far – that he is strictly winning by default. In essence, he is not winning Christine's heart; he is only winning her reluctant body. She is offering herself as a sacrifice to save Raoul's life. Her heart belongs to Raoul. So the Phantom lets them both go. Raoul and Christine sing of their love and this nightmare is finally over for them. The Phantom sits on his throne and disappears into thin air, leaving only his mask on the throne. The N has been resolved, and the Phantom moves on to a new, changed world. "The Phantom's Lair" is the GM.

The ground plan of the musical

The Phantom is forcing Christine to make a choice in her life. She must choose between him and Raoul. Raoul, of course, wants Christine to choose him over the Phantom. Ultimately, Christine must make the decision. She is N, and the Phantom and Raoul are LF. The overall Ground Plan of this show is:

$$LF \leftarrow N \rightarrow LF$$

Like *Oklahoma!*, this is another "*The Choice*" ground plan. Like Laurey, Christine is being pulled in two separate directions, and she is the only one who can decide what is right for her. It is her unfulfillment and yearning, and only what is in her own heart that will make the correct decision. It matters not how much magical power the Phantom has. The heart is ultimately in control.

LF Phantom	N Christine	LF Raoul	N Opera Company
		ACT I	
	←N2		1. Dress Reh of Hannibal N2
3. Angel of Music LF3	2. Think of Me N1	→LF2	→N1
5. The Phantom of the Opera LF1	→N1		→N1
6. The Music of the Night LF5	4. Little Lotte/The Mirror N1	→LF2	
8. I Remember/ LF1	→N2		
Stranger Than You Dreamt LF2	7. I Remember N1		
			9. Magical Lasso N1
←LF5		←LF1	10. Notes N2
		←LF2	11. Prima Donna N1
			12. Poor Fool N2
	←N2	13. Why Have You Brought LF1	
	14. Raoul I've Been There N1	→LF2	
	←N1	14. All I Ask of You LF2	
15. All I Ask of You – Reprise LF2	→N1	→LF2	
		ACT II	
	←N1	←LF1	15. Masquerade N2
16. Why So Silent LF1			
17. Notes/Twisted LF5	→N1	→5/1	→N2
	18. A Music Call N1	→LF5	→N2
	19. Phantom of the Opera-Reprise N1		
	20. Wishing You Were Somehow N1		
21. Christine Wandering LF5	→N1	→LF2	
22. Before the Premiere LF1		→LF1	→N2
			23. Don Juan Triumphant N2
24. The Point of No Return LF5	→N1		
25. Down Once More LF1/2		→LF1	→N2
26. The Phantom's Lair	→	→	→

A: The Mirror
GM: The Phantom's Lair
Ground Plan: LF←N→LF "The Choice"

Dramatic Question: *"Will the Phantom or Raoul win the heart of Christine?*

Figure 69 *The Phantom of the Opera*: Final.

Note

1   Rich, *The New York Times*, 27 January 1988.

18

1990s – The Voice of a New Generation

Rent

A sign of the times

There are draughts in everything we do. We have draughts in good movies, books, innovative food, and even in fun dating. It is no different with musical theatre. In the desert of the 1990s, suddenly *Rent* became the thirst-quencher. Ben Brantley, reviewer of *The New York Times* puts it this way: "*… this show restores spontaneity and depth of feeling to a discipline that sorely needs them.*"[1] Again, it took new ideas, innovations, and a then unknown rookie composer-lyricist to open our eyes, and the investor's pocketbooks, to show us the way. Brantley continues, "*People who complain about the demise of the American musical have simply been looking in the wrong places. Well done, Mr. Larson.*"[2] *Rent* proves that taking a risk on an unknown quantity can both be financially rewarding as well as artfully fulfilling.

Credits

Music, Lyrics, and Book by Jonathan Larson
Based on the opera *La Bohème* by Giacomo Puccini
Directed by Michael Greif
Choreographed by Marlies Yearby
Produced by Jeffrey Seller, Kevin McCollum, Allan S. Gordon, and the New York Theater Workshop

History at a glance

With spectacle theatre now well established into the mainstream consciousness of theatregoers, the financial success that goes along with it suddenly opens the ears of new investors. New York decides to literally clean up Broadway after years of social and economic neglect, and in doing so, entices major corporations to invest dollars into closed, run-down theatres. From American Airlines to the mega-company Disney, corporate support started theatre renovations, and Broadway continued to grow. But who would have thought that a little Off Broadway show about a cast of young people plagued with HIV would be the hottest ticket in New York? *Rent* started off-Broadway, but due to public demand and some savvy producers, the show moved to Broadway in 1996. While squeaky clean shows like *Beauty and the Beast* and *The Lion King* are the focal point of tourists, *Rent* has a cult following that will not let the show go unnoticed. It is bringing awareness to the national AIDS epidemic. Its gritty rock music and uncensored plot of HIV-stricken neo-bohemians not being able to afford their rent spoke to an unheard new generation in ways never done before. *Rent* was a social phenomenon, and except for maybe *Bring in 'Da Noise, Bring in 'Da Funk*, it was an unexpected anomaly and gift, in an otherwise less than inspiring decade in Broadway history.

THE ANALYSIS
Create the dramatic question

What makes this show so powerful is the fact that we know from the get-go that there isn't much hope for these young people who have contracted HIV. We know what their outcome will eventually be. Yet, it's an incredibly upbeat show that gives us hope in humanity. Their lives are doomed, yet they want to live it, short as it could be, with as much zest for life as possible. We envy them because we know that many times we diddle our lives away on unimportant things. That is what makes this show so powerful, and why we want to see the end. We want to be assured that their lives are indeed lived to the fullest.

Dramatic Question: *"Will this group of friends seize their time together and live their Bohemian lives to the fullest?"*

Figure 70 *Rent*: The Dramatic Question.

Dramatic Question: *"Will this group of friends seize their time together and live their Bohemian lives to the fullest?"*

Mark   Roger   Collins   Angel   Mimi   Benny   Joanne   Maureen   Company

Figure 71 *Rent:* List of Characters.

List all analytically important characters

This is the epitome of an ensemble show. Each character in the group has a sizable amount of songs to sing and has a very individualized character. We should list all of them in the diagram. There is, however, a smaller group of actors in the show who cover important nameless roles, as well as strengthen the big chorus numbers. We can list these folks under the Company category.

List all of the songs under the character's name

Figure 72 *Rent:* List of Songs.

Lyrically analyse all of the songs

Mark

Mark is a poor, struggling artist, who lives hand to mouth and certainly doesn't have enough money for rent. He's in **trouble**. He is **yearning** to find his artistic voice through film, but finds that he has to choose between doing his art or "selling out" and working for a company in order to pay his bills. He gets dumped by Maureen. His biggest fear: that when finished, his film project that shows the glorious memories of his friendships, will indeed go unseen by the very people who made the memories. Mark is N.

Roger

Roger fears his own mortality, knowing he has AIDS. He desperately **yearns** to write that one great song before he dies, and at this point, that great song seems to be out of his reach. He's poor, can't pay the bills, and wants more to his life than what exists right now. He's **yearning** for a life filled with music, love, and excitement. He's **unfulfilled**. He longs for Mimi but can't get over his past. Roger is N.

Collins

Collins has HIV. He's a college professor who doesn't want to go through that daily grind anymore. He has dreams of opening a restaurant in "Santa Fe" – he's **unfulfilled** in life. Collins **yearns** to create a new, honest, real life with Angel. Collins is N.

Angel

Angel "*dresses his wounds*" and saves Collins after a mugging. She brings money to the guys to celebrate Christmas with some food. She is **larger than life** and a **central driving force** to all of them, by giving them support and optimism – **a vision and credo** – even though she too has AIDS. She wears extravagant clothing and is incredibly extroverted – **attractive to be with**. Even after Angel dies, she is still helping the group by giving Mimi strength to pull out of her fever and unconsciousness. Angel is LF.

Mimi

Mimi is a drug addict who desperately wants to belong and have a relationship with Roger. She is so **yearning** for a different life – one where she is clean and her life fruitful. She is **unfulfilled**. She has to work in a sleazy sex club, dancing in order to pay her bills. Her addiction gets her in **trouble**. She **dreams of getting away** from her life of pain. Mimi is N.

Benny

Benny is a friend of the group, but unfortunately, is on the outs with them. He has "sold out" to corporate America. He controls the rent district and tries to manipulate Roger and Mark to end Maureen's protest by offering them free rent. "You'll See" is the real deal – with conditions. He is a **central driving force** to their problems and a representative of the rich and powerful. He's **attractive to be with** and **larger than life**, shown through his callous, yet elegant traits of corporate America. Benny is LF.

Joanne

Joanne is a successful lawyer. She's meticulous in her work and private life. Sound's LF? She's not. She loves Maureen and she is desperate to have her in her life, yet tired of the mesmerizing love tango that Maureen dances. She is **unfulfilled** without her. Yes, she has standards, and she states them very clearly to Maureen. But when Maureen doesn't follow her desired path, Joanne comes undone. She is uncomfortable with Maureen's former lover – Mark. Joanne is N.

Maureen

Maureen is a woman who constantly seeks attention. She has this insatiable need to flirt in order to get people to notice her. She can't help it that "*everybody stares*" at her. She loves Joanne, but wants it both ways – her love but also the continued flaunting of herself to others. Her flirting is almost like heroin – she's addicted to it. Maureen is **unfulfilled** and has an insatiable **yearning** for love and attention. She is N.

Company

The company can be a bit confusing since they play so many multiple characters. But, as an ensemble, they really do support the N energy cast in their songs throughout. They are the support group who have contracted HIV in "Will I," **yearning** for the answer to the inevitable question of whether "*someone will care?*" They are the ones who open Act II with "Seasons of Love" – supporting the preciousness and shortness of life. They are the voices of all of those who fall victim in any capacity to HIV. They are N. See Figure 73.

Musically analyse all of the songs

This is a rock opera that has very little dialogue. Therefore, some songs go through sequences and events within one titled number. Sometimes, you'll see in the musical analysis that those pieces have changes in levels because

Dramatic Question: *"Will this group of friends seize their time together and live their Bohemian lives to the fullest?"*								
N Mark	**N** Roger	**N** Collins	**LF** Angel	**N** Mimi	**LF** Benny	**N** Joanne	**N** Maureen	**N** Company
			ACT I					
1. Rent	→	→		2. You Okay Honey? →	→	→		→
	3. One Song Glory 4. Light My Candle							
←	←	←	5. Today 4 U		6. You'll See	→		
7. Tango:Maureen								8. Life Support
←		←	←					
	10. Another Day ←			9. Out Tonight →				11. Will I?
←	←	12. Santa Fe	→ ←					
			13. I'll Cover You			14. We're Okay		
←	←	←	←					15. Christmas Bells
							16. Over the Moon	
17. La Vie Boheme →	18. I Should Tell You	→	→	→ →	→	→	→	→
←	←	←	←	19. La Vie → Boheme B		→	→	→
			ACT II					
←	←	←	←	←	←	←	←	20. Seasons Of Love
21. Happy New Year	→	→	→	→		→	→	→
22. Happy New Year B	→	→	→	→	→	→	→	→
						←	23. Take Me Or Leave Me	
24. Seasons of Love Reprise	→	→	→	→		→	→	→
	←			25. Without You				
←	←	←	←	←	←	←	←	26. Contact
←	←	27. I'll Cover You Reprise	←	→	→	→	→	→
28. Halloween								
←	29. Goodbye Love	→	→	→	→	→	→	→
30. What You Own	→	→	→		→	→	→	→
←	←	←	←		←	←	←	31. Finale A
	32. Your Eyes							
33. Finale B	→	→	→	→	→	→	→	→

Figure 73 *Rent:* List of Character Energies.

of this. It's basically having more than one song within the body of the one song.

You'll also notice that there are two N Level 4–The Struggle songs. One is Roger singing "Another Day." He is screaming for her to leave him alone, but deep inside, he is truly wanting her. What makes this a struggle versus a Protest Too Much song is the fact that within the song, he actually does sing the lines "I should tell you. I should tell you. No!" He is struggling with himself between what logic says and what his heart says.

The other Struggle song is Joanne singing "We're Okay." She is trying to talk herself and everyone else into thinking that she has things under control. But she doesn't. She's frantic and almost at her wit's end. She's juggling three telephone and cell lines at once. Who can multi-task that much? This also is not a Protest Too Much song because she really is handling this pressure-cooker situation of being a lawyer, daughter, and producer/girlfriend simultaneously.

Dramatic Question: *"Will this group of friends seize their time together and live their Bohemian lives to the fullest?"*

N Mark	N Roger	N Collins	LF Angel	N Mimi	LF Benny	N Joanne	N Maureen	N Company
			ACT I					
1. Rent N2	→N2	→N2 ←N1		→N2	→LF1	→N2		→N2
			2. You Okay Honey? LF2					
	3. One Song Glory N1							
	4. Light My Candle N2			→N2				
←N2	←N2	←N2	5. Today 4 U LF1					
←N2	←N2	←N2	←LF1		6. You'll See LF1			
7. Tango:Maureen N2						→N2		
←N1		←N1	←N1					8. Life Support N1
	10. Another Day N4 ←N1			9. Out Tonight N2 →N1/2				→N1/2 11. Will I? N1
←N2	←N2	12. Santa Fe N2 ←N1	→LF1 13. I'll Cover You LF1					
←N2	←N2/1/2	←N1/2	←LF2/1	←N1/2		14. We're Okay N4		15. Christmas Bells N2
17. La Vie Boheme N2	→N2	→N2	→LF1	→N2	→LF1	→N2	16. Over the Moon N2 →N2	→N2
	18. I Should Tell You N1			→N1				
←N2	←N2	←N2	←LF1	19. La Vie Boheme B N2		→N2	→N2	→N2
			ACT II					
←N1	←N1	←N1	←LF2	←N1	←LF2	←N1	←N1	20. Seasons Of Love N1
←N2	←N2	←N2	←LF1	21. Happy New Year N2		→N2	→N2	→N2
←N2	←N2	←N2	←LF1	←N2	←LF1	←N2	22. Happy New Year B N2	→N2
						←N2	23. Take Me Or Leave Me N2	
←N1	←N1	←N1	←LF2	←N1	←LF2	←N1	←N1	24. Seasons Of Love N1
	←N1			25. Without You N1				
←N2	←N2	←N2	←LF1	←N2	←LF1	←N2	←N2	26. Contact N2
←N1	←N1	27. I'll Cover You Reprise N1		→N1	→LF2	→N1	→N1	→N1
28. Halloween N1								
←N1	29. Goodbye Love N1 →N1	→N1		→N1	→LF2	→N1	→N1	→N1
←N2	←N2	←N2			←LF1			30. What You Own N1
←N2/1	←N2/1	←N2/1		←N1		←N2/1	←N2/1	31. Finale A N2
	32. Your Eyes N1							
33. Finale B	→	→	→	→	→	→	→	→

Figure 74 *Rent*: List of Music Truths.

The Alignment energy

Early on in the show, when the song "Rent" is sung, we have been introduced to all of the N characters, plus the LF character Benny. However, Benny is more anti-LF than anything. He is not the person that we would like to think was going to solve the problems of the group. He could solve the financial part, but Benny is pro-establishment – a credo that doesn't mesh with the group of neo-bohemian artists. It is not until Angel enters, rescues Collins, and then surprises the group with cash at a time that the group really needs it. Once Angel is there, we have LF that counteracts the LF of Benny, and we then see a potential road for resolution to the dramatic question. The alignment is "Today 4 U."

The Growth Moment energy

Roger sings "Your Eyes" to a dying Mimi in front of all of his friends. After the song, Mimi's fever then breaks, causing great celebration. Roger and Mimi will be together, Mark will finish his art film, Maureen and Joanne will work out their troubles after now learning about how precious life is, and Collins will always have the support of all of his friends. It is true that some of them still may die of HIV, however, they all have learned to hold dear each moment going forward. The GM is "Finale B."

The ground plan of the musical

We are introduced to a community of N characters with the song "Rent." Benny and Angel are outsiders, both being LF. They enter into the N community. Could this be the N characters again choosing between two LF possibilities? Not really. They never considered following Benny's advice and they never would. However, Benny is an outside influence. He even paid for Angel's funeral. In spite of that, the friends stood their ground on their dream and vision.

With this in mind, the ground plan is:

$$LF \rightarrow N \leftarrow LF$$

This is the same ground plan as *Les Misérables*. Interesting!

Dramatic Question: *"Will this group of friends seize their time together and live their Bohemian lives to the fullest?"*

N Mark	N Roger	N Collins	LF Angel	N Mimi	LF Benny	N Joanne	N Maureen	N Company
			ACT I					
1. Rent N2	→N2	→N2		→N2	→LF1	→N2		→N2
		←N1	2. You Okay Honey? LF2					
	3. One Song Glory N1							
	4. Light My Candle N2			→N2				
←N2	←N2	←N2	5. Today 4 U LF1					
←N2	←N2	←N2	←LF1		6. You'll See LF1			
7. Tango:Maureen N2						→N2		
←N1		←N1	←N1					8. Life Support N1
				9. Out Tonight N2				
	10. Another Day N4			→N1/2				→N1/2
	←N1							11. Will I? N1
←N2	←N2	12. Santa Fe N2	→LF1					
		←N1	13. I'll Cover You LF1					
						14. We're Okay N4		
←N2	←N2/1/2	←N1/2	←LF2/1	←N1/2				15. Christmas Bells N2
							16. Over the Moon N2	
17. La Vie Boheme N2	→N2	→N2	→LF1	→N2	→LF1	→N2	→N2	→N2
	18. I Should Tell You N1			→N1				
←N2	←N2	←N2	←LF1	19. La Vie Boheme B N2		→N2	→N2	→N2
			ACT II					
←N1	←N1	←N1	←LF2	←N1	←LF2	←N1	←N1	20. Seasons Of Love N1
←N2	←N2	←N2	←LF1	21. Happy New Year N2		→N2	→N2	→N2
←N2	←N2	←N2	←LF1	←N2	←LF1	←N2	22. Happy New Year B N2	→N2
						←N2	23. Take Me Or Leave Me N2	
←N1	←N1	←N1	←LF2	←N1	←LF2	←N1	←N1	24. Seasons Of Love N1
	←N1			25. Without You N1				
←N2	←N2	←N2	←LF1	←N2	←LF1	←N2	←N2	26. Contact N2
←N1	←N1	27. I'll Cover You Reprise N1		→N1	→LF2	→N1	→N1	→N1
28. Halloween N1								
←N1	29. Goodbye Love N1	→N1		→N1	→LF2	→N1	→N1	→N1
←N2	←N2	←N2			←LF1			30. What You Own N1
←N2/1	←N2/1	←N2/1		←N1		←N2/1	←N2/1	31. Finale A N2
	32. Your Eyes N1							
33. Finale B	→	→	→	→	→	→	→	→

A: Today 4 U
GM: Finale B
Ground Plan: LF → N ← LF

Figure 75 *Rent*: Final.

Notes

1   Brantley, *The New York Times*, 14 February 1996.
2   Ibid.

19

2000s – Corporate Broadway: Gems in the Rough

Spring Awakening

A sign of the times

I think perhaps Charles Isherwood is my all-time favourite *New York Times* theatre reviewer. Personally, I loved his thought pattern and his way with words. Isherwood's *Spring Awakening* review is one of my favourites. He so zings theatrical trends and still surprises the hell out of you with his finishing point. He starts off in luring you into the bland, predictable, and recycled direction of the Broadway musical: "*The great American art form. Karaoke nightmare. Bring the kids, leave the I.Q. at home. Another op'nin, another revival.*"[1] It is wonderful when a reviewer finds that morsel of truth within theatrical history and then makes a point of it by ending with, "*Probably nobody thinks: pure sex.*"[2] *Spring Awakening* took us all to a new level of sexual perception and understanding.

Credits

Music by Duncan Sheik
Lyrics and Book by Steven Sater
Based on the play by Frank Wedekind
Directed by Michael Mayer
Choreographed by Bill T. Jones

Produced by Ira Pittelman, Tom Hulce, Jeffrey Richards, Jerry Frankel, the Atlantic Theater Company, Jeffrey Sine, Freddy DeMann, Max Cooper, Mort Swinsky, Cindy and Jay Gutterman, Joe McGinnis, Judith Ann Abrams, ZenDog Productions, Jennifer Manocherian, Ted Snowdon, Harold Thau, Terry Schnuck, Cold Spring Productions, Amanda Dubois, Elizabeth Eynon Wetherell, Jennifer Maloney, Tamara Tunie, Joe Cilibrasi, StyleFour Productions, CarJac Productions, and Aron Bergson Productions

History at a glance

Looking above to see more than two dozen producers in *Spring Awakening* certainly supports evidence that the Broadway musical is no longer for the weak at heart investor. Broadway had entered a phase that is still evident in the early 2020s: Broadway is big money. Spectacle musicals reign – audiences now demand to be wowed in the same way that movies have wowed them with computer-generated special effects. Corporations are fully involved, with big money support, and big money gains. But when money gets so involved, suddenly creativity can take a backseat to ideas that are more safe: title familiarity and revivals. But, at times, special original musicals prove to be so good that they are destined to make it to Broadway, for instance, *Light in the Piazza*, *Next to Normal*, and *Spring Awakening*. Smaller producers are willing to take the risk. These great shows work contrary to the formulaic shows of the time. Solid, meaty creative books, deeper, thoughtful lyrics, and new trends in music from neo-Classical to Alternative Rock are the foundation of these shows. They are indeed the Gems in the Rough, but also the pride of theatre.

THE ANALYSIS
Create the dramatic question

In this ensemble show, it is again hard not to feel for all of the youth. They are brought up in a society that will not have conversations about sexuality. The youth are left alone, making naïve assumptions and feeling ignorant and

> Dramatic Question: *"Will the kids fight the oppressive society they live in and succeed in attaining the sexual understanding and awakening that they so desperately demand and need?"*

Figure 76 *Spring Awakening*: The Dramatic Question.

guilty about their true feelings. We want them all to have the freedom to learn and explore sexual realities. We want this because we know in this century, sexual enlightenment is not only a natural part of life, it is also healthy. We want these kids to be free of oppression and suppression from their parents, their teachers, and society as a whole.

List all analytically important characters

This is the same as *Rent*, in that all of the characters are important to list. I just happen to list four characters into two couples since they're a bit smaller in size and likely similar in their analysis. Also, in this show I'm listing the company separately: by boys and girls. Since each gender fundamentally have different solo songs and perspectives in this show, I think in the long run, it would make it easier for analysis to keep them separate.

> Dramatic Question: *"Will the kids fight the oppressive society they live in and succeed in attaining the sexual understanding and awakening that they so desperately demand and need?"*
>
> Melchior   Moritz   Wendla   Ilse   Martha   Otto/Georg   Hanschen/Ernst   Girls   Boys

Figure 77 *Spring Awakening*: List of Characters.

List all of the songs under the character's name

Dramatic Question: *"Will the kids fight the oppressive society they live in and succeed in attaining the sexual understanding and awakening that they so desperately demand and need?"*								
Melchior	**Moritz**	**Wendla**	**Ilse**	**Martha**	**Otto/Georg**	**Hanschen/Ernst**	**Girls**	**Boys**
				ACT I				
		1. Mama Who Bore Me						
		2. Mama Who Bore Me Reprise					→	
3. All That's Known					→	→		→
←	4. The Bitch of Living				→	→		→
←	←	5. My Junk	→	→	→	→	→	→
6. Touch Me	→	→	→	→	→	→	→	→
←		7. The Word of Your Body						
			←	8. The Dark I Know Well				→
					9. The Word of Your Body			
	10. And Then There Were None						→	
←								11. The Mirror Blue Night
←	←	←	←	←	←	←	12. I Believe	→
				ACT II				
←	←	13. The Guilty Ones	→	→	→	→	→	→
14. Don't Do Sadness								
			15. Blue Wind					
16. Left Behind	→		→	→	→	→	→	→
17. Totally Fucked	→		→	→	→	→	→	→
←		←	←	←	←	18. The Word of Your Body	→	→
		19. Whispering						
←	21. Those You've Known	→						
←		←	22. Song of Purple Summer	→	→	→	→	→

Figure 78 *Spring Awakening*: List of Songs.

Lyrically analyse all of the songs

Before I examined each character individually for their energies, I really needed to think about the overall design and make-up of this show. It is so unique in its structure. When I first started analysing this musical, I knew it would be one that falls into the structure line of *West Side Story* or *Fiddler on the Roof*. After all, all the singing characters were *kids* – no adults sing in this show except for the very end of "Totally Fucked" and the very last song. None of these kids have power. They are all taken care of or controlled by their parents, and they are certainly oppressed by the cultural mores of a closed-minded and archaic society. How could any of them be anything but N?

But the dilemma is there are no adult LF figures in this show. No adults individually sing in this musical. One male and one female adult actor play the roles of all the adults, from parents of multiple kids, to the teachers. They can't be the LF in this show. That leaves the LF represented either through the use of theatrical imagery, like *West Side Story*, or through some other plane, like the religious belief system of tradition in *Fiddler on the Roof*.

I first considered theatrical imagery, since they pulled out microphones and had light changes in many of their songs. I thought perhaps the "rock song dreams" that they were portraying on stage was their LF persona, considering that they are very poetic, emotional state-of-being songs versus plot-driven songs. Further justification is that the pulling out of microphones is in the stage directions of the script. Unfortunately, there wasn't a consistent connection between the mikes, the light shifts, and the lyric analysis of each song in the show. Therefore, I had no choice but to throw out the use of this convention as theatrical imagery.

With this in mind, the show had to have the LF somehow embedded in each N character. The question then became, what is that inner ego connected to?

They have two things fighting in their souls – one is instinctual and the other is societal. I again studied the dramatic question and then it hit me. The kids have two states that they're living in and dealing with. The first state, the N, is when the oppressive cultural society is telling the kids what to do, how to think, and what to say and feel. Societal rules and mores through the adults will not give the information needed to the kids in order to deal with their sexual awakenings. They consider those topics bad, unthinkable, and unspeakable. Therefore, the kids are truly trapped because of these archaic rules. All of the kids are N.

The second state, the LF, are the kids revolting and telling the oppressive societal culture that they are wrong. The kids are speaking from their instinctual and natural feelings of desire and need. The kids *know* deep down inside that there is nothing wrong with what they are feeling. (Except perhaps for Moritz, who is so overwhelmed and confused by it all that he just can't handle it.) The kids' quest for knowledge and truth is why they are fighting back. It is within their rights and beliefs to be fully educated and affirmed. They recognize that the societal *system* is wrong – they know this because they can instinctually feel it. They did not ask for these feelings, nor did they have anything to do with putting them there. The societal rules make no sense and the kids get that.

Therefore, all the kids are both N and LF depending on which plane they are singing from:

N – The oppressive society is telling the kids

1 "The Bitch of Living" – "*Don't have those feelings – they don't exist.*"
2 "Touch Me" – "*Don't talk about it, don't feel it – it's unspoken.*"
3 "The Word of Your Body" – "*You don't do this – it's sinful.*"
4 "The Dark I Know Well" – "*Don't disobey your father.*" "*Spare the rod, spoil the child.*"
5 "And Then There Were None" – "*You'll get over it – your parents are right.*"
6 "The Mirror-Blue Night" – "*Just don't think about it and it won't exist.*"
7 "Don't Do Sadness" – "*Pull up your bootstraps.*"
8 "Blue Wind" – "*You made your bed, now live with it. We don't care.*"

LF – The kids are telling the oppressive society

1 "Mama Who Bore Me" – "*Your job is to educate me about such things.*"
2 "All That's Known" – "*Your rules and laws are misinformed – your way is wrong.*"
3 "My Junk" – "*This is who I am – live with it.*"
4 "I Believe" – "*This is our credo and it is right.*"
5 "The Guilty Ones" – "*I am awakened and this is good – this is who I am now.*"
6 "Left Behind" – "*This happened because of your mores, rules, and ignorance.*"
7 "Totally Fucked" – "*You may think you have me, but you don't – you can't squash my soul and truth.*"
8 "Whispering" – "*This is what I learned and it is good.*"

So now you already know how the analysis turns out! Keep in mind, however, that only a unique, amazing, and depth-filled show such as *Spring Awakening* can pull off something like this. This type of energy sharing is definitely not the norm and not easy to write or execute.

Melchior

I would say that Melchior leans more towards the LF side of a character than on the N side, and that makes sense. He is the most intelligent of all of the youth – **attractive to be with**. He questions, explores, and philosophizes, knowing there's a lot *"more to find"* – **vision** and **philosophy**. He is more mature, with more charisma than all the others. He is a leader that the boys follow, and the girls swoon over – a **central driving force**. He, however, also falls to the uncontrollable needs and desires of sexual awakening, pleading to be touched – **yearning**, **unfulfillment**. He gets into severe trouble for his views – **trouble**. He eventually considers taking his own life – **trouble** and **pressure**. Melchior is N/LF.

Moritz

Where I would say Melchior is the strongest LF influence, I would suggest that Moritz is the strongest N influence in the boys. He lags behind in studies – **trouble**. He has uncontrolled exotic dreams and insurmountable desires – **yearning**. He has no informational outlet to answer questions – **unfulfillment**. He commits suicide, with no one listening to the signs – **mental illness** and **troublesome pressures**. But he also has philosophical moments and observations, such as singing in "I Believe" – **credo**. He also comes back as a ghost and guide to Melchior at the end of the show – **larger than life**. Moritz is N/LF.

Wendla

Although a bit more naïve than Melchior, she is a good match for him in energies. She is strong in her questioning of things, as in "Mama Who Bore Me," and the exploring of truths – **philosophy**. She leads her group of girls – **central driving force**. Her honesty and purity allow her to be forward in her questioning and leading – **attractive to be with**. She also comes back as a ghost and guide to Melchior – **larger than life**. On the other side, she too has sexual desires, singing of her *"words of wanting"* – **yearning**. She wants and needs to know the ways of the world – **unfulfilled**. She gets pregnant – **trouble**. Wendla is N/LF.

Ilse and Martha

Ilse and Martha are sexually abused children, consoled by predators who justify their evil by stating that Christ "*won't mind.*" Martha is trapped at home and Ilsa is cast out of the house to an artist colony – **deep trouble**. They too have sexual awakening and desires – **yearning**. They also, however, have the awareness that they have been wronged and that judgement day will come. They are aware of the societal injustices of it all, knowing that everybody "*has junk*" – **philosophy and vision**. They are both N/LF.

Otto, Georg, Hanschen, and Ernst

All of these boys have individuality and uniqueness, however, they all have the same basic N and LF tendencies. They all have sexual desires – **yearning**. They are **unfulfilled** in their quest for knowledge and know-how. They're stuck in this hopeless "Bitch of Living." They sit in the middle as Hanschen so well explained: you can have the status quo defeat you, like Moritz, they can destroy you if you try to rock the boat, like Melchior, or you can just buy time. These four are buying time, just trying to survive. Their LF is their united front of **credo**, **philosophies**, and what is instinctually right in the "*totally fucked*" life of a teenager. They are all N/LF.

The other girls and boys

They have the same dealings as all of the above girls and boys, since they never sing a song without the others – never one alone. They are supporting representatives in the energies, therefore share the same energies at that moment. They are N/LF. See Figure 79.

Musically analyse all of the songs

All of the songs in this show, by design and lyric, are "state of being" songs for the characters. That is, no song ever really progresses the plot along – it's very non-Sondheim! That is why the lyric analysis for the songs are so difficult to analyse since all of them are quasi-poetry versus lyric plot progression. This is also why all the songs stem in truth – either the societal truth of the matter or the kids' inner, instinctual truth. Therefore, all but one song are either N or LF level 1 or 2 songs.

Dramatic Question: *"Will the kids fight the oppressive society they live in and succeed in attaining the sexual understanding and awakening that they so desperately demand and need?"*								
N/LF Melchior	N/LF Moritz	N/LF Wendla	N/LF Ilse	N/LF Martha	N/LF Otto/Georg	N/LF Hanschen/Ernst	N/LF Girls	N/LF Boys
				ACT I				
		1. Mama Who Bore Me						
		2. Mama Who Bore Me Reprise					→	
3. All That's Known					→	→		→
←	4. The Bitch of Living				→	→		→
←	←	5. My Junk	→	→	→	→	→	→
6. Touch Me	→	→	→	→	→	→	→	→
←		7. The Word of Your Body						
			←	8. The Dark I Know Well				→
					9. The Word of Your Body			
	10. And Then There Were None						→	
←								11. The Mirror Blue Night
←	←	←	←	←	←	←	12. I Believe	→
				ACT II				
←	←	13. The Guilty Ones	→	→	→	→	→	→
	14. Don't Do Sadness							
			15. Blue Wind					
16. Left Behind	→		→	→	→	→	→	→
17. Totally Fucked	→		→	→	→	→	→	→
←			←	←	←	18. The Word of Your Body	→	→
		19. Whispering						
←	21. Those You've Known	→						
←	←	←	22. Song of Purple Summer →			→	→	→

Figure 79 *Spring Awakening*: List of Character Energies.

The one song that differs is Moritz's song, "Don't Do Sadness," which is a N Level 5–Protest Too Much song. Moritz has been so distraught that he says he can't feel sadness or regret because of such parental injustice. Moritz *is* feeling extreme sadness. He is so sad, and sees so little choice in his life, that he feels he needs to self-destroy it – commit suicide. This is the utmost example of sadness one can experience – total depression. So, he believes he's not feeling sadness, but we know he's totally breaking down in it.

In "All That's Known," Melchior is LF in this song as explained above, however, the other students are N. This is because Melchior is the only one singing about his credo and philosophy on society's views on things. The other boys are just doing their Latin recitation as told to do by the instructor. See Figure 80.

The Alignment energy

Since each song is a state of being, the A can only happen after both the LF and N energies have been introduced. The first three songs: "Mama Who Bore Me," "Mama Who Bore Me Reprise," and "All That's Known" are all LF.

Dramatic Question: "Will the kids fight the oppressive society they live in and succeed in attaining the sexual understanding and awakening that they so desperately demand and need?"

N/LF Melchior	N/LF Moritz	N/LF Wendla	N/LF Ilse	N/LF Martha	N/LF Otto/Georg	N/LF Hanschen/Ernst	N/LF Girls	N/LF Boys
ACT I								
		1. Mama Who Bore Me LF2						
		←LF1						
							2. Mama Who Bore Me Reprise LF1	
3. All That's Known LF2					→N1	→N1		→N1
←N2	4. The Bitch of Living N2				→N2	→N2		→N2
←LF1	←LF1	5. My Junk LF1	→LF1	→LF1	→LF1	→LF1	→LF1	→LF1
6. Touch Me N1	→N1	→N1	→N1	→N1	→N1	→N1	→N1	→N1
←N1		7. The Word of Your Body N1						
				←N2	8. The Dark I Know Well N2			→N2
					9. The Word of Your Body N1			
	10. And Then There Were None N2							→N2
←N1							11. The Mirror Blue Night N1	
←LF1	←LF1	←LF1	←LF1	←LF1	←LF1	←LF1	12. I Believe LF1	→LF1
ACT II								
←LF2	←LF2	13. The Guilty Ones LF2	→LF2	→LF2	→LF2	→LF2	→LF2	→LF2
	14. Don't Do Sadness N5							
			15. Blue Wind N1					
16. Left Behind LF2	→LF2		→LF2	→LF2	→LF2	→LF2	→LF2	→LF2
17. Totally Fucked LF1	→LF1		→LF1	→LF1	→LF1	→LF1	→LF1	→LF1
←N1	←N1		←N1	←N1	←N1	18. The Word of Your Body Ernst N1 Hanschen LF5	→N1	→N1
		19. Whispering LF2						
←	21. Those You've Known	→						
←	←	←	22. Song of Purple Summer	→	→	→	→	→

Figure 80 *Spring Awakening*: List of Music Truths.

At this point, we understand not only how the kids feel but also we have understood the format of this show, complete with handheld mikes and light changes. But we haven't quite experienced the societal oppression on the group through song, until "The Bitch Of Living." It is at that point that we get everything: the oppression, the rebellion, and the theatrical formatting and design of the show. The A is "The Bitch Of Living."

The Growth Moment energy

Our strongest LF character is Melchior, and when he finds out Wendla is dead, his world totally falls apart. He's ready to give up his life: surrender to the insurmountable pressures of the society he lives in. But Moritz and Wendla – à la Angel in *Rent* – rise from the dead to guide him, encourage him to move on, and continue to fight the fight. His realization of the importance of continuing on is the GM of the show – that vision to persevere against all odds for the greater good. The GM is "Those You've Known."

The ground plan of the musical

Since the kids are both N/LF, we need to be able to show those two planes within all of the characters. With the instinctual feelings coming from deep within, it seemed logical to have that LF energy embedded within the womb of their N energy.

The Womb

Figure 81 *Spring Awakening* Ground Plan.

Dramatic Question: *"Will the kids fight the oppressive society they live in and succeed in attaining the sexual understanding and awakening that they so desperately demand and need?"*

N/LF Melchior	N/LF Moritz	N/LF Wendla	N/LF Ilse	N/LF Martha	N/LF Otto/Georg	N/LF Hanschen/Ernst	N/LF Girls	N/LF Boys
			ACT I					
		1. Mama Who Bore Me **LF2**						
		←**LF1**					2. Mama Who Bore Me Reprise **LF1**	
3. All That's Known **LF2**					→**N1**	→**N1**		→**N1**
←**N2**	4. The Bitch of Living **N2**				→**N2**	→**N2**		→**N2**
←**LF1**	←**LF1**	5. My Junk **LF1**	→**LF1**	→**LF1**	→**LF1**	→**LF1**	→**LF1**	→**LF1**
6. Touch Me **N1**	→**N1**	→**N1**	→**N1**	→**N1**	→**N1**	→**N1**	→**N1**	→**N1**
←**N1**		7. The Word of Your Body **N1**						
			←**N2**	8. The Dark I Know Well **N2**				→**N2**
					9. The Word of Your Body **N1**			
	10. And Then There Were None **N2**							→**N2**
←**N1**							11. The Mirror Blue Night **N1**	
←**LF1**	←**LF1**	←**LF1**	←**LF1**	←**LF1**	←**LF1**	←**LF1**	12. I Believe **LF1**	→**LF1**
			ACT II					
←**LF2**	←**LF2**	13. The Guilty Ones **LF2**	→**LF2**	→**LF2**	→**LF2**	→**LF2**	→**LF2**	→**LF2**
	14. Don't Do Sadness **N5**							
			15. Blue Wind **N1**					
16. Left Behind **LF2**	→**N1**		→**N1**	→**N1**	→**N1**	→**N1**	→**N1**	→**N1**
17. Totally Fucked **LF1**	→**LF1**		→**LF1**	→**LF1**	→**LF1**	→**LF1**	→**LF1**	→**LF1**
←**N1**		←**N1**	←**N1**	←**N1**	←**N1**	18. The Word of Your Body **Ernst N1 Hanschen LF5**	→**N1**	→**N1**
		19. Whispering **LF2**						
←	21. Those You've Known **GM**	→						
←	←	←		22. Song of Purple Summer →	→	→	→	→

A: The Bitch of Living
GM: Those You've Known
Coda: Song of Purple Summers
Ground Plan:

"The Womb"

Figure 82 *Spring Awakening*: Final.

Notes

1   Isherwood, *The New York Times*, 11 December 2006.
2   Ibid.

20

2015 to ... What Will the Future Bring?

Hamilton

A sign of the times

What *will* the future bring to the theatre world? I believe that Ben Brantley's review of *Hamilton* in *The New York Times* summarizes it best by saying that *Hamilton* is " ... *proof that the American musical is not only surviving but also evolving in ways that should allow it to thrive and transmogrify in years to come.*"[1] We can't project the future. But we can take heart in listening to people in the business who sense that the theatrical future of our musical theatre genre is in good hands. Being a long-time Dramatist Guild member, I will attest to that. God knows we have a plethora of talented, new writers coming up the ranks to take charge of this musical beast and steer it in another unexpected, yet welcome direction!

Credits

Music, Lyrics, and Book by Lin-Manuel Miranda
Inspired by the book *Alexander Hamilton* by Ron Chernow
Directed by Thomas Kail
Choreographed by Andy Blankenbuehler
Produced by Jeffrey Seller, Sander Jacobs, Jill Furman, and The Public Theatre

History at a glance

I love the way Ben Brantley writes about the future of Broadway in his review of *Hamilton*. It's not about future musicals now following the footsteps of rap-based shows, but it's more about innovation and evolution of theatre. That's where it lies. As in anything else, we must evolve and change. If we don't, things become stagnant and uninspiring, because the "new" is only new for that moment. The constant repeating of a new genre creates predictable formula, less creative, and milk-toast work. Lin-Manuel Miranda's *Hamilton* opened our world to the voice of revolutionaries, personified through the use of a multicultural/race cast. That is one of the theatrical changes that *should* continue constantly as the theatre evolves – this notion that different cultures and races *can* play traditional white, historical roles. For while musical theatre has evolved greatly through its ninety-year existence, we still have a long way to go before there is true equity in culture, race, and gender, both in writing as well as in performance. *Hamilton* took our hand and led us through the next door of theatre, into what may be a whole new dimension.

And what better way to change not only theatre but also society for the better, than through the power of the artistic pen?

THE ANALYSIS
Create the dramatic question

In looking at the show *Hamilton*, I found interesting similarities between the dramatic question of this show and of the show *Evita*. First, both musicals have the main character as the title. Second, both have strong-willed, feisty characters. Thirdly, we as audience members are rooting for both of those characters to succeed in their lives. And finally, both Hamilton and Eva can never seem to be totally satisfied with where they are in their lives at the moment. They both have this insatiable appetite for more power and more change. When is enough, enough? We can interpret their rise to power and fame as both heroically strong or realistically flawed and weak, depending on

Dramatic Question: *"Will Alexander Hamilton ever accomplish enough to satiate his own appetite for change and legacy?"*

Figure 83 *Hamilton:* The Dramatic Question.

the individual circumstances and outcome. Hamilton is incredibly driven, intelligent, and outspoken. But his work and drive will also eventually take him to a level of self-destruction. Thus, we are hoping that he takes that right path in life.

List all analytically important characters

This show has a large ensemble cast that needs to be listed individually, due to their affiliations with Hamilton. I list separately character roles that actors play multiply in the show, again due to the importance of the storyline, as well as having songs: Jefferson/Lafayette are obvious due to their size, but also Peggy/Maria and John/Philip. The character list is large, but I feel they are all necessary in the analysis. Notice there is a list for each act – again due to the changing characters.

Dramatic Question: *"Will Alexander Hamilton ever accomplish enough to satiate his own appetite for change and legacy?"*

ACT I

Hamilton Burr Eliza Peggy Angelica Washington Jefferson Madison Lafayette Laurens Mulligan King Ensemble

ACT II

Hamilton Burr Eliza Maria Angelica Washington Jefferson Madison Lafayette Laurens Mulligan King Philip Ensemble

Figure 84 *Hamilton*: List of Characters.

List all of the songs under the character's name

Dramatic Question: *"Will Alexander Hamilton ever accomplish enough to satiate his own appetite for change and legacy?"*

ACT I

Hamilton	Burr	Eliza	Peggy	Angelica	Washington	Jefferson	Madison	Lafayette	Laurens	Mulligan	King	Ensemble
←	1. Alexander Hamilton →	→		→	→	→		←	←	→		2. Aaron Burr Sir
3. My Shot →						←	←	←	←			
4. The Story of Tonight	5. Schuyler Sisters	→	→							←		6. Farmer Refuted
←	←										7. You'll Be Back	8. Right Hand Man
9. Winter Ball	←	←		←	←			←	←	←		→
10. Helpless →		→		→				←	11. Satisfied →			
←	←			←					12. The Story Of Tonight Rep			
←	13. Wait For It	14. Stay Alive →		→		→	→		←			→
←	←											15. Ten Duel Commandments
16. Meet Me Inside →				→					→			→
←	17. That Would Be Enough											
←	18. Guns & Ships				→	←	←	→	→			
←					19. History Has Its Eyes On You							20. Yorktown
←					←	←	←	←			21. What Comes Next	
←	22. Dear Theodosia →		→	→	→	→	→					
	23. NonStop											

ACT II

Hamilton	Burr	Eliza	Maria	Angelica	Washington	Jefferson	Madison	Lafayette	Laurens	Mulligan	King	Philip	Ensemble
←	←				←	←	→						24. What'd I Miss?
←		26. Take A Break	→	→	25. Cabinet Battle #1	→							
←	27. Say No To This →											→	→
←	28. The Room Where It Happens				→	→	→						
←	←	←											29. Schuyler Defeated
←					30. Capital Battle #2 →	→	→						→
32. One Last Time	31. Washington On Your Side				→	→	→						→
←	34. The Adams Administration										33. I Know Him		
35. We Know →						→	→						
36. Hurricane →	←	→	→	→	→	→	→						37. Reynold's Pamphlet →
←		38. Burn									39. Blow Us All Away		→
←		←									←		40. Stay Alive Rep →
←	←			41. It's Quiet Uptown		←	←						42. Election Of 1800 →
←	43. Your Obedient Servant	44. Best Of Wives, Best Of Women											
←	←			←							←		45. World Was Wide Enough →
	←	←			46. Who Lives → Who Dies..?	→		→					→

Figure 85 *Hamilton*: List of Songs.

Lyrically analyse all of the songs

Hamilton

Hamilton is a poor, orphaned immigrant with no status. He, however, is a very driven and intelligent man, who has definite ideas as to how things should be done. He is constantly seeking ways to wiggle into the system in order to get his agenda produced. This may seem like LF, but unfortunately, it is as if the man can't ever be satisfied with what he's done. His efforts are insatiable. He's almost an addict, needing his next hit to be temporarily okay for the moment. He has a legacy to build. He claws his way to the top by desperate motivation to survive. He is constantly **yearning** for more; he's almost uncontrollable in his need for ideological reform and change. He's **unfulfilled** without that constant drive pushing him. Therefore, his thirst for getting things the way they "have to be," gets him more and more into **trouble**, especially with his friend Burr, and his wife Eliza and son Philip. He's so determined to make it that he's an out-of-control mega workaholic, having to take advantage of "*his shot*," although his shot is a never-ending carrot. He has an **unfulfillable dream/vision** to control and write his destiny and legacy. Hamilton is N.

Burr

Aaron Burr is an elite lawyer, well tested, well educated. He knows how the system works, and he uses it to his advantage. The difference between his escalation to power and change is that he is more tempered. He knows what he wants, and he knows how to get it – through basic political manoeuvring. His desires are not uncontrolled and insatiable – they are calculated points to a precise endgame. Therefore, Burr is LF. He's a player in the system, knowing in his mind that you just have to be patient and "*wait for it*" – a **central driving force** and **credo** for gaining power. He has power, intelligence, and savvy – **attractive to be with.** He continues to gain momentum and power, and knows how to work the system to gain advantage – **larger than life**.

Eliza

Eliza loves Hamilton whole-heartedly, and her main desire is for them to live happily together *safely*. She **yearns** for a normal life, a family together. She constantly is trying to convince Hamilton to slow down and smell the roses. She asks for little, and wants the best for Hamilton, although she knows he will never find it or achieve it. But for her, just having Hamilton "*would be enough.*" Eliza is N.

Peggy/Maria

Peggy is a sister who **yearns** to find a man to have in her life who "knows things." Maria is fleshed out more – she has an abusive, cheating husband who leaves her destitute. She is in dire straits – **in trouble.** She **yearns** for security and love in a man and finds it in Hamilton. Peggy and Maria are N.

Angelica

Angelica is the oldest of the three sisters, and she feels obligated, like the other two, to find a rich man to take care of her. She falls in love with Hamilton, love at first sight, yet she sacrifices her own feelings for her sister Eliza's happiness. She will always have undying faithfulness to Eliza. Throughout the show, Angelica yearns for Hamilton, and even tries to set up an affair with him, yet she will survive without him, willing to "*never be satisfied*" in life. She is a strong, independent woman who knows and understands the way it is – she is **attractive to be with** and **larger than life**. She is similar to Eponine in *Les Mis*. She is LF.

Washington

Washington is a general and then the first President of the United States – **larger than life, attractive to be with**. He has charisma, power, he listens, he's smart, and he's a leader – **persuasive**. He's a **central driving force** in winning the war and leading this newborn nation. He is LF.

Jefferson and Madison

Jefferson and Madison represent the south and are both powerful men, as well as allies to each other and Aaron Burr – **central driving force**. They form a force against Hamilton and his agenda. Jefferson becomes the Secretary of State under Washington – he's **larger than life**, and he knows it by reminding people in the song "Cabinet Battle #1" who wrote the Declaration of Independence. Both Madison and Jefferson are savvy, intelligent, and they know how the political system works – they are **persuasive**. It obviously works to their advantage with Jefferson becoming President after Adams. Madison and Jefferson are LF.

Lafayette, Laurens, and Mulligan

These three men are allies to Hamilton as well as good friends. Lafayette represents the French revolutionaries, leading the attack on the Redcoats, while Laurens stays home supporting the anti-slavery movement through writing essays. Mulligan is a spy in the British community, smuggling information to/for the United States. All three are pragmatic, hard-working, American revolutionaries fighting for the cause of freedom and liberty – **credo**. They are **central driving forces** to the winning of the revolution. They are all LF.

King George

King George is a king. He controls England, and at the beginning of the show, controls the colonies. He is pompous, egocentric, rich, and powerful – **larger than life, attractive to be with**. Oh, and by the way, "*when push comes to shove*," he'll kill anyone who gets in his way. King George is LF.

Phillip

Philip is the son of Hamilton, who feels ignored by his father. Yet he tries to live up to his father's grandeur and fame. Finally, to prove his love and bravery, Philip fights in a duel to uphold *the great name of his father*, Hamilton. He's a **child** who **yearns** for the attention and love of his father. He is N.

Ensemble

The ensemble reflects and magnifies the goings-on of that moment on stage. They are characters that support the song at that specific juncture in the show. So each of their characters need to be supportive and allies to the characters who are singing that specific song. They, however, are observers and participants in the scene, as if they are narrators already knowing what is going to happen. This clairvoyance gives them the traits of LF – **larger than life**, and **persuasive** in their support. They are the exclamation point to each song. The ensemble is LF. See Figure 86.

Musically analyse all of the songs

This rap musical is the beginning of something very new and different. Musically, it offers challenges to the "traditional" thinking of music in musical theatre. Can this type of music translate into the same music energy levels as past musicals did? I believe it can, with the exception of one ideological change of perception within the Need energy music characteristic paradigm. Rap, in and of itself, is rhythmic in nature due to the poetic accents of the lyrics. If looked at from a traditional, basic level of general music characteristics, this would then lead to the conundrum of all the rap music sounding a bit Life Force through its very rhythmic nature. Therefore, is there really a N Level 1–Tell It Like It Is rap song? If we look at the comparison of rap upbeat music to rap slow music, I think we can find that new level N difference. Of course, music is going to constantly evolve and change, and our listening

Dramatic Question: *"Will Alexander Hamilton ever accomplish enough to satiate his own appetite for change and legacy?"*

ACT I

N Hamilton	LF Burr	N Eliza	N Peggy	LF Angelica	LF Washington	LF Jefferson	LF Madison	LF Lafayette	LF Laurens	LF Mulligan	LF King	LF Ensemble
	1. Alexander Hamilton											2. Aaron Burr Sir
3. My Shot												
4. The Story of Tonight												
	5. Schuyler Sisters											6. Farmer Refused
											7. You'll Be Back	8. Right Hand Man
	9. Winter Ball											
10. Helpless												
									11. Satisfied			
									12. The Story Of Tonight Rep			
	13. Wait For It											
		14. Stay Alive										15. Ten Duel Commandments
16. Meet Me Inside												
		17. That Would Be Enough										
	18. Guns & Ships											
					19. History Has Its Eyes On You							20. Yorktown
											21. What Comes Next	
	22. Dear Theodosia											
	23. NonStop											

ACT II

N Hamilton	LF Burr	N Eliza	N Maria	LF Angelica	LF Washington	LF Jefferson	LF Madison	LF Lafayette	LF Laurens	LF Mulligan	LF King	N Philip	LF Ensemble
													24. What'd I Miss?
					25. Cabinet Battle #1								
		26. Take A Break											
	27. Say No To This												
	28. The Room Where It Happens												
												29. Schuyler Defeated	
					30. Capital Battle #2								
	31. Washington On Your Side												
32. One Last Time													
												33. I Know Him	
	34. The Adams Administration												
35. We Know													
36. Hurricane													37. Reynold's Pamphlet
		38. Burn										39. Blow Us All Away	
													40. Stay Alive Rep
				41. It's Quiet Uptown									42. Election Of 1800
	43. Your Obedient Servant	44. Best Of Wives, Best Of Women											
													45. World Was Wide Enough
					46. Who Lives Who Dies..?								

Figure 86 *Hamilton*: List of Character Energies.

then needs to move with it. Songs like "Satisfied" or "Alexander Hamilton" definitely have a driving beat to them and are rhythmically accented in line, however, in the context of comparison, I would say that they are more in the spirit of a traditional N song. Is this subjective? Absolutely. Could my interpretation be contrary to other interpretation? Absolutely. Does this make the music levels invalid? I think not. We still have the basis of our theories working for us. It's just that the music gauge has shifted a bit from what we've traditionally been listening to. And, of course, we know that *Hamilton* is anything but traditional.

Sondheim was one to point out that *"lyrics need some air in them for the audience to understand what's going on, so it's the rigidity of form ... that helps convey power."*[2] This is a major challenge in a very word-dense work like *Hamilton*. Therefore, many songs in the show really aren't hugely fast in tempo, even though the lyrics are on rapid fire. This is another important concept to consider when analysing slower numbers in this show. It makes perfect sense that the first number, "Alexander Hamilton," is at a slow tempo. We need to truly understand and register this first onslaught of information in the show – for if we miss something in that first song, we miss the important background to the main characters. Likewise, it gives the audience some start-up time to adjust to this type of listening and viewing. Can you imagine what it would've been like as a first time audience member to listen to the opening number "Alexander Hamilton" with a tempo of "The Ballad Of Sweeney Todd?" We would've been lost and had given up immediately on the show.

Finally, you'll notice that this again is a show with all but one LF and N Level 1 and 2 music truths. No one in this show is "evil" per se, and no one is hiding her/his true feelings. This show is about political confrontations of ideology and everyone in the show has a stand. (Except for Burr, according to Hamilton.) This sets the sides clearly and definitively. See Figure 87.

The Alignment energy

In the first song, "Alexander Hamilton," many of the characters already align with their energies, including Hamilton and Burr. This first song not only fills us in on some background information, but also gives us a clue as to what to expect in rest of the show. There is so much information, however, that it is difficult to assimilate it all in one dose – especially whether Hamilton is N or LF. We need to see him make friends with Burr, Lafayette, Laurens, and Mulligan, and then give us a sense of his incessant drive and hunger for

Dramatic Question: *"Will Alexander Hamilton ever accomplish enough to satiate his own appetite for change and legacy?"*												
N Hamilton	LF Burr	N ElizaF	N Peggy/Maria	LF Angelica	LF Washington	LF Jefferson	LF Madison	LF Lafayette	LF Laurens	LF Mulligan	LF King	LF Ensemble
					ACT I							
←N1	1. Alexander Hamilton LF2	→N1	→N1	→N1	→LF2	→LF2	→LF2		→LF2	→LF2		→LF2
←N2	←LF1							←LF1	←LF1	←LF1		2. Aaron Burr Sir LF1
3. My Shot N2 →LF1								→LF1	→LF1	→LF1		→LF1
4. The Story of Tonight N1								→LF2	→LF2	→LF2		→LF2
	5. Schuyler Sisters LF1	→N2	→N2	→LF1								→LF1
←N2	←LF2									←LF2		6. Farmer Refuted LF5
											7. You'll Be BackLF1	
←N2	←LF1	←N2	←N2	←LF1	←LF1			←LF1	←LF1	←LF1		8. Right Hand Man LF1
←N2	9. Winter Ball LF1								→LF1			→LF1
10. Helpless N2 →LF1		→N2		→LF1				←LF2				→LF2
←N1		←N1		←LF2								
←N2/1	←LF1/2							←LF1				→LF2
									12. The Story Of Tonight Rep LF1			
13. Wait For It LF2		14. Stay Alive N1		→LF2	→LF2			→LF2	→LF2	→LF2		→LF2
←N1									←LF1			15. Ten DuelLF1 Commandments
←N2												→LF1
16. Meet Me Inside N1 →LF1					←LF1				→ LF1			
←N1		17. That Would Be Enough N1										
	18. Guns & Ships LF1							→LF1				→LF1
←N1					19. History Has Its Eyes On You LF2				→ LF2	→ LF2		→LF2
←N2					←LF1			←LF1	← LF1	← LF1		20. YorktownLF1
											21. What Comes Next LF1	
←N1	22. Dear TheodosiaLF2							←LF1	← LF1	← LF1		
←N2	23. Non-Stop LF1	→N1/2		→LF2/1	→LF2/1			←LF1	← LF1	← LF1		→LF1
N Hamilton	LF Burr	N Eliza	N Maria	LF Angelica	LF Washington	LF Jefferson	LF Madison	LF Lafayette	LF Laurens	LF Mulligan	LF King	N Philip	LF Ensemble
					ACT II								
←N2	←LF1				←LF1	←LF1	←LF2						24. What'd I Miss? LF1
←N2					25. Cabinet Battle #1 LF1	→LF1	←LF1						
←N1		26. Take A Break N1		→LF2								→N1/2	
←N1	27. Say No To This LF2		→N1										→LF2
←N2	28. The Room Where It Happens LF1				→LF1	→LF1	→LF1						←LF1
←N2	←LF1	←N2										29. Schuyler Defeated N2	
	30. Capital Battle #2 LF1				←LF1	→LF1	→LF1						
	31. Washington On Your Side LF1					←LF1	→LF1						←LF1
32. One Last Time N2/1					←LF1/2								→LF1
											33. I Know Him LF1		
←N2	34. The AdamS Administration LF1					←LF1	←LF1						
35. We Know N2→ LF1						←LF1	←LF1						
36. Hurricane N1→ LF2		→N1	→N1	→LF2	→ LF2								→LF2
←N2	← LF1			←LF1		←LF1	←LF1						37. Reynold's Pamphlet LF1
	38. Burn N1											39. Blow Us All Away N2	→LF1
←N1		←N1										←N1	40. Stay Alive Rep LF2
←N2		←N1		41. It's Quiet Uptown LF2									→LF2
←N2	← LF1					←LF1	←LF1						42. Election Of 1800 LF1
←N2	43. Your Obedient Servant LF1												
←N2		44. Best Of Wives, Best Of Women N1											45. World Was Wide Enough LF1/2
←N2/1	←LF1/2			←LF2									
←	←	←		←	46. Who Lives→ Who Dies..?	→	→						→

Figure 87 *Hamilton*: List of Music Truths.

change. That happens in "My Shot." At that point, we get it and know that we are rooting for Hamilton to succeed. "My Shot" is the A.

The Growth Moment energy

In the song "The World Was Wide Enough" we witness in growing anticipation and dread the final duel between Hamilton and Burr. The gun goes off and we capture the flash of thoughts of Hamilton in his last seconds of life. Here he analyses and questions all of his achievements and regrets. He dies in the arms of Eliza and Angelica, with Burr also feeling the huge sense of weight and regret in how this played out. The song, however, doesn't give us final closure. We don't have a sense of completion yet – the reaction to his death. It takes the final song "Who Lives, Who Dies, Who Tells Your Story" to give us that closure, as well as the final bookend to the piece. We needed to know that Hamilton didn't die totally in vain and that he did leave a legacy to be proud of. "Who Lives, Who Dies, Who Tells Your Story" is the GM.

The ground plan of the musical

There are two camps in this show: the allies, Washington, Lafayette, Laurens, and Mulligan, versus the foes, Burr, Jefferson, and Madison. These two forces are opposite each other, trying to change the perspective and power of the brilliant Hamilton. Interestingly enough, Eliza really isn't a part of this final ground plan, mainly due to the fact that she really isn't involved in the dramatic question. If Hamilton had ever resolved the dramatic question sooner, Eliza and company would have then fallen into place in the life of Hamilton. But alas …

Hamilton

$$LF \rightarrow N \leftarrow LF$$

Community of   Community of

Foes   Allies

Figure 88 *Hamilton:* The Ground Plan.

Figure 89 *Hamilton* Act I: Final.

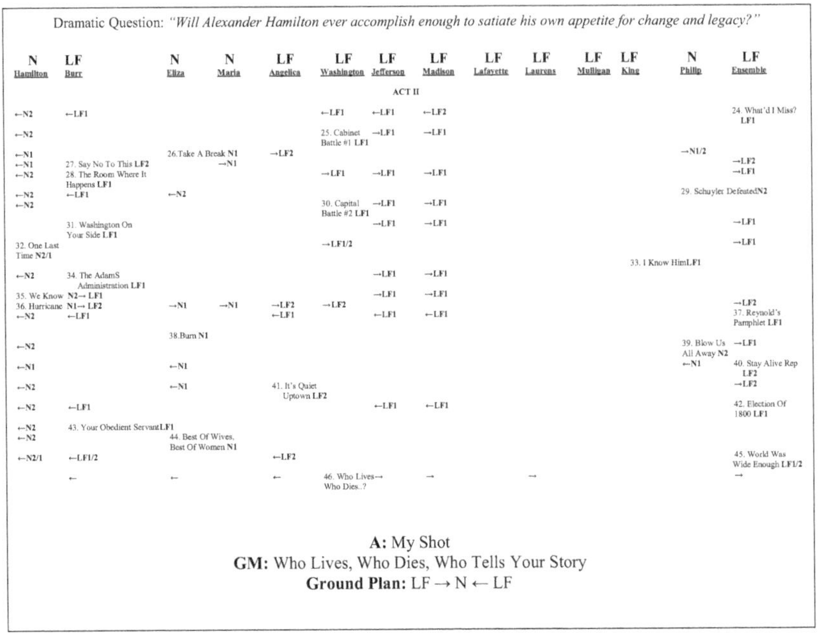

Figure 90 *Hamilton* Act II: Final.

Notes

1   Brantley, *The New York Times*, 6 August 2015.
2   Carnelia, "Stephen Sondheim," 19.

Conclusion

As stated previously, I taught these theories of energies for over thirty years to high school and university classes. Inevitably, when we first started, students had great difficulty analysing the first couple of musicals that we did. They got frustrated because they tended to overthink the process. They also feared being wrong. I too still approach unanalysed musicals with great anxiety and trepidation. Oh my God, what if I can't figure it out? What if I get it wrong? I'm supposed to know this stuff! I'll be such a loser!

Don't let your fear take over. When I start to get all worked up about this, all I need to do is first settle myself down and remind myself that there is a process: figure out the dramatic question, write out the instrumental characters, assign the songs to the characters, and then slowly go through the grunt work of lyric and music analysis. It *will* work out, and it will make sense. The bottom line is you're putting work into the analysis of the show and your understanding of the show will increase, regardless whether you get it totally "right" or not.

The most common comment now that I receive from my former students usually begins with a smile, followed by the line "Jim, I hate you." They then continue to speak about their frustration as to how they can no longer "just sit back and enjoy" watching a musical anymore. Now, they see problems in performances that they hadn't seen before. They can't just let shows totally

Figure 91 Working in class at Casper College.

ride on its entertainment merits anymore. They are being an educated and discretionary audience. They aren't just saying that every show is great. They also aren't just saying that a show sucks anymore, after seeing something they didn't like. They are following it up with solid, structural, and analytical justification. They now see how a production potentially could have been better if that show had just known about the energy theories. These students are now *critical thinkers*.

As I listen to them, I begin to smile inside, knowing that our theatre community, one by one, is getting more informed. They are appreciating the arts in a much deeper way and I'm okay with that. There's never anything wrong with an intelligent, discretionary audience. As a matter of fact, that is what pushes all of us as artists to the next level, and that is exciting.

May the life force be with you!

Contributors

Richard Burk is a professional director and actor, and Coordinator of Acting at Casper College, Casper, Wyoming.

Arthur Giron is a nationally known playwright, with plays published at Concord Theatricals, and was Chair of the Playwriting Department at Carnegie-Mellon University, Pittsburgh, Pennsylvania.

Charles Willard was a Broadway theatrical producer and manager and an assistant professor in the Drama Department at Carnegie-Mellon University, Pittsburgh, Pennsylvania.

Abbreviations

A	Alignment (energy)
GM	Growth Moment (energy)
LF	Life Force (energy)
LF1	Life Force Energy Level 1–Tell It Like It Is
LF2	Life Force Energy Level 2–The Affirmation
LF3	Life Force Energy Level 3–The Lie
LF4	Life Force Energy Level 4–The Struggle
LF5	Life Force Energy Level 5–The Tactical
N	Need (energy)
N1	Need Energy Level 1–Tell It Like It Is
N2	Need Energy Level 2–The Affirmation
N3	Need Energy Level 3–The Lie
N4	Need Energy Level 4–The Struggle
N5	Need Energy Level 5–Protest Too Much

Bibliography

Amusements, "'Show Boat' Proves Fine Musical Show," *The New York Times*, 28 December 1927. Available online: https://www.nytimes.com/1927/12/28/ archives/show-boat-proves-fine-musical-show-distinguished-audience-finds-new.html?searchResultPosition=1 (accessed 10 June 2021).

Atkinson, Brooks, "Theatre: The Jungles of the City," *The New York Times*, 27 September 1957. Available online: https://timesmachine.nytimes.com/ timesmachine/1957/09/27/84767567.html?pageNumber=14 (accessed 10 June 2021).

Brantley, Ben, "Theater Review; Rock Opera A la 'Boheme' and 'Hair,'" *The New York Times*, 14 February 1996. Available online: https://www.nytimes.com/1996/02/14/theater/theater-review-rock-opera-a-la-boheme-and-hair.html (accessed 10 June 2021).

Brantley, Ben, "Review: 'Hamilton,' Young Rebels Changing History and Theater," *The New York Times*, 6 August 2015. Available online: https://www.nytimes.com/2015/08/07/theater/review-hamilton-young-rebels-changing-history-and-theater.html (accessed 10 June 2021).

Carnelia, C., "In Conversation With Stephen Sondheim," *The Dramatist*, 19 (2007).

Close Encounters of the Third Kind [Film] Columbia Pictures Industries, Inc. All Rights Reserved. Courtesy of Columbia Pictures. 1977, © renewed 2005.

Flinn, Denny Martin, *Musical! A Grand Tour* (New York: Schirmer Books, 1997).

Gäntl, Kurt, *The Musical, A Concise History* (Boston, MA: Northeastern University Press, 1997).

Isherwood, Charles, "Sex and Rock? What Would the Kaiser Think?," *The New York Times*, 11 December 2006. Available online: https://www.nytimes.com/2006/12/11/theater/reviews/11spri.html (accessed 10 June 2021).

Kerr, Walter, "'The Wiz' Misses," *The New York Times*, 12 January 1975. Available online: https://www.nytimes.com/1975/01/12/archives/the-wiz-misses.html (accessed 10 June 2021).

Kerr, Walter, "Is 'Sweeney' on Target?," *The New York Times*, 11 March 1979. Available online: https://archive.nytimes.com/www.nytimes.com/ books/98/07/19/specials/sondheim-sweeney.html (accessed 10 June 2021).

Nichols, Lewis, "'Oklahoma!' A Musical Hailed as Delightful, Based on 'Green Grow the Lilacs,' Opens Here at the St. James Theatre," *The New York Times*, 1 April 1943. Available online: https://timesmachine.nytimes.com/timesmachine/1943/04/01/88524844.html?pageNumber=27 (accessed 10 June 2021).

Rich, Frank, "Stage: 'Phantom of the Opera,'" *The New York Times*, 27 January 1988. Available online: https://www.nytimes.com/1988/01/27/theater/stage-phantom-of-the-opera.html (accessed 10 June 2021).

Stempel, Larry, *Showtime, A History of the Broadway Musical Theatre* (London: W. W. Norton & Company, Inc., 2010).

Taubman, Howard, "Theater: Mostel as Tevye in 'Fiddler on the Roof,'" *The New York Times*, 23 September 1964. Available online: https://www.nytimes.com/1964/09/23/archives/theater-mostel-as-tevye-in-fiddler-on-the-roof-sholem-aleichem.html (accessed 10 June 2021).